GROWING IN VIRTUE

Recent Titles from the Moral Traditions Series

David Cloutier, Andrea Vicini, SJ, and Darlene Weaver, Editors

The Structures of Virtue and Vice
Daniel J. Daly

Consumer Ethics in a Global Economy
Daniel Finn

The Aesthetics of Solidarity: Our Lady of Guadalupe and American Democracy
Nichole M. Flores

Radical Sufficiency: Work, Livelihood, and a US Catholic Economic Ethic
Christine Firer Hinze

Humanity in Crisis
David Hollenbach, SJ

Tragic Dilemmas in Christian Ethics
Kate Jackson-Meyer

The Fullness of Free Time: Leisure and Recreation in the Moral Life
Connor Kelly

Beyond Biology: Rethinking Parenthood in the Catholic Tradition
Jacob M. Kohlhaas

Reimagining Human Rights: Religion and the Common Good
William O'Neill, SJ

Reenvisioning Sexual Ethics: A Feminist Christian Account
Karen Peterson-Iyer

Tomorrow's Troubles: Risk, Anxiety, and Prudence in an Age of Algorithmic Governance
Paul Scherz

Wealth, Virtue, and Moral Luck: Christian Ethics in an Age of Inequality
Kate Ward

GROWING IN VIRTUE
AQUINAS ON HABIT

WILLIAM C. MATTISON III

GEORGETOWN UNIVERSITY PRESS / WASHINGTON, DC

Cataloging-in-Publication data is on file with the Library of Congress.

ISBN 978-1-64712-327-7 (hardcover)
ISBN 978-1-64712-328-4 (paperback)
ISBN 978-1-64712-329-1 (ebook)

♾ This paper meets the requirements of ANSI/NISO Z39.48-1992 (Permanence of Paper).

24 23 9 8 7 6 5 4 3 2 First printing

Printed in the United States of America

Cover design by Nathan Putens. Cover image from Jorisvo, Dreamstime.com
Interior design by BookComp, Inc.

To my students, in gratitude

The pages of this book are littered with
the fruits of our shared search for wisdom

CONTENTS

ACKNOWLEDGMENTS

This book is dedicated to the students with whom I have journeyed in twenty years of teaching. As much as my time teaching Catholic elementary school helped me learn as much about my faith as any other experience, my undergraduate and graduate teaching has helped me learn as much about virtue and happiness as anything else.

This is true of the hundreds of undergraduates, masters of theological studies students, seminarians, and ministerial students with whom I have shared invigorating classroom conversation. They have helped me hone my grasp of the material, at times through challenging questions and critiques that corrected my thinking, and at times through the demand for concrete examples of the dynamics described in these pages.

It is especially true of the doctoral students with whom I have been blessed to work, to whom this book is dedicated in particular. Doctoral seminars are the crockpot where ideas are gathered, mixed together, and tenderized. And there is no more robust example of this dynamic than directing a student's dissertation. I have learned an enormous amount from James Stroud, Matt Tapie, Andrew Kim, John Meinert, John Makdisi, Andrew Whitmore, and Marc Rugani. There are significant sections of this book that I would not have been able to write without them or walking with them through their research. Through James Stroud and John Meinert I came to learn far more about the dynamics of grace and the gifts of the Holy Spirit than I had in my own formation. Drew Kim took on the seemingly impossible task of defending the connectivity of the virtues today, and I learned a tremendous amount from that study while he helped me to affirm a position I intuitively held but did not yet fully understand. Andrew Whitmore's project on the disposition/habit distinction in Thomas Aquinas echoes through nearly every chapter.

Speaking of scholars to whom I owe a great debt of gratitude, we live in a time when there is vigorous and erudite scholarship on Thomas Aquinas's thought on moral theology, and on virtue and grace in particular. Alasdair MacIntyre would say that a tradition is truly alive when its participants have enough common commitments to ground their at times vociferous disagreements, all in humble service to the tradition itself and to its lived (in this case ecclesial) reality in communities. To name but two outstanding scholars whose work I have at times reacted against but from whom I have learned more than I will ever be able to repay, my gratitude to Steven Jensen and David Decosimo.

The most beautiful level of such scholarly community is when it is marked not only by excellence and shared commitment but also by friendship. I have been blessed to have peers in the field who are first and foremost friends, such as Joe Capizzi and David Cloutier, among others. But in this specific area of Thomistic thought on grace and virtue, three people stand out. Patrick Clark has generously read and suggested revisions on two of my previous books, and those are far better thanks to him. In a manner reminiscent of Servais Pinckaers, OP, Patrick's spirituality reverberates through all of his theological scholarship and communication. David Elliot also read and commented on those books with an incisiveness, eloquence, and vision that is unsurpassed. The field will be blessed to read his books for decades to come. Last, but certainly not least, my unending gratitude to Angela Knobel. There is literally nothing I have written on this topic that she has not read, critiqued, and improved. Her razor sharp mind and scholarly generosity astound me over and over again. Everyone should be so fortunate to have a friend such as Angela.

Jean Porter is not mentioned in this group only because it is hard for me to characterize her as anything other than a mentor, though I am grateful to now have her as a colleague and friend. No one has been more influential on my own work. As her doctoral student in the 1990s I did a course paper on dead faith (which she saw as significant before I did, even after I wrote the paper) and a comprehensive exam question on the infused cardinal virtues (a completely unsolicited suggestion from her!). As evident in these pages, her influence continues to shape me and my work. Serge-Thomas Bonino, OP, once told me that Jean Porter's *Nature as Reason* was the most influential book to the International Theological Commission subcommittee that wrote the 2009 document on natural law, *In Search of a Universal Ethic.* I would use comparably singular terms to describe Jean's impact on the field, particularly the formation of scholars of Catholic moral theology in the past quarter century.

Thank you to Department Chair Tim Matovina, the Department of Theology, and the University of Notre Dame for support in writing this book, especially in the form of a sabbatical in fall 2021. Thank you also to Cait Duggan for her excellent work on the index.

Bridging the professional and personal, thanks to my friend Shea Gibbs, a friend on the basketball court and softball field for years before I learned what an outstanding editor he is. He made significant improvements to portions of this text.

Finally, I am eternally grateful to my wife, Courtney, and sons, Billy and Jack, in more ways than can be said. Our family life influenced this book in a different manner, as the lived venue where accustomization, habituation, and (God willing) growth in virtue happen in the day to day. I am grateful for their love and their being the very heart of my life.

It is a joy and a gift to express my gratitude to all mentioned here, without whom this book would not have been possible.

INTRODUCTION

Virtue is back. In recent years, popular books on virtue have flooded the market, whether they be coffee table books about virtuous lives or practical self-help books on developing good habits. In moral philosophy, a deluge of virtue scholarship published over the past few decades has led to an evolution in college ethics courses, from focusing on the "big two" (Kantian deontology and utilitarianism) to including virtue among the "big three."

In Catholic moral theology, virtue was almost completely absent from scholarly discussion as recently as twenty-five years ago. Today it is impossible to imagine a graduate-level introduction to the field failing to devote extensive attention to virtue. In many cases virtue now provides the structure to such courses.

Virtue's ascendency in recent moral philosophy, theology, and popular literature affirms that it matters not simply what we do but also who we are. These two are not the same, but they are intricately intertwined. Furthermore, while "who I am" in one sense provides a stability that guards a person's singular lifelong identity, in another sense "who I am" signals a person's character, which is not fixed even as it retains a certain stability. A turn to virtue is a turn to this stable but not unchangeable character which is somehow related to a person's identity on the one hand and to particular actions on the other.

Despite heightened attention to virtue, the current philosophical and theological literature has failed to offer detailed analyses of how people attain and grow in the good habits we know as the virtues. Though popular literature focuses on virtue growth, it lacks careful scholarly analysis on which to base its accessible accounts. What's more, the popular literature commonly depends on a behaviorist model of virtue that rightly focuses on changes in observable actions but only mechanically so, in a manner less concerned with the goals of those actions from the perspective of the acting person and with the relation of those actions to other goals in a person's life. The behaviorist model is one from which virtue scholars are always quick to distance themselves. We're left with a need for guidance on growing in virtue.

Julia Annas recognizes the topic's importance in a recent book: "We cannot understand what virtue is without coming to understand how we acquire it."[1] She continues, "Understanding the process of ethical education is a part of virtue ethics," not something "merely practical" or "extraneous to theory." Any account of virtue that does not attend to how virtue is attained or increased is inadequate. Indeed, explaining how people attain and grow in virtue requires a precise account of habits, as virtues are good habits. In other words, any account of growing in virtue must reflect some understanding of habit.

Though any approach to morality assumes some account of moral education, the assumption is particularly important when examining virtue. A virtue approach should focus on individuals' socially situated goals and practices from their own perspective. Virtue formation recognizes that a person is in some important senses already formed, but in other ways is engaged in a continual process of formation. A person's ends, desires, plans, projects, and character traits are not the mere matter on which some "right-making" feature of human action supervenes and renders them within the scope of morality.[2] A person's everyday practices reflect and continually refine her character, the formation of which is an ongoing process.

Though the past half-century has produced extensive scholarship on "moral development," particularly in the field of psychology, the relatively recent turn to virtue necessitates a distinct take. Philosophers are outpacing theologians in updating their thinking on moral development, but the social sciences are leading them both. Some current social science literature recognizes the classical tradition of thought on virtue, most commonly with respect to Aristotle but, due in part to its distinct disciplinary methodology, the accounts have ignored many of the resources on virtue from classical thought. While this book does not directly engage the social sciences, its account of growing in virtue can contribute to this important work.[3]

Because this book provides a Thomistic account of growing in virtue, its focus requires a precise explanation of what habits are, why they are needed, and what they supply once possessed. This work begins with a technical analysis of habit based on the thought of Thomas Aquinas, then examines the attainment of and growth in virtue. In line with Aquinas's work, it addresses the relevance of both natural or "acquired" virtues as well as supernatural or "infused" virtues and concludes with an appendix focused on the relationship between acquired and infused virtues.

Why should we focus on Aquinas's writings on virtue? The primary intention is neither to convince readers of the value of a virtue approach to morality over other approaches nor to justify Aquinas's thinking to those not already open to his importance. The focus on Aquinas is in part due to the untapped yet enormously valuable resources his writings offer on habit and growing in virtue. While Aquinas is prominent in contemporary moral theology, his examination of several types of habits and dispositions, the various ways they are attained, and their relationships to each other are relatively unexplored in recent virtue scholarship.

Additionally, Aquinas's attention to both acquired and infused virtue is essential for a *theological* treatment of growth in virtue. Reflective of the scholastic dictum that grace perfects nature—rather than obliterating it or leaving it untouched—no Christian thinker offers a more extensive or more penetrating analysis of habit's natural dynamics and especially the continuities and discontinuities between acquired and infused virtues. The commonalties and differences between natural and supernatural virtues are a central consideration here, and Aquinas's thought is an invaluable resource.

Finally, both the comprehensive character of Thomistic thought and its frequency of use as an arena for philosophical and theological debate warrant a focus on Aquinas. We find in this thinker's corpus both untapped virtue resources and an understanding of their relation to classical moral topics, like law, passion, and grace. We thus find that an account of growing in virtue has implications for a variety of scholarly debates, including the spontaneity of virtuous passions, the gifts of the Holy Spirit, and the function of the "last end" in morality.

Who comprises this book's intended audience? One obvious audience is Thomistic scholars. Another is those interested in Catholic moral theology, for whom the topic of virtue and Thomistic thought serve as valuable resources. Debates among such scholars are routinely and extensively engaged, and anyone broadly interested in the graced life of discipleship will find a careful account of the transformation wrought by God's grace at the nexus of divine and human agency. Those interested even more broadly in virtue and morality will find arguments with ready points of contact to philosophical virtue ethics.

The analysis in this book also ultimately will inform anyone committed to raising children, particularly in schools and especially in the context of faith. Readers rarely think of Aquinas as offering a theory of education. Yet expanding the scope of schooling and education to the breadth indicated by the term "formation," we can see virtue and habituation play a crucial role. After all, habits describe who we are, that is, who we are in a stable though not unchangeable way. The panoply of habits a person possesses might be called her character. Thomistic thought on the types of dispositions and habits and the ways they are attained and grow, all within a communal context, undergirds a robust and eminently practical vision of education.

Since any account of growing in virtue will assume some operative vision of habit, the book begins with a Thomistic explanation of the concept. Chapter 1 relies on the classic description of habit as "second nature," to explain the sense in which habits are not our first nature yet are still natural. The discussion situates habits between the person and her activity, and presents habits as stable specifications of a person's natural powers toward certain activities. As such, habits are intimately related to but not reducible to either individuals or their activities.

Chapter 2 examines a neglected Thomistic distinction between dispositions and habits. What "qualifies" a habit as being distinct from a disposition is both its stability and the specification of its end through rationality. Absent either condition, the trait is merely a disposition to action, even if it may be relatively stable, complex, or both. Because dispositions can be possessed to increasing degrees on the way toward habit formation, the distinction supplies a crucial resource for an account of growth in virtue.

Aquinas repeatedly identifies four causes of dispositions and habits. Chapter 3 examines the first two: nature and custom. For Aquinas, nature and custom are crucial in habit formation but, properly speaking, they cause a person to possess dispositions, not habits. The chapter therefore functions as a hinge between the discussion of the characteristics of dispositions and habits examined in chapters 1 and 2 and the discussion on attaining and growing in virtues in ensuing chapters. Aquinas distinguishes customs from properly human habits, despite both being caused by repeated activity. Scholars often neglect Aquinas's account of custom's role in habit formation. Once recognized, it provides virtue-engaged Thomists a way to incorporate social theory on communal practices and social structures into a discussion of human agency.

Chapter 4 examines Aquinas's third cause of habits and dispositions, human acts. By "human" he means actions engaging a person's reason and will. The analysis explains why repeated acts are needed to engender the habits known as acquired virtues. Because repeated acts also lead to custom dispositions, the analysis addresses what differentiates customs from acquired virtues. The key differentiator is rational rather than merely sensory specification of the habit's object or end. The chapter closes by touching on the difference made by rational specification "within" a virtue, "across" virtues, and regarding one's life "as a whole." These sections address, respectively, the relationship between acquired virtue and practical reasoning, the connectivity of the virtues, and the last end.

Chapter 5 offers an account of growing in acquired virtue. It begins with a basic discussion of virtue growth from childhood in a manner sensitive to the distinction between dispositions and habits, and the social context of formation. It then addresses a popular topic in virtue formation, the existence of and lessening or removal of contrary dispositions within the virtuous person. Despite the common experience of lessening contrary dispositions, this is not the primary manner of virtue's growth. The next section examines how growth in virtue most properly occurs: in a manner not limited to lessening contrary dispositions. The final section turns away from growth and examines loss of virtue and the persistence of residual dispositions. Though the primary focus is on growth in virtue, descriptions of habits often apply to vice as well, which is pertinent to the chapter's treatment of virtue's loss.

Chapter 6 turns to Aquinas's fourth cause of virtue: grace. A major theme of this project is the continuity yet difference between graced and natural virtues. Therefore chapters 6 and 7 parallel the structure of chapters 4 and 5. Chapter 6 begins with an explanation of why the infused virtues are needed. The infused virtues, like the acquired virtues, are habits and remain such even as they are oriented to an ultimate end beyond humanity's unaided reach. Then comes an examination of how God's grace makes an impact within virtues, culminating with an extensive look at the gifts of the Holy Spirit. An ensuing section probes the difference grace makes across virtues, with a focus on how charity connects the infused virtues. The final section explores the difference grace makes for a person's life as a whole, analyzing how a person clings to her last end in charity and how charity plays its role as "form of the virtues."

Chapter 7 offers an account of growth in infused virtue. By examining two lives, those of the baptized infant and the adult convert, the discussion explores the similarities and important discontinuities between infused and acquired virtue. Echoing chapter 5, the next section addresses the persistence of contrary dispositions in the graced life, a common topic in scholarship on infused virtue. Granting significant differences, the chapter lays out the case that infused virtue shares more similarity with acquired virtue than commonly thought. As with the acquired virtues, a decrease in contrary dispositions does not constitute the primary locus of growth in infused virtue. Thus the following section describes growth in infused virtue, illustrating how Aquinas's account of habitual ordering depicts "room for growth" in acquired as well as infused virtue. The final section examines the loss of infused virtue, paying special attention to the phenomenon of "dead faith."

The concluding appendix addresses the recent scholarly debate on the relationship between the acquired and infused virtues and whether they can in fact coexist within the same person. Interlocutors, relying heavily on Thomistic thought, have questioned whether the same person can possess both infused and acquired virtues. Based on the Thomistic account of virtue offered here, I claim they cannot. But this argument appears as an appendix rather than a chapter for two reasons. First, though the position I articulate there is closely related to the preceding arguments about virtue, my position in the recent debate is distinguishable from those claims. In other words, one could conceivably concur with the account of growing in virtue offered in the chapters and yet disagree with the concluding argument. The second reason the argument is placed in an appendix is its different format from the main chapters. The appendix is written in the form of a medieval "disputed question," which readers of Aquinas will immediately recognize. The disputed question format provides a way to "map" the various arguments leveled in debates over the possibility of coexistence of acquired and infused virtue in the same person.

This book offers a scholarly account of Thomistic thought on growing in virtue. As such it is at times technical and its treatment of recent academic disputes is geared toward scholars of morality and Aquinas. Still, no topic is more applicable to daily life than growth in virtue. Perhaps one day this work will in some way inform the efforts of those focused on human formation, particularly among children. In the shorter term, I hope readers will see the dynamics of dispositions and habits in their own lives and further their own ongoing journey of growing in virtue.

NOTES

1. Annas, *Intelligent Virtue*, 21.
2. For a description of an acting person's ends and activities, see Vogler, *Reasonably Vicious*, 102. For a rejection of some "right-making" feature of human action distinct from a person's ends and activities, see Annas, *Intelligent Virtue*, 48, in which Annas relies on Hursthouse, *On Virtue Ethics*, 25–87.
3. For a recent book that does engage the social and natural sciences in relation to virtue, see Sullivan, *Habits and Holiness*.

CHAPTER 1

HABITS

Second Nature Perfections of Personal Potential

Theologian and ethicist Stanley Hauerwas looks back at his work on virtue in a 2017 essay. While many consider his early writing on virtue groundbreaking, Hauerwas uses the essay to acknowledge his own "failure to develop the significance of habit for any account of the virtues."[1] Hauerwas is not alone. Contemporary scholars of morality consistently neglect careful analysis of habits in their examination of virtue.

In Thomas Aquinas's Aristotelian account, virtues are habits that make their possessor good. Vices, conversely, are habits that make their possessor bad. Yet scholars rarely reflect on what exactly habits are and how they relate to individual selves or to their activities.[2] Some scholars distance virtues from acts, either endorsing virtue ethics as an improvement on "act-centered" morality or criticizing it for failing to account for "right action."[3] Others have distanced virtue ethics from natural law.

The following Thomistic account of habit explores how habits perfect individuals by stably changing individuals and therefore influencing their activities. Habits are related to both the individual on one hand and the individual's activities on the other. Habits are not unchangeable features of who a person is; yet habits are far more stable than a person's particular activities. Conversely, they are "deeper" than particular acts yet still intimately related to specific actions. Thus habits are presented here as a middle ground, or level, residing between a person and her acts. We might imagine three levels: level one is the person; level two is the person's habits (and dispositions); and level three is the person's actions. Each level is orientated toward the person's ends, or goals, in an increasingly specific way.

Through this examination we will arrive at a Thomistic definition of habit as the stable specification of a person's powers to do certain activities in certain ways. To reach the conclusion we engage in a two-part analysis of the description of habits—and thus virtues as good habits—as "second nature." Why are habits *second* nature (level two), rather than simply *nature* (level one)? Many scholars fail to recognize habits as qualifications of natural human powers. If habits are second nature, a virtue morality approach must attend to nature; thus we repudiate the chasm often suggested between a virtue approach and natural law.

The second part of our analysis examines why habits are second *nature*. If habits are not nature, why call them "second" nature? Why are they more akin to nature than particular activities are? Why are they needed, that is, why does nature alone not suffice for guiding individuals to act, flourish, and attain their ends? The second part offers an account of how habits (level two) contribute to activities (level three) and in the end perfect the person (level one). It addresses which features render some human powers in need of habituation, what such habits provide to those human powers, and why habits are natural.

SECOND NATURE

Why are habits a person's second nature, rather than simply her nature? Aquinas claims in the *Summa Theologiae* that habits are "qualities."[4] The English cognate is helpful. Habits qualify what already exists.

In Aristotelian terminology, an entity is defined by its "substantial form." Also known as essence or nature, an entity's substantial form cannot change without the entity ceasing to be itself. Aristotle says entities have many "accidental" features (or "forms") that can change without altering their essence.[5] Being tall or hungry or brave are human characteristics that can and do change, even as the characterized person remains the same person "underneath," we might say.

Aristotle enumerates various categories of accidental forms. Qualities are one category, and habits are one quality type.[6] Critically, habits (level two) are not substantial forms (level one). Why does Aquinas begin each of his virtue treatises by making this Aristotelian distinction? Because his contemporaries commonly misunderstood virtue and confused virtues (i.e., good habits) with the entities they qualified. Indeed, it is in the context of his addressing growth in virtue that Aquinas offers his most extensive treatment of the point. He offers a warning, which is applicable today: "Many make mistakes about *forms* [such as virtues] by treating them as if they were substances. This seems to happen because forms are described by using nouns, just as substances are, albeit abstract nouns, such as whiteness or virtue."[7]

Aquinas goes on to say, virtues do not "give their subject its being as a substance, as the substantial forms do." Rather, he says, virtues qualify what already exists. His description of what happens when a person attains a habit is perhaps more precise: "The process of coming into being (which concludes with there being a form) [such as a virtue] does not belong to the form, but to the subject."[8] When we talk about habits and virtues we are also talking about what they qualify—that is, people and their powers to act. Attaining a habit is a qualification, a change, a stable specification of a person's power to do a certain activity a certain way.[9] As Aquinas says, "A form is said to come into being not because it itself comes into being, but because something comes to be it."[10] For example, when you tell your friend that his son has "gotten tall," you are acknowledging that the son is the same person both before and after becoming tall. Yet now that same person (level one) has taken on a new quality of tallness (level two). He has not so much "gained" tallness as he has *become* tall. He is still who he was before (level one), but he is that person in a new, specific, and stable way. Similarly with virtue, although it would not be inaccurate to say a person *gains* temperance, it would be less misleading to say the person—or, more exactly, her sensual desires—has *become* temperate. Her sensual desires, which existed before and after the "arrival" of the habit, have become stably ordered toward a more specific way of sensually desiring.

If habits are second nature and only qualify what already exists, what exactly do they qualify? They qualify the sort of creature their possessor is. Any living creature possesses a nature that is inclined to certain activities as expressed through particular "powers," to use Aquinas's term. We might also refer to these powers as capacities, or personal potential. A human person, for instance, is ordered by nature to various activities, such as eating, making decisions, communicating, resisting threats, and so on. These powers are not wholly open-ended. They are specified so as to incline their possessor toward certain activities to achieve certain ends or goals. To use an obvious example, a person is not ordered simply to eat but to eat in a manner that is nourishing, relationship-building, and so forth. By nature (level one) a person already aspires to the goals or ends of her power's activities with some degree of specificity, although that specification is still quite underdetermined. Regarding animals, we commonly use the term "instincts" to refer to the way natural powers are specified. For humans, we more commonly use the term "inclinations."[11] Aquinas calls these beginnings of virtue that a person possesses by nature "seeds."[12]

Prior to possessing any habit, therefore, a person is by nature already inclined toward certain activities. David Decosimo addresses the point with reference to eating and temperance: "Note well, though, habit does not *cause* the appetitive power to desire food—that desire, instead, is what habit works upon, shapes, and perfects. The subject [that] habit perfects always has an initial but insufficiently determined [i.e., specified] direction or inclination, [an] inchoate, underdetermined beginning. . . . The habit itself is not this beginning but what habit presupposes."[13] Habit does not supply an individual's initial inclinations and the ends toward which they are directed, but rather further specifies those ends.

Following Aristotle, Aquinas calls habits *qualities* because they *qualify* what is already present. Habits qualify a person's nature or, more specifically, a person's distinct natural powers or various ways a person has potential to act. A person is inclined toward various activities that together, in a manner unified by its soul, enable it to flourish.[14] Habits qualify various powers to give more specificity to their ends. When stable specification that is provided by habit is conducive to a person's flourishing, it is a virtue. When it impedes that flourishing, it is a vice. An account of habits must therefore attend to how habits qualify a person's natural inclinations and dynamisms such that the latter are actualized more specifically.

Why should we begin a consideration of how to grow in virtue by claiming that habits (level two) are not a person's nature (level one)? Because when an individual gains a virtue, the person does not gain the power to act toward some end supplied by nature. Rather, the power to act changes so that its end is pursued in a more specific way. Aquinas claims a virtue "is said to come into being not because it itself comes into being, but because something comes to be it."[15] A virtue is like a tool, augmenting or perfecting a person's power for a certain activity. Yet a virtue is also unlike a tool in that it is not an artifact. There is no distance between a person's power and the way that power is qualified. When a person gains or loses a virtue, the individual does not gain or lose the power to act toward a goal at hand; she simply gains or loses the power's qualification to act in a specific way toward that goal.

Furthermore, habits are not agents. Habits do nothing on their own. They qualify a person's powers so the individual performs activities in a certain way. Thus, temperance does not act; rather, the person, whose sensual desires might be temperate, acts.[16] Understanding that habits are qualifications of a person's already possessed potential is critical for constructing an account of growth in virtue.

In moral theology, a discussion of nature requires consideration of natural law. Despite some important scholarly protestations, a natural law approach to moral theology is too often distanced from, contrasted with, or even excluded from a virtue approach.[17] Contrast may actually apply to certain less adequate conceptions of natural law or approaches to virtue. For instance, if we do not accept that the negative and positive norms of natural law specify activities incompatible with or constitutive of ends supplied by a person's nature and further specified by virtues, it is possible to imagine a natural law ethic that ignores virtue. Conversely, if we conceive of virtue as an ideal toward which a person can act without impacting the specification of particular actions, we can endorse a virtue ethic while rejecting natural law. However, if we accept that a natural law ethic identifies continuity between a person's nature (level one) and a person's activity (level three), attention to habit (level two) necessarily complements natural law.

An adequate virtue approach to moral theology is, in fact, unintelligible without taking some account of the virtuous agent's nature.[18] Virtues are second nature and thus qualify and perfect their subject's nature. Scholars commonly disagree about what is "natural," particularly with regard to areas like human sexuality. They contest both which activities (level three) are in accord with human nature (level one) and how to describe human nature itself. I do not claim that the role of natural law in relation to virtue is to supply a self-evident foundation. In fact, many seem to repudiate natural law's relationship with virtue precisely due to exactly this poor operative definition of natural law. Nevertheless, some recognition of a subject's nature and the flourishing toward which nature orients the person is indispensable for a Thomistic virtue account.[19] Rather than offer such an account of nature or specific arguments about natural inclinations, I consider a creature's nature only to situate a virtue approach to moral theology as integrated with natural law properly understood.

Habits are not nature, but second nature. They qualify a person's already existing nature. This conception does not denigrate the importance of habit. To the contrary, as is evident in the following section, habits are crucial for actualizing a person's natural potential.

SECOND *NATURE*

Granting that habits are qualifications but not the same as the powers they qualify, why are habits needed? Why can't individuals simply operate in constant interaction with their environments? In other words, if a person's nature (level one) orients her toward activity constitutive of flourishing (level three), where do habits fit in?

Having examined the relationship between nature and habits, we now consider the relationship between habits and activity: What characteristics of human powers make them amenable to possessing habits? What does habit possession provide for the powers' activities? How are these qualifications second nature?

Aquinas addresses the need for habits several times in his corpus. While these treatments do not contradict each other, they do offer different emphases.[20] In his discussion of underdetermination, Aquinas suggests habits are needed when it is possible to act in various ways, as opposed to simply acting or not acting.[21] When does this situation *not* occur? God, for example, does not need habits. God has no potentiality or imperfection, and His activity is His essence.[22] Or consider the lack of underdetermination in human bodily and nutritive powers. Though unlike God, these natural powers can be moved or prompted by outside influences; the acts prompted by these powers are toward one end. They are already stably specified toward one act and thus do not require habits to stably specify them.

Aquinas suggests that habituation-amenable powers are not only underdetermined; they also are not solely determined by whatever prompts or moves them. The power is not only moved but also a mover. In other words, the specification of the power's activity is not provided wholly from the outside. Aquinas claims this condition rules out the exterior senses as needing habits.[23] Though underdetermined in that what a person sees or hears can activate the exterior senses in different ways, they are specified solely by whatever moves her to act. For Aquinas, there "is not in them . . . some form that is immanent in its possessor" playing a causal role in specifying activities. The exterior senses' powers and their interaction with the environment suffice to specify activities. If all a person's powers operated in the way Aquinas understood exterior senses to operate, we would have no need for habits.[24]

Aquinas says the activities of habituation-amenable powers entail "many things coming together," which can be "measured out in various ways."[25] Though the claim in part reaffirms underdetermination, Aquinas claims underdetermined powers not only entail various ways of being measured but also that they can dispose of their subject "well or poorly," an important characteristic.

So, what characterizes human powers that can be habituated? These human powers are prompted from the outside—unlike God, but like natural capacities and exterior senses—and their activities are neither determined toward one act (as with natural powers) nor wholly specified by exterior movers (as with exterior senses). Some mediating cause influences the activation and specification of the power's activity beyond, but also including, the person's own natural principles and the outside impetus. Thus, habituation-amenable powers toward certain sorts of activities can be actualized in diverse ways and can be done well or poorly.

Aquinas concludes that powers needing habits "are fulfilled for activity through the help of something extra; that, however, is in them in the manner not of passive experience, but of a form that rests and remains in its possessor."[26] This causal influence, or "something extra," is habit. His conclusion implies two characteristic features of habits.

First, habits are forms—the specifications—of a power to do an activity in a certain way. In other words, though a person's powers are inclined by nature to certain specified goals or ends, habits provide further specification. A person by nature has a dynamic inclination toward eating. Nature supplies the goal of eating with some specificity. People are not inclined to eat rust, but rather nourishing food. This end of nourishment is underdetermined by nature, however, and made more specific in the process of habituation: a temperate person has the natural inchoate end of eating for nourishment, but that end is further specified by habit in terms of nutritional value, amount of food, and setting for eating. The specification is not nature, but second nature. It is not activity, but aids activity. Any activity that occurs out of habit is an instantiation and further specification of the habit, which is itself a further specification of a person's natural ends.[27] Hence, the habit (level two) specifies the more inchoate ends supplied by the person's nature (level one) in pursuit of the end in particular activities (level three).[28]

Second, Aquinas's description of the "something extra" supplied by habit indicates its critical feature of stability. Aquinas says habit as a form "rests and remains" in a person; it becomes part of the person.[29] Stability, however, does not indicate a shift in nature because habits are changeable. Their stability, however, prompts the description "second nature."

Most of the present discussion addresses how habits are attained or grow (or lost or diminish, for that matter). However, it is first crucial to address what exactly habits are. Habits are qualifications of a person's powers toward certain types of activities. They stably specify the powers with more particular ends than supplied by nature so their possessor is inclined to do activities in a certain way. Before turning to how they aid a person's activity (level three), two brief points are in order.

Exactly which human powers are habituated? We have addressed the necessary features of habituation-amenable powers: underdetermination, moved-mover, exercised well or poorly. But we have not identified the powers themselves. How we enumerate the powers that are able to be habituated results in the list of habits (virtues or vices) that can qualify them. Part of the answer to what one scholar calls the "enumeration problem" depends on an account of human nature (level one), or which human capacities possess the features of habituation-amenable powers.[30] For Aquinas the habituation-amenable powers are the human dynamisms toward knowing the truth (apprehension) and pursuing the good (appetite), both of which have their object supplied by or at least informed by reason. Aquinas therefore enumerates the four cardinal virtues, in line with the long tradition of Plato, the Old Testament, Cicero, and early church thinkers. Aquinas regards the cardinal virtues as qualifying the habituation-amenable powers—namely, practical intellect, will, irascible passions, and concupiscible passions—so that their resulting activities are more readily done well. The hesitance in modern moral philosophy to offer a robust account of human nature has dissuaded many from being as specific as Aquinas, though when they do it usually approximates the four cardinal virtues.[31] If we understand the cardinal virtues as encompassing the moral life accessible to unaided reason, the various activities toward which they are directed lead us to create lists of more specific virtues.[32] For example, if the general virtue temperance broadly qualifies a person's sensual desires, the power's distinguishable objects can lead to virtues like sobriety or chastity. The myriad ways to delineate activities (level three) leads to further lists of virtues. Yet while we need not completely enumerate the virtues, including what Aquinas calls the "parts" of general virtues, it is important to note that this enumeration problem pertains to both the various morally significant facets of a person's nature (level one) and the various ways activities can be differentiated (level three).[33]

Having situated habits between individuals and their acts, we must next address a critique of this level's very existence. Dubbed the "situationist challenge" to virtue by Nancy Snow and advanced by John Doris and Gilbert Harman, this critique rejects the existence of character traits and their impact on activity. These scholars claim the features of a situation, not stable habits, cause a person's activities.[34] Situationism, whose history extends back at least half a century, has several distinct variations, each essentially suggesting that habits (level two) do not exist as a distinct causal influence residing between individuals and their activities.[35] Snow and others have ably defeated this critique, generally by distinguishing poor "trait psychology" targeted by situationists from a more psychologically sophisticated account of habits.[36] While this task is far beyond the scope of this project, the situationist challenge is noted here simply to "situate" it with regard to Aquinas's argument on why habits (level two) are needed and what they causally contribute to activity (level three).

Concluding his most extensive treatment of the subject, Aquinas offers three reasons why virtues as good habits are needed to perfect habituation-amenable powers.[37] He does not describe the features of human powers that make them amenable to habituation, but instead and relatedly what habits supply to the powers and their activities. Though the context is his treatment of virtue, what Aquinas says virtuous habits provide are actually features of habits more generally, and thus they occur also in the case of vices as bad habits (a topic addressed later).

The first feature that habits supply to the powers they qualify is consistency of activity, or *uniformitas*. Aquinas makes it clear he is referring to stability: "For those things depending solely on activity are easily changed, unless they be stabilized by habitual inclination."[38] Assuming a power is amenable to habituation, the stability of the habitual inclination grants the activity of that power consistency in its activity.

The second feature a habit grants is promptness. Aquinas says the cause of promptness is the specificity habits supply to a person's natural, less specific ends: "Unless the rational power is in some way inclined to one thing by habit, it will always be necessary when we act that inquiry precede activity. . . . Things done right away are from habit."[39] Aquinas suggests that habits, rather than nature, provide promptness to activity by supplying a person's potential with a more specific or particular end. Activity can then proceed from the power more readily. Indeed, promptness or "automaticity" is perhaps the feature most commonly associated with habit.[40]

The third feature habits provide is the ability for goals to be "pleasantly accomplished."[41] Activity proper to a person's nature is pleasant or delightful, since "fittingness is a cause of delight." We commonly call this attainment of ends "enjoyment" or "fulfillment." Fulfilling is actually a more apt designation. Though generally accompanied by pleasure, there are occasions when such pleasure can be thwarted (discussed in chapters 5 and 7). Since a habit qualifies a power with a more specific end inclining a person toward activity (level three), it is a "sort of nature" (*per modum cuiusdam naturae*). Activity instantiating that end in a particular context constitutes a fruition that is quasi-natural (i.e., second nature) and thus pleasant.[42] Habits make activity in accordance with a person's habit connatural and thus pleasant. In sum, habituation enables a person's activity to be consistent, to be more readily done, and to "feel" right.

Having addressed what characterizes habituation-amenable human powers and identified what habituation provides, how are habits second *nature*? Consider three reasons. Our operative definition of habit is the stable specification of a person's power to do some sort of activity in a particular way. Habits are therefore a "sort of nature" because they are stable and abiding. They equip a person with ends more specific than ends supplied by nature alone, albeit still requiring instantiation in particular actions (level three). Such ends rest or remain stably in the possessor, even if they may increase, decrease, or even be lost. As second nature, habits and virtues may not be as stable as their possessor's nature but they qualify the powers of nature in an enduring manner that is "difficult to change."[43]

Habits also qualify undetermined human powers and enable a person to attain perfection or completion through their contribution to activity or the attainment of ends. Aquinas follows Aristotle in claiming that "because potency is said with reference to act, a potency is fulfilled when it has its complete activity."[44] Habits enable human powers to operate consistently, promptly, and pleasantly. Since "a thing is good insofar as it has a complete ordering to its end . . . virtue makes one having it good and makes his work good."[45] Thus "virtue . . . points to the perfection of a power."[46] Virtue is not simply natural in its stability; it is also so in its enabling individuals to attain their ends or reach their potential. Virtues are not an "add-on" to nature; rather, they are actualizations and perfections of nature. In the same way an individual's spoken language ability is an actualization, not an add-on to her nature as a linguistic animal, virtues bring fulfillment to a person's nature.

"Natural" is a notoriously difficult word to define. It can have a variety of meanings, from possessed at birth, to commonplace ("to err is human"), to distinct from reason (such as the biological), among others. In fact, each of these three senses are addressed in one article where Aquinas examines whether or not vice is natural.[47] Yet, as pertaining to humans and their actions as rational animals, Aquinas claims that "natural" properly means "according to the order of reason." Thus a third reason habits are natural is that they enable a person to act according to the order of reason, in a manner constitutive of human flourishing. This conception of nature is similar to the previous definition, where habits are described as natural because they enable human power perfection through activity.[48] Added here is that it is not simply the exercise of the person's rational powers but their accurate exercise.

This raises the question of whether or not vices are natural. Are vices perfections of a person's powers? Vices as habits are stable specifications of a person's potential toward certain activities, and they grant an activity stability, promptness, and pleasure. Aquinas is clear that individuals can become accustomed to activities not in accordance with the ends supplied by nature, and when he mentions how this happens he lists causes that may also engender virtues.[49] Hence the importance of good formation, the dynamics of which are the focus here. However, in the fullest sense of natural as constitutive of a rational human person's flourishing, vices are unnatural.[50] They deform the person, deploying the natural dynamics of habituation in a manner corrosive to flourishing.[51] They qualify the person such that certain activities are connatural, even though the activities in reality do not constitute attainment of ends supplied by nature.

In both vicious and virtuous individuals, habit formation and practical reasoning informed by a person's habits share similarities. Candace Vogler argues in *Reasonably Vicious* that, shorn of a "substantive account of the good," we cannot make the case that viciousness is a failure of practical reasoning.[52] She relies on the work of scholars like Philippa Foot and James McDowell to address how "metaphysics of value" arguments can be made in contemporary moral philosophy.[53] This inquiry is far beyond the scope of this book. Our task is not to offer a justification of particular virtues or depict which activities truly constitute happiness. Rather, we address the mechanics of growing in virtue, including virtues' status as habits, their manner of attainment, and how they increase and decrease. Given that virtues are habits, most of the dynamics described also apply to vice.[54] We do find differences, but a useful analysis of virtue can help us understand how vices as habits are attained or lost and can increase or decrease.[55]

Habits are natural. They are necessary, since the human person possesses certain powers that are underdetermined and motivated by outside influences (even if not wholly determined from the outside). Habits are stable specifications of human powers with more particular ends than those supplied by nature. Their ends neither necessitate nor determine particular actions; rather, they contribute to human activity by providing consistency, promptness, and pleasure. Since virtues as habits enable a person to flourish in a stable manner, they are rightly called natural, albeit second nature.

The common description of habit as second nature helps delineate in the ways a habit is a qualification of, and therefore distinct from, a person's nature and the ways that qualification is nonetheless "natural" to the person, since it stably orders the person toward activity commensurate with the habit. Thus habits (level two) are "in between" a person (level one) and her activity (level three). We have established an operative definition of habit: the stable specification of a person's powers that are amenable to habituation, ordering the person toward activity commensurate with the habit. When such habits incline her toward activities constitutive of happiness, these qualifications are virtues. Next we will examine two different but related ways a person can be qualified, ways that are distinguished precisely by the degree of stability and the origin of specification. But in closing I offer, with some trepidation, an attempt to visually depict these three levels.

Since reference to these three levels will persist throughout this project, a visual depiction of this schema may be of service—but is offered with some hesitation, knowing that any visual metaphor will be beset by as many disanalogous features as analogous ones. Recognizing the potential of any visual depiction to mislead, I nevertheless offer an accessible one that has the potential to illuminate the dynamic of the levels and provides a ready tool to address questions about, or debates over, them. If the image must eventually be revised (or even discarded), still, my hope is that it will advance the discussion by clarifying why any such change would be needed.

The two archers represent differently qualified individuals. Level one refers to the natural powers of the person. These powers have ends, but those ends are only beginnings and most underdetermined. Level two refers to habits: the stable specifications of a person's natural powers but with more particular ends that aid, even though they neither determine nor necessitate, action. The different ways the archers are habituated is represented by their varying musculature, grooming, and outfits. Their actions, proceeding from who they are and have been qualified to be, are represented by the arrows, which are aimed toward a target and hit that mark with varying degrees of success.

Some insights (and certain inadequacies) likely leap out from this image, so it is important to clarify what the image is intended to depict (the relationship between the three levels) what it does not depict, how it does both, and which aspects of it can be misleading.

Each sketched archer (person) and her natural powers do have ends, but these are least specified. Though there are two archers and they are variously qualified and habituated, notice that their natural ends (level one) are the same. The archers are qualified (here in two different ways) in a manner that further specifies the ends they have. The various specifications of the archers' ends are depicted by degree of physical fitness, apparel, and presentableness—the (virtuous) archer with good habits and the (vicious) archer with bad habits are indicated by the variation in clothing, musculature, and being well kempt or unkempt. The archers are depicted as distinct yet overlapping persons to indicate there is no distance, if you will, between each person and her qualifications. This is not meant to indicate that in real life we can observe a delineation between a person's natural ends (level one) and her habits (level two). The figure depicts both that there is a nature "underneath" the person's habits (the spatial metaphor being obviously inadequate) and also no distance between the person and her habits, even though habituation can change with the same person (again, inadequately) underneath.

The array of shots each archer has taken toward the target indicates the person's activity (level three). Given the contingent nature of practical action, it is not the case that all the virtuous archer's shots hit the target perfectly, nor that the vicious archer's shots all fail completely. Nevertheless, the virtuous archer clearly hits the mark more frequently and accurately, while the reverse is true of the vicious archer.

What does this visual depict? It visually depicts the three levels in a related yet distinguishable manner. They are all oriented toward the same end, with increasing specificity. Habits are depicted between a person and her acts, inclining her well or poorly toward the target. Particularly through clothing and fitness, there is a certain stability to that specification of the archer's ends, even while that stable specification can change. Though the habituation (level two) of the archer facilitates (virtue) or impedes (vice) good shooting, such habituation neither necessitates that both archers shoot, nor how well they shoot. More is required for particular actions than the possession of habits, namely, a person's concrete instantiation of an end through practical reasoning (level three). Specific end-oriented activity is influenced by her habits, though not determined by them.

Where to start with all the aspects of habituation that this visual does *not* depict! Despite the enormously important distinction between habits and dispositions, both at level two, this distinction is not depicted here. Perhaps it could be shown with the degree of acuity (or fuzziness) at level two, or varying vibrancy (or fadedness) of color. Nor is there any depiction here of the different reasons a disposition does not qualify as a habit. Relatedly, there is no indication of the (efficient) cause of dispositions or habits, another crucial topic for this project. Finally, there is no statement regarding natural versus supernatural targets, and how they are related to each other.

In addition to certain aspects of habituation *not* depicted, there are also some potentially misleading features of this visual. Clothing seems an inaccurate portrayal of habits since what we wear is more obviously external to who we are. The better depiction on that front is the musculature of each archer, since there are no muscles separate from how they are toned, even though their tone may increase or decrease. Similarly, depictions of poor habituation by disheveled hair and wrinkly clothes can suggest habits are less stable, and more easily changeable, than they are. Despite protestations that habits are not artifacts or tools, the use of the archer visual requires a bow and a quiver of arrows, and these instruments are (rightly) not readily placed at level one or level two.

This visual also fails to depict the various types of virtues or vices and their relation to various natural powers. It is not true, for instance, that one arm is temperance, one leg is fortitude, and so on. The visual aptly depicts good and bad habituation on the whole, rather than the distinctions and relationships between different habits and their relationship to different natural powers.

All these qualifications notwithstanding, this visual is offered in an effort to depict how the most underdetermined ends of a person and her powers supplied by nature are, to different degrees and from a variety of causal influences, habituated well or poorly so as to be her second nature. The stable specification provided by habits toward a person's various ends issues forth, though not deterministically, into most particular concrete actions that hit the mark to varying degrees.

NOTES

1. Hauerwas, "Habit Matters." For Hauerwas's role in the late-twentieth-century resurgence in virtue scholarship, see Cloutier and Mattison, "The Resurgence of Virtue in Recent Moral Theology."
2. There are exceptions, including a classic work on habit from a Thomistic perspective: Klubertanz, *Habits and Virtues*. Recently scholars have begun to remedy the neglect. See Decosimo, *Ethics as a Work of Charity*; Austin, *Aquinas on Virtue*; Miner, "Aquinas on *Habitus*"; Kahm, *Aquinas on Emotions' Participation in Reason*; Knobel, *Thomas Aquinas on the Infused Moral Virtues*; and Sullivan, *Habits and Holiness*.
3. For an example of the former, see Salzman and Lawler, *Virtue and Theological Ethics*: "Our method is a virtue ethical method. It focuses primarily not on the acts a person must do to be ethical, but on the person and his/her character, and only secondarily on the acts he/she must do to be virtuous" (6). For a dismissal of this contrast, see Russell, *Practical Intelligence and the Virtues*, 1–2. For an examination of the common contrast between virtue ethics and act-centered morality, see Hursthouse, *On Virtue Ethics*, 25–29. For the capacity of virtue ethics to account for right action, see Hursthouse, *On Virtue Ethics*, 25–42; Russell, *Practical Intelligence and the Virtues*, 37–71; and Solomon, "Internal Objections to Virtue Ethics," 437–39.

4. Aquinas, *Summa Theologiae* I–II 49,1. Aquinas begins his two most important treatments of virtue by saying virtues are habits, which are therefore qualities. See also *Summa Theologiae* I–II 55,1; and Aquinas, *Disputed Questions on Virtue,* a. 1. All *Summa Theologiae* texts (hereafter ST) are taken from Leonine Commission Critical Edition (Latin) and the Dominicans' translation (English). The passages cited from *Disputed Questions on Virtue,* both Latin and English, are generally taken from the Ralph McInerny translation. There are five such disputed questions: the first, "on Virtue in General," is cited here as *De virt.*; the second, "on Charity," is cited as *De car.*; and the fifth, "on the Cardinal Virtues," is cited as *De virt. card.* See also E. M. Atkins's English translation of all five disputed questions in Aquinas, *Disputed Questions on the Virtues* (which, when used, are identified as Atkins).
5. For Aristotle's account of accidents and the substantial forms they characterize, see "Categories," Book *viii,* 23–28.
6. It is not necessary for our purposes to explain the differences between the various categories of accidents nor the various types within the particular category of "quality." How a habit qualifies a person (i.e., what it means to possess a habit) is addressed later. Chapter 2 addresses differences between habits and dispositions, which Aristotle groups into one category.
7. *De virt.* a. 11 (Atkins).
8. *De virt.* a. 11 (Atkins). In *Summa Theologiae,* Aquinas says: "This distinction is not to be understood as implying that the form has a being outside its matter or subject" (ST I–II 52,1).
9. Conversely, the loss of a habit is a disqualification or requalification.
10. *De virt.* a. 11 (Atkins).
11. For a comparable treatment of given ends being supplied by instincts, relying on both Immanuel Kant as well as Aristotle, see Korsgaard, *Self-Constitution,* 104–7. For an exploration of Aquinas's increasing use of *instinctus* late in his career to refer to both human spiritual dynamics and supernatural dynamisms, particularly the gifts of the Holy Spirit, see Stroud, "*Instinctus* and the Gifts of the Holy Spirit"; and Pinckaers, "Morality and the Movement of the Holy Spirit." For a recent exploration of instinct in reference to natural law, see International Theological Commission, *In Search of a Universal Ethic,* particularly Mattison, "Part of the 'New Look' at Natural Law." For another look at several recent approaches to natural inclinations, see Levering, "Natural Law and Natural Inclinations."
12. For examples, see Aquinas, *Disputed Questions on Truth* (hereafter *De ver.*), XIV.2; and ST I–II 63,2 ad 1.
13. Decosimo, *Ethics as a Work of Charity,* 86–87. For a similar point, see Annas, *Intelligent Virtue.* Annas describes acquiring virtues as "forming the unformed motivations that we start with" (10).
14. Aquinas addresses the connection between one's soul and one's powers in ST I 77,1 and 77,6. For more on why habits qualify a creature's powers or capacities, not its soul, see Kahm, *Aquinas on Emotions' Participation in Reason,* 101–16. Kahm notes that an exception is grace, an accidental form qualifying the soul as well as its powers.
15. *De virt.* a. 11 (Atkins).
16. See chap. 4 for treatment of a mistranslation in the popular Dominicans' version of *Summa Theologiae* I–II 65,1, where prudence is ascribed agency.
17. For examples of distancing natural law from virtue, see Hursthouse, *On Virtue Ethics,* 211; as well as Salzman and Lawler's claim that they focus "primarily not on the acts a person

must do to be ethical [which act-based emphasis they associate with natural law], but on the person and his/her character" (*Virtue and Theological Ethics*), 6. For recent moralists insisting on virtue and natural law's compatibility, see Hibbs, *Virtue's Splendor*; Porter, *Nature as Reason*; and Rhonheimer, *The Perspective of Morality*. For a more dynamic account of natural law readily relatable to virtue, see the recent Vatican document on natural law in International Theological Commission, "In Search of a Universal Ethic."

18. Consider two possible manners of contrasting natural law and virtue. The first suggests incompatibility between virtue and "norm-based" natural law. For a repudiation of the dichotomy, see Annas, *The Morality of Happiness*. Hursthouse's influential treatment of the relationship between virtue and right action in *On Virtue Ethics* is endorsed and expanded in Russell, *Practical Intelligence and the Virtues*, 37–142; see also Hibbs, *Virtue's Splendor*, Porter, *Nature as Reason*; and Rhonheimer, *The Perspective of Morality*, for more recent repudiations of the dichotomy. The second stems from Christian ethics and moral theology and contrasts natural law morality with a grace-elevated Christian life, which the virtues more readily capture. For examinations with attention to Protestant natural law critiques, see essays by Jennifer Herdt, David Cloutier, Gilbert Meilaender, and Livio Melina in Berkman and Mattison, *Searching for a Universal Ethic*.
19. Despite many contemporary moral philosophers' adverse reactions to natural law, attention to the "givens" of the human person is essential if one accepts that virtues are habits and thus qualities. Hursthouse distances her project from "natural law theory" (*On Virtue Ethics*, 211) but recognizes the need for an "objective account of human nature" and offers such an account (192–216). See also Korsgaard, *Self-Constitution*, 33–43, 104–8. For criticism of Michael Slote on virtue as failing to attend to deliberate activity (level three) and nature (level one), see Russell, *Practical Intelligence and the Virtues*, 98.
20. For the three most important treatments, see *De virt.* a. 1; ST I–II 49,4 and 50,1; and ST I–II 55,1. *De virt.* a. 1 begins with fifteen objections, the first eight of which propose that virtues (as habits) are acts or activities. For objections that virtues are powers rather than qualities see ST I–II 49,4 obj. 1–3, and 55,1 obj. 1.
21. Underdetermination is crucial for establishing a need for habituation. In Aquinas's shorter treatments of the need for habituation, underdetermination is the only feature mentioned that renders human powers in need of habituation mentioned. See ST I–II 55,1. Aquinas does not claim that the powers are determined to nothing, but rather to "many things" (*ad multa*) and thus requiring further specification that comes through possession of habit.
22. See *De virt.* a. 1; and ST I–II 49,4. For God, we make no distinction between the entity (level one) and His activities (level three), thus there is no need for habits (level two) to aid in perfection.
23. See *De virt.* a. 1; and ST I–II 50,3 ad 3. ST I–II 56,5 addresses the ways the interior senses can be habituated (or, more properly, disposed): by implication denying exterior sense habituation.
24. For an in-depth treatment of the exterior senses' complexities, see Pasnau, *Thomas Aquinas on Human Nature*, 278–95.
25. See ST I–II 49,4. The Dominicans' translation uses the more mechanical "adjusted" rather than "measured out": "*Quod plura concurrant ad disponendum subiectum ad unum eorum ad quae est in potentia, quae diversis modis commensurari possunt.*" The claim is repeated later in the same article in reference to the person and activity: "Since there are

many things for whose natures and operations several things must concur which may vary in their relative adjustability [*quae diversis modis commensurari possunt*], it follows that habit is necessary."

26. *De virt.* a. 1 (trans. Atkins). The passage continues as follows: "Action belongs to them as powers which are in a sense rational and these powers are completed in acting by something superadded . . . in such a way, however, that by it the power is not necessitated to one, since then the power would not have dominion over its act. The virtues of these powers are not the powers themselves, nor passion, as with sensitive powers, nor qualities acting necessarily, like the qualities of natural things. Rather, they are habits thanks to which one can act when he likes."
27. Aquinas recognizes that a person can possess a habit and yet act in a manner not proceeding from that habit. See, e.g., *De virt. card.*, a. 6 ad 12. This is a crucial point for making changes to habits.
28. Aquinas quite explicitly describes habits as existing between nature and activity; see ST I–II 49,3 and 49,4, and I–II 54,2.
29. The latter term, *manet*, is often translated as "stays" or "abides."
30. See Russell, *Practical Intelligence and the Virtues,* 145–236.
31. Scholars who provide a robust account have typically approximated the four cardinal virtues. See Annas, *Intelligent Virtue,* 98. Russell also arrives at a "cardinality" solution to the enumeration problem but says naming the cardinal virtues is largely up to the virtue theorist (*Practical Intelligence and the Virtues,* 151–58). He notes that one contemporary social scientific account of character, Seligman's VIA (Values in Action) Project, offers a list of virtues with a cardinality approach (156). For another example of contemporary social science arriving at claims similar to premodern anthropology, see Snow's support of virtue using the cognitive affective personality system (CAPS), which is fundamentally a connection of cognition (Thomistic apprehension) and affect (Thomistic appetite), in Snow, *Virtues as Social Intelligence,* 20, 38. Russell relates CAPS to an account of virtue (*Practical Intelligence and the Virtues,* 247–62).
32. For an examination of Aquinas's understanding of general and particular virtues, see Houser, *The Cardinal Virtues,* 66–82; and Houser, "The Virtue of Courage (IIa–IIae qq. 123–140)." See also Porter, "The Virtue of Justice (IIa–IIae qq. 58–122)."
33. For a summary of the different types of parts of virtue and as applied to prudence, see ST II–II 48. See also Houser, *The Cardinal Virtues,* 51–82. It is this dynamic that has led to the often long and varied lists of virtues, a dynamic that can make a virtue approach to ethics more supple and attuned to cultural contexts even if more "messy." As a point of contrast, that Stoics' claim that there is only one morally significant part of the human person (level one) leads to their claim that there is only one virtue (level two), namely, *phronesis*. For a helpful introduction to this issue see Annas, *Morality of Happiness,* 73–84, esp. 80.
34. See Harman, "Moral Philosophy Meets Social Psychology." See also Doris, *Lack of Character.*
35. For an examination of the debate, see Snow, *Virtue as Social Intelligence,* 1–13. To understand situationists' various claims, see Miller, "Virtue Cultivation in Light of Situationism." See also Miller, *Moral Character,* 1–26.
36. For a situationism rebuttal, see Snow, *Virtue as Social Intelligence;* and Snow, "Notes Toward an Empirical Study of Virtue." Snow offers an "empirically adequate" virtue account (38) and details the features of "automaticity" characterizing virtues (39–62).

Her account of virtue as social intelligence is similar to what is described by others as skill. Like Snow, Russell relies on a CAPS account of personality to respond to the situationist challenge in *Practical Intelligence and the Virtues*, 239–331, though Russell grants situationists more than Snow does (e.g., agent construal).

37. *De virt.* a. 1.
38. *De virt.* a. 1: "*Ea enim quae ex sola operatione dependent, facile immutantur, nisi secundum aliquam inclinationem habitualem fuerint stabilita*" (author's translation).
39. *De virt* a. 1: "*Nisi enim potentia rationalis per habitum aliquo modo inclinetur ad unum, oportebit semper, cum necesse fuerit operari, praecedere inquisitionem de operatione; . . . repentina sunt ab habitu*" (author's translation). The last phrase is a citation of Aristotle's *Nic. Eth.* iii.8, 979. While the second feature is commonly described as promptness, Aquinas clearly says it results from specificity. If one were to always act promptly in one area of activity but not promptly toward a specific sort of activity, the person would not possess the habit. Austin describes the phenomenon in *Aquinas on Virtue*, 28–29: "A habit reduces complexity to unity and orders a power or capacity of the soul to a single act."
40. Snow labels promptness "goal dependent automaticity" (*Virtues as Social Intelligence*, 39) and provides features of automaticity (43). Her work can easily be connected to Aquinas's account of virtual ordering (ST I–II 1,6 ad 3).
41. *De virt.* a. 1.
42. For more on types of pleasure, see Klubertanz, *Habits and Virtues*, 166.
43. ST I–II 49,2 ad 3.
44. *De virt.* 1.
45. *De virt.* a. 1.
46. *De virt.* a. 1.
47. ST I–II 71,2.
48. See Porter, *Nature as Reason*, 176: "If the [level one] inclinations are to function in such a way as to promote the agent's true good, they must be directed by appropriate [level two] dispositions toward [level three] action—and this is precisely what the virtues are."
49. ST I–II 31,7. For a contemporary reflection, see Vogler, *Reasonably Vicious*, 54–56. Vogler describes a drastic example of how vices can make certain activities connatural, as when individuals can be habituated such that erotic knife play becomes second nature.
50. See the culminating article of Aquinas's treatise on habit, ST I–II 70,4 ad 1: "Works of virtue are connatural to reason, while works of vice are contrary to nature." A case can be made that the text is the culmination of Aquinas's treatise on happiness and virtue. For the initial claim, see Pinckaers, "Beatitude and the Beatitudes in Aquinas's *Summa Theologiae*," 115–29; and Berkman and Titus, *The Pinckaers Reader*, 124. For further exploration and defense, see Mattison, "Beatitude and the Beatitudes in the *Summa Theologiae* of St. Thomas Aquinas."
51. They do not, of course, obliterate the "form" of the person, as in nature (level one). But they are forms (level two) that are deforming in that they do not in reality conduce to the fulfillment of naturally supplied ends.
52. Vogler, *Reasonably Vicious*, 5, 193, 199. Though I endorse Vogler's recognition of the importance of a substantive account of the good, it is not the case that a "theological frame" alone can supply such an account (see *Reasonably Vicious*, 41; compare 67 and 199). Other scholars claim vice is a failure of practical reasoning, either on neo-Kantian

grounds (see Korsgaard, *Self-Constitution*, 179) or because vices lack some characteristic feature of virtue (see Annas, *Intelligent Virtue*, 104).

53. See Vogler, *Reasonably Vicious*, 192.
54. The obvious important exception concerns the infused virtues caused by God's grace.
55. One example of such a difference is how the virtues connect to one another in a manner that the vices do not.

CHAPTER 2

DISTINGUISHING HABITS AND DISPOSITIONS

Stability and Rationality

It is customary in scholarship on habit and virtue to address at some point the difference between the term "habit" as it is used colloquially and the term "habit" as it is used in the technical moral theological or philosophical sense. This distinction is important enough that a major influence on the current discussion, Fr. Servais Pinckaers, OP, titled one of his first publications "Virtue Is Not a Habit."[1] Pinckaers obviously means that virtue, in the Thomistic sense, is not a habit in the colloquial sense, since a virtue is indeed a habit on Aquinas's (or Aristotle's) terms. Yet it is not a habit if by that is meant an automatic, repetitive activity that does not engage a person's rationality. This potentially confusing difference between Aquinas's sense and the colloquial understanding is not only frequently noted in scholarship but even drives some to use the Latin term *habitus* for the richer sense of habit that characterizes a virtue approach to morality.[2] This practice is not adopted here, though the caveat is certainly true; by the end of this chapter it will be clear what is accurately captured by the colloquial sense of habit and yet what is lacking.

Our task is to offer a Thomistic account of the difference between habits and dispositions. Despite the heavy reliance on the thought of Aquinas in the recent resurgence in attention to virtue, there has been a stunning lack of attention to Aquinas's distinction between disposition and habit. A grasp of this distinction is important simply for a complete grasp of Aquinas's account of habit. Yet it is also important in a treatise on growth in virtue, since in one sense attaining a virtue or growing further in virtue entails movement from disposition to habit and because once a habit is possessed its growth can include the lessening or elimination of contrary dispositions. Finally, an additional reason the distinction between disposition and habit is important is that it serves as a valuable resource in facilitating connections between a

Thomistic account of habit and other literatures on (and the situationist critique of) habit.[3] Though such a dialogue is not undertaken in this project, an examination of the distinction between disposition and habit is a crucial resource in that endeavor.

This chapter begins with an examination of the classic text in Aquinas's work on distinguishing habits and dispositions. It notes different possible positions, based on this text, regarding the distinction between habits and dispositions. It turns out that the two candidates that serve as bases for this distinction result in different answers to the question, "Can dispositions become habits?" The next section offers a constructive account of the distinction between habits and distinctions based on the thought of Aquinas; this account reduces to neither of the two positions already stated. The third section returns to the question of whether or not dispositions can become habits and examines the ramifications of whether or not dispositions become habits (based on the account of what distinguishes habits and dispositions) as well as the broader topic of growth in virtue. Though extended attention to the processes of growth in virtue comes in ensuing chapters, this chapter proposes how an accurate grasp of the difference between dispositions and habits provides an invaluable resource for treatment of growth in virtue.

HABITS AND DISPOSITIONS: POSSIBLE BASES FOR DISTINCTION

The relationship between habits and dispositions is addressed by Aquinas at the beginning of his treatment of habits in the *Summa Theologiae*. As to the question of whether or not habit is a distinct species of quality, Aquinas responds to an objector who addresses the phrase "difficult to change" as a feature of habit.[4] Though it is a long quote, it is worth hearing Aquinas's reply:

> This difference, "difficult to change" (*difficile mobile*) does not distinguish habit from the other species of quality, but from disposition. Now disposition may be taken in two ways; in one way, as a genus of habit, for disposition is included in the definition of habit. . . . In another way, according as it is divided against habit. Again, disposition, properly so called, can be divided against habit in two ways: first as perfect and imperfect within the same species; and thus we call it a disposition, retaining the name of the genus, when it is had imperfectly, so as to be easily lost; whereas we call it a habit, when it is had perfectly, so as not to be lost easily. And thus a disposition

> becomes a habit, just as a boy becomes a man. Secondly, they may be distinguished as diverse species of one subaltern genus: so that we call dispositions, those qualities in the first species, which by reason of their nature are easily lost, because they have changeable causes [*causas transmutabiles*], e.g., sickness and health; whereas we call habits those qualities which, by reason of their very nature, are not easily changed, in that they have unchangeable causes [*causas immobiles*], e.g., knowledges and virtues. And in this sense, disposition does not become a habit.[5]

In one sense disposition can be considered a genus that includes both species of disposition and habit.[6] In this sense there are two types of dispositions, namely, habits and (mere) dispositions. (This meaning of disposition is uncontested, and here, for clarity's sake and except where explicitly noted, "disposition" does not refer to the genus containing both habits and dispositions. Rather, "inclination" is used as the genus term to include both species of dispositions and habits.[7])

However, in another sense, and the far more relevant one here, disposition is distinguished from habit, such that a habit is *not* a disposition. In this meaning of disposition as distinct from habit, there are two ways to understand the relationship between habit and disposition. First, a disposition could be something imperfect that is of the same sort as habit and "on the way" to becoming a habit even though not yet there.[8] Second, a disposition could be of a different kind than a habit, in which case it cannot become a habit (nor can a habit become a disposition).

Given that Aquinas goes on to say that it is in this last sense that Aristotle understood the relationship between disposition and habit, scholarship on this topic commonly addresses not only what Aristotle's position in fact was but also whether Aquinas adopts Aristotle's position or rather is simply identifying Aristotle's view.[9] Aristotle's view, and its conformity (or not) to Aquinas's view, is not the focus here. The focus here is how best to understand the relationship between habits and dispositions in a manner relying on Aquinas's thought on habit.[10]

One possible basis for making a distinction between habit and disposition is stability. Indeed, Aquinas opens by stating that their being "difficult to change" distinguishes habits from dispositions. If it were stability alone that distinguished habit and disposition, then *any* (level two) more particular specification of a human power's end or goal (level one) with a high degree of stability would constitute a habit, whereas a disposition would be any such more particular specification (level two) that was less stable. To use Aquinas's examples, virtue, knowledge, health, and beauty would all be habits if they were more stable, but dispositions if less stable. Furthermore, any disposition could become a habit if it were to become more stable.[11]

Yet in the same passage Aquinas mentions another possible basis for distinguishing habits from dispositions, namely, their "causes." Dispositions (Aquinas's example is health) have "changeable causes" (*causas transmutabiles*), whereas habits (Aquinas's examples are knowledge and virtue) have "unchangeable causes" (*causas immobiles*). Note that the claim here is not that the (level two) disposition or habit is changeable or unchangeable; as second nature all habits (and certainly dispositions) are changeable even if they have *causae immobiles*. The claim is that the "*causa*" is *transmutabilis* or *immobilis*.

More detailed inquiry into what Aquinas means by the "cause" of a habit or disposition is forthcoming. For now it suffices to note that the *causa immobilis* refers to the person's soul, whereas *causa transmutabilis* refers to the person's body.[12] Given this difference, it is clear why dispositions and habits are two different sorts of things, and dispositions cannot become habits, or vice versa. While it may be the case that dispositions (whose more particular specificity is supplied by bodily causes) are generally less stable and habits (whose more particular specificity is provided by the immaterial soul) are generally more stable, on this view of the distinction it is not the degree of stability per se that distinguishes dispositions from habits but rather the origin of the specification.

Once this difference of cause of specification is understood, it is more obvious why there is a question as to whether or not dispositions can become habits or vice versa. On the one hand, it would seem impossible, since they have different causes. On the other hand, it would seem that people can grow from having a less stable disposition toward some activity to having a more stable habit toward that activity (or vice versa). Thus we not only have a question as to how to read Aquinas's texts on this matter; we have a conceptual issue on the distinction between habit and disposition that has ramifications for how we describe growth (or decline) in virtue. There are two possible ways of understanding the relationship between disposition and habit and what Aquinas means by their causes, leaving an opening to the question of whether or not dispositions can become habits.

AQUINAS'S DISTINCTION BETWEEN HABIT AND DISPOSITION

What is the best understanding of the relationship between dispositions and habits? Aquinas adopts neither of the aforementioned approaches based *solely* on degree of stability *or* on cause of specification, but rather he offers a combination of the two. In other words, the best reading of Aquinas's mature work on this distinction is this: in order to "qualify" as a habit and not (merely) a disposition, *both* stability ("difficult to change") *and* specification by the rational soul are necessary.

First, Aquinas identifies degree of stability as requisite for something to be a habit rather than merely a disposition. This, of course, follows from the understanding of habits as the perfection of human powers. One of the things that habits supply to powers that are amenable to habituation is consistency, and that consistency is the result of stability.[13] Indeed, this emphasis on the importance of stability to qualify as a habit is evident in the passages treating the relationship between habit and disposition. Aquinas makes several references to dispositions that clearly have a *causa immobilis*, such as knowledge (*scientia*), yet nonetheless are inchoate or imperfect. In his previous article, he distinguishes between "dispositions which are in course of formation and not yet arrived at perfect usefulness" and "perfect dispositions which are called habits."[14] His examples are "knowledge and virtue": each has as *causa immobilis* in the person's rational soul. Thus dispositions can be imperfect as to stability even though they have *causae immobiles*. Indeed, in the very reply with the extended quotation, Aquinas claims: "Supposing a man to have a knowledge imperfectly, so as to be liable to lose it easily, it is better to say that he is disposed to knowledge rather than that he has knowledge [*scientiam habere*]."[15] It thus seems that on Aquinas's terms, stability is not merely a tangential feature associated with a habit, with the real defining feature of habit being its cause. Rather, stability is a necessary condition of a habit. Indeed Aquinas goes on to say that "the word 'habit' implies a certain lastingness; the word 'disposition' does not."[16] Whatever its origin of specification, absent stability, any quality is a disposition, not a habit.

Is it then the case that stability alone renders a quality a habit rather than a disposition? No, because a *causa immobilis* as the origin of specification is also required in order for a quality to be a habit. Habits have their causes, or sources of specification, in the soul, not simply in the body. This claim requires more unpacking, first in understanding what is meant by "soul" as distinct from "body," and second in what is meant by the cause of specification being either *immobilis* or *transmutabilis*. Only then can we turn to examine whether such a *causa immobilis* is requisite for a habit as distinct from a disposition.

One consistent claim in recent scholarship, that the difference in cause between habits and dispositions pertains to soul and body, respectively, is true—in a sense. But it can be misleading if it is taken to mean that bodily dispositions are unrelated to the soul. This is untrue. In Aquinas's anthropology, soul informs body. One contemporary Thomist puts it this way: "Body is constituted as *body*, by soul; it is matter informed by soul. This is why Thomas holds that at death the 'body,' properly speaking, is no longer a body but a corpse. Body's nature is the soul—in soul's capacity as form."[17] The writer goes on to say that "whether subjected in a power [of the soul] or a body, every habit is somehow related to the soul."[18] Thus in a sense all dispositions and habits (including "bodily" dispositions such as health and beauty) are related to the soul.

So why are causes *immobilis* and *transmutabilis* aligned with soul and body, respectively?[19] The context for Aquinas's treatments of habit and virtue is the human person's activity, and thus it is proper to understand "soul" in these conversations as "rational soul."[20] Therefore, within the description of a habit having a *causa immobilis* is the claim that a habit properly so-called engages the person's rationality. With the recognition that by *causa immobilis* Aquinas is referring to a person's rational soul, we can examine whether or not a habit or disposition can be "caused" by the rational soul.

Aquinas uses cause in various ways in his work on virtue, so it is important to clarify exactly what he means. For instance, later chapters examine various causes of virtue, in the sense of efficient cause, namely, the processes whereby virtues (as habits) come to exist in a person. But here cause refers to the source or origin of the more particular specification of the end of the power qualified. Both habits and dispositions are specifications (level two) of ends of activity that are more particular than the more general and inchoate ends of activity supplied by nature (level one). These more specified ends (level two) of underdetermined powers facilitate a person's attaining even more particular ends during activity (level three). In Aquinas's understanding of inclination and activity toward an end, the end is given its specificity (at any level) through the person's cognitive apprehension, whether that be rational or merely sensory apprehension. However the person cognitively apprehends the end causes the habit or disposition (level two) ultimately influences action (level three). What different possible origins of specification of end are there for the human person?

Regarding the human powers that can be habituated (unlike, say, how a human joint moves or how food is digested), the specification of the end of a habit or disposition can be supplied simply by a person's senses or in a manner engaging her rationality. Aquinas's distinction between *causa transmutabilis* and *causa immobilis* is thus a distinction between the specification of a disposition's or habit's end (level two) simply through the senses or in a manner engaging the person's rationality, respectively. Explaining what differentiates specification through the senses from specification through reason, as well as how each is brought about, is in some sense a major task of our analysis.

Consider one brief example to illustrate this point. A person's power to eat (sensory appetite) is supplied by nature (level one) with an end, namely, nourishment to sustain the physical body. Though that end is not wholly indeterminate, it is also quite underdetermined. Through childhood a person is brought up to eat certain kinds of foods and in certain manners of eating. These types of food and manners of eating become connatural to the child, such that the child eats in a more specific way consistently (stably) and "feels like" doing so. (A later discussion addresses why we say the child is "accustomed to," or gets used to, such ways of eating, and how the child becomes more or less stably inclined to eat in a specific manner through repeated activity.) There can be many ways the child's underdetermined natural end to eat becomes more particularly inclined, and these differ based on culture, family, and other factors. Situational factors, of course, influence whether or not, and if so, how so, the child's more or less stable inclination to eat in that more specific way (level two) is actualized through particular actions (level three). Furthermore, different specifications at level two may be better or worse at facilitating certain activities (level three) that truly attain the person's end in a manner constitutive of flourishing.

The point here is that a young child does not have a rational grasp of the ends of eating nor understand the more specific ways of eating in relation to other and further ends in life. If the child did have a rational grasp of the end at hand (*causa immobilis*), and if that end were stably specifying the child's power to eat, the child would possess a habit. But, instead, at an early age, the more particular way of eating inculcated through upbringing is a connaturalization or specification (level two) of sensory appetite (level one), and a grasp of this more particular end (whether the child is able to articulate it or not) is supplied by the *causa transmutabilis* of the child's senses. Thus the child possess a disposition—not a habit—to eat in that manner. Note that when we distinguish the cause of specification as the rational or sensory, we are not evaluating the goodness or badness of either. Indeed, either origin of specification can be done well or poorly (as was a condition for a power to be amenable to habituation). Rather, we are addressing whether the end supplied to the habit or disposition (level two) engages the person's rationality or simply emanates from the senses.

Regarding the relationship between habits and dispositions, the claim here is that not only stability, but also a specification of the more particular end informed by a person's rationality, is requisite for an inclination (level two) to be a habit rather than a mere disposition. In any texts does Aquinas claim that absent specification of the end with rationality, an inclination (even a stable one) can only be a disposition and not a habit? Indeed, he does.

A first set of texts emphasizes that natural dispositions are not habits in the proper sense of the term "habit" because the specification provided by nature is "ordered to one" activity, and thus only a "beginning of virtue." This inclination to one sort of activity precludes natural dispositions from being considered habits in the proper sense of the term. Aquinas claims that the "rational power relates to opposites whereas nature is ordered to one. Obviously then the perfection of virtue is from reason not nature."[21] Though he claims a disposition within an individual person "is a kind of beginning of virtue [*inchoatio virtutis*]," nonetheless it "is not perfected virtue because for perfected virtue the governance of reason is needed."[22] What exactly do dispositions caused by nature lack? Aquinas describes this in detail: "Intellectual and moral virtues are in us by way of a natural aptitude, inchoatively, but not perfectly, since nature is determined to one, while the perfection of these virtues does not depend on one particular mode of action, but on various modes, in respect of the various matters, which constitute the sphere of virtue's action, and according to various circumstances."[23] This statement is crucial, not only in its claim that dispositions are different from habits but also in its naming that what is supplied in a full-blown habit is a more particular end that is attuned to "various modes, in respect of various matters . . . according to various circumstances."

Given the human rational ability to consider a particular action in light of various circumstances and further ends, any power that is able to be habituated is only truly habituated (rather than merely disposed) to "its utmost reach" when the stable specification (level two) is supplied with the involvement of a person's rationality.[24] Aquinas offers a particularly vivid image to explain the need for the involvement of reason for an inclination to qualify to be a virtue (or habit, more broadly), involving a horse:

> There are some wholly imperfect virtues which exist without prudence, not attaining right reason, such as the inclination which some have to certain works of virtue even from their birth. . . . Such inclinations are not all at once in everybody, but some have an inclination to one and others to another. Such inclinations do not have the character of virtue, however because . . . a person can use such inclinations badly and harmfully if he acts without discretion, much as a blind horse bangs into things harder the faster it runs. . . . Hence these inclinations without prudence do not fulfill the definition of virtue.[25]

The specification of the end of activity provided by an innate disposition might prompt a person in generally positive ways, as toward chastity or meekness.[26] And such natural dispositions might even be rather stable. Health and beauty are possible examples of the latter, as they may be consistent throughout a life.[27] But, even in these cases, "they have not the nature of habit perfectly, because their causes, of their very nature, are easily changeable."[28] And of course as Aquinas's stark image indicates, a natural disposition to acts—like meekness and chastity—can impede the acts of other virtues and thus be destructive for her ability to live virtuously with regard to various circumstances in life. It is precisely the specification of an end in relation to other ends that is gained when a person's rationality in the specification of the habit's more particular end is involved.

Before returning to the issue of the distinction between habit and disposition, it is worth noting how commonly in recent moral philosophy this contribution to habit from a person's rationality is referenced. For instance, Julia Annas distinguishes virtues as "intelligent" in that they "take account of all relevant factors," as opposed to an "inarticulate knack," which does not do so.[29] In a phrase that echoes Aquinas's "various modes . . . and according to various circumstances," Annas claims that "practical intelligence gets things right in very diverse circumstances."[30] In his illuminating Aristotle-inspired account of *phronesis,* Daniel Russell claims: "Virtues in the strict sense . . . involve practical reasoning, since virtue in the strict sense involves integration and balance of diverse demands."[31] Rosalind Hursthouse claims that children, even those with good natural traits and good upbringing, do not have habits in the proper sense since they lack an overall "concept of goodness" and thus the ability to act "from reason."[32] Annas claims a person's rationality supplies not only a grasp of what is good and attends to various factors but also a "commitment to goodness," that is, a pursuit or striving that describes the will.[33]

Aquinas is quite clear that stability alone does not suffice for a quality to be a habit rather than a disposition. There must also be a *causa immobilis* of the specification of the inclination's end (level two), and the *causa immobilis* is rightly understood as the rational soul. One further word is in order in clarifying the involvement of the person's rationality. For Aquinas, the human person is rational in both her ability to know the truth (which Aquinas calls apprehension) and her ability to pursue the good (which he calls appetite). It is important to note that Aquinas claims that a habit in the properly human sense involves both rational apprehension (in this case practical reason) and rational appetite (will). It is already clear from the previous discussion that rational apprehension, or reason, is requisite for specification of the power's end (level two) in order for there to be a habit. It is through practical reason that a person grasps the ends of her actions in relation to other ends. While this does not preclude the influence of other sources of specification (e.g., natural dispositions), if they are not governed by reason there is not a habit in the proper sense.[34]

What about the role of the rational appetite, or will? Aquinas treats this topic when he addresses whether or not there can be habits in the sensitive powers we share with animals. He claims that when these powers are actualized simply by "natural instinct," they cannot be habituated in the proper sense. But habits properly understood can inhere in these powers when they act at the command of reason. This is a claim about reason supplying the object of the acts of these powers (addressed in detail in chapter 4). The interesting thing for our purposes now is what he goes on to say about the nature of a habit.

Aquinas recognizes that animals can be trained by humans so as to become accustomed to certain acts, and this is a habit, "in a certain way." He cites Augustine to recognize that animals can, for instance, be trained to be kind and gentle, such that there develops a "custom" in them. However, Aquinas then observes that the habit is incomplete, as to the use of the will, for animals have not that power (*dominium*) of using or of refraining, which seems to belong to the notion of habit (*ad rationem habitus pertinere*), and therefore, properly speaking (*proprie loquendo*), there can be no habits in them.[35] Though trained animals (and presumably pre-rational children) evidence stable specification of underdetermined powers, Aquinas claims there is something essential to habit (*ratio habitus*) that is lacking in them, namely, the use of the will. Since it pertains to the essence (*ad rationem*) of a habit to have the ability (*dominium*) to use or not use the habit, properly speaking (*proprie loquendo*) animals do not have habits. They instead have dispositions.

A human quality is therefore only a habit in the proper sense when the rational powers not only of reason but also of will are involved in the specification of a more particular end (level two). This claim about the will is perhaps unsurprising since the will is simply the person's appetitive response to what is apprehended by reason. With a properly human habit an end is grasped as to its "various modes, in respect of various matters . . . according to various circumstances." A person's appetitive inclination is toward that end in relation to various (and including further) ends. The person grasps (through reason) their end (level two) in a broader context and is stably inclined toward it (through rational appetite, or will) as part of that larger whole. This is why when habits are virtues they both make a person's activity good and make the person good.[36] The engagement with a person's rationality that is requisite for the existence of a habit refers both to reason (as rational apprehension) and will (as rational appetite).

As evident from the source of many of the quotations used to substantiate this argument, reflection on the nature of (and need for) habit and its distinction from disposition leads directly to the need to clarify which human powers can be habituated in the proper sense of the term habit. Aquinas treats the former topics in *Summa Theologiae* Questions 49 and 55, on habit and virtue, respectively, and the latter in Questions 50 and 56, on habit and virtue, respectively. Given the dual requirements of stability and *causa immobilis,* the obvious answer to the question of which human powers can be habituated is that it is those that can be stably specified in a manner informed by rationality. What would that *not* include? Aquinas claims the body is not a subject of habits, because it is solely moved and not itself a mover, and it is not underdetermined but ordered to one act.[37] He also adduces the exterior senses as not subjects of habits in the properly human sense, since they are given their specification wholly from the outside.[38] As noted earlier, Aquinas does not think the body or senses have nothing to do with the rational soul, but they are nevertheless not stably more particularly specified in a manner that is informed by rationality.

Which human powers *are* able to be stably more specifically specified through the influence of rationality? Most obviously, these would be acts of the intellect, or rational apprehension.[39] Some qualifications will need to be made (in a later chapter) but, generally speaking, the intellect can be habituated. So, too, can rational appetite, or the will.[40] (This claim will also require more in-depth treatment, also in a later chapter.) And the sensitive appetite, whose movements are called passions, may also be habituated.[41] This may seem surprising since Aquinas claims that human persons share the sensitive appetite in common with animals, which clearly do not have rational powers. However, Aquinas (like Aristotle) claims that in the human person the sensitive appetite can "participate in reason" or act at the "command of reason." When it does not, it is *not* the subject of properly human habits. But when it does, it can be habituated in the full sense of the term.

On the basis of Aquinas's claims about what is requisite for a habit in the properly human sense, the argument offered here is that habits are rightly distinguished from dispositions because habits are characterized *both* by greater stability and by the specification of the end supplied by a *causa immobilis,* namely, the rational soul.

HABITS AND DISPOSITIONS: RAMIFICATIONS FOR GROWING IN VIRTUE

The previous discussion identified the basis for making a distinction between habits and dispositions—not only as a topic worthy of inquiry in itself but also as a crucial resource in developing an account of growth in virtue. Having established the necessity of the more particular end to be possessed both stably and with the rational soul as *causa immobilis* for the existence of a habit in the proper sense, as distinct from a disposition, we turn back to the relevance of that position for a Thomistic account of growth in virtue.

Recall that one central question regarding the distinction between habits and dispositions was whether or not a disposition could become a habit, or vice versa. The answer seems to be yes, if the distinction is based on stability, yet no, if based on cause. Yet the previous argument is that both stability and engagement with a person's rationality are requisite. So how to answer the question of whether or not dispositions can become habits?

Recall that dispositions and habits are both qualities, not substantial forms. Though we might say that a person gains temperance, it is even more precise to say that a person's sensual desires become temperate. Properly speaking, a person gains temperance not because temperance "comes into being" but because the person's sensual desires become temperate.[42] Whether they become disposed or habituated to temperate acts depends, in addition to the degree of stability, on whether the origin of specification of the end (level two) comes simply from her senses (the body, a *causa transmutabilis*) or involves her rationality (the rational soul, a *causa immobilis*). Therefore, it is not precise to say that a disposition becomes a habit (or vice versa). Rather, a person's sensual desires, which had been *disposed* temperately, become sensual desires that are *habituated* temperately.

This is what Aquinas means when he says habits and disposition are "diverse species" and that "a disposition does not become a habit."[43] It is also what contemporary Thomists emphasize as the qualitative difference between disposition and habit. David Decosimo describes this as a "bright line" between a disposition and habit;[44] Robert Miner claims that habits are not "on the same plane as dispositions."[45] What happens in the attainment of a virtue is not a disposition becoming a habit. Rather, the power that is previously "disposed" (even if stably so) is "habituated" through the stable, more particular specification of the habit's end, which is supplied in a manner informed by rationality. As Miner puts it, with reference to Aquinas's own "boy becomes a man" example in examining dispositions and habits, a boy does not become a man so much as a human being who was a boy becomes a human being who is a man.[46] People commonly speak of dispositions becoming habits, and that dynamic is indeed true. However, properly speaking, dispositions do not become habits; rather, a person's powers that had been disposed become habituated.

Yet it is also true to say that a person can grow from having a *disposition* of temperance to having a *habit* of temperance. When this occurs, there is not only greater stability but the engagement of the person's rationality. But what continuity is there in such a change? Said differently, is there anything of the previous disposition that persists when a person comes to possess a proper habit? This question will be addressed later, but several things can be said now. First and foremost, the main thread of continuity is that it is the same human power toward the same type of activity (e.g., the irascible appetite to occasions of anger, or the sensory appetite toward occasions of eating) that is continuous between the previously held disposition and the new habit. This continuity is more obvious to see when a person goes from being disposed to activities that engage her rationality (such as a beginner in knowledge or virtue) to being habituated to knowledgeable or virtuous activities. In such cases there is not only continuity in type of activity but also in the (rational) source of specification. What is lacking is stability. Even in cases where a person goes from being disposed to acts of temperance without the specification provided by the involvement of her rationality (and provided instead by, say, upbringing) to being habituated such that the specification is informed by her rationality, the sorts of actions that are performed (in this case the temperate desiring of pleasures) may be observably the same.[47] Thus, the main enduring continuity when someone who is disposed becomes someone who is habituated is not the disposition but the power it qualifies.

Does anything remain of the power's previous disposition? In other words, granting that the disposition had a nonrational source of specification, what happens to such sensory influence on specification? Does the disposition's sensory specification persist in any way as the habit's specification comes to be provided by the *causa immobilis* of a person's rationality? Since we are talking about the relationship in the human person between the sensory powers of apprehension and appetite on the one hand and the rational powers of apprehension and appetite on the other, we would benefit from consulting Aquinas's position on the so-called plurality of forms debate during the Middle Ages.

An in-depth examination of the context of and various positions taken in this debate is well beyond the scope of this project.[48] The basic issue was how to account for the fact that the human person has several different types of powers, which reflect the human person's continuity with yet also distinction from other creatures. Medievals (influenced by Aristotle) referenced the various "souls" of the person, namely, nutritive (in common with plants), sensory (in common with animals), and rational (distinct to persons).[49] The question for the medievals was how to describe the ongoing presence of all of these in a human person, yet in a unified manner. While some medievals affirmed in the human person a position called the "plurality of forms" (i.e., souls) to explain these various types of activities, Aquinas endorsed a "unicity of form" position, whereby the human person possesses just one (rational) soul, which "contains" or, we might say, "includes" the other forms. Aquinas explains his view using a geometric analogy and Socrates as an example: "Therefore, as a surface which is of pentagonal shape, is not tetragonal by one shape and pentagonal by another, since a tetragonal shape would be superfluous as contained in the pentagonal, so neither is Socrates a man by one soul, and animal by another, but by one and the same soul is both animal and man."[50]

Aquinas goes on to say that the intellectual soul "contains" whatever belongs to both the sensitive soul and the nutritive soul, and this unicity of forms position is crucial for two reasons that are relevant to our inquiry. First, Aquinas thought that without maintaining a unicity of forms position, the person would not be one.[51] Second, and relatedly, the plurality of forms position "is shown to be impossible by the fact that when one operation of the soul is intense it impedes another, which could never be the case unless the principle of action were essentially one."[52] Aquinas therefore thought that his position on the unity of forms rightly describes both the reality of possible interference (or, presumably, consonance and mutual support) between the sensory and rational within the same person and the fundamental unity of the human person, a unity falling "under," so to speak, the rational soul.

What has this seemingly obscure medieval anthropological debate have to do with the relationship between habits and dispositions? As noted earlier, one reason dispositions do not attain the *ratio* of a habit is that they do not engage the person's rationality. Aquinas's description of such dispositions indicates that the specification of the end of the disposition is supplied simply by the senses. A person is unified by and through the rational soul, including the senses. Thus there are other non- or pre-rational sources of (more or less stable) specification of the ends of a person's powers within even the rational human person. Therefore, any Thomistic account of how various sources of specification relate to one another should be compatible with Aquinas's thought on the relationship between "souls" in the plurality of forms debate. Given that Aquinas claims the human person's sensory soul is not a separate soul from the rational soul but is "contained" by or included in the person's rational soul as source of unity, it is reasonable to assume this same understanding of the relationship between rational powers and sensory powers when examining the person's possession of a disposition or habit.

Even if it is the case (as argued here) that nonrational sources of specification *cannot* cause human habits properly understood (but rather cause more or less stable dispositions), we should also assume that a Thomistic account of properly human habits will not simply include the stable specification provided by rationality. That sensory specification is not inherently rational but is indeed united to the rational in a manner echoing Aquinas's position on the unicity of forms. For example, consider a child who grows up getting used to certain ways of eating. Even before understanding the more specific goals of eating in relation to other ends, the child's physical senses become "used to" eating in certain ways. This connaturalization of senses is normally part of any more rationally informed habituation that will presumably come in due time. In other words, the source of specification of the child's activity in dispositions will continue to exert causal influence over activity once that person possesses a habit. The influence can dispose the person toward acts that are observably the same as the specification provided by the rational powers. We can expect that there also may be occasions where this sensory specification of human power will exercise an influence that opposes the *causa immobilis,* that is, practical reasoning. This is why contrary dispositions are compatible with the possession of a habit.[53] While a person's powers toward the same activities can only be qualified by one habit in the proper sense of the term, it is possible that contrary dispositions can persist, where the source of specification of the disposition may be, say, the repeated actions in her upbringing (a topic addressed in chapter 3). Interestingly but unsurprisingly given Aquinas's position on the unicity of forms, when the causal influence of sensory specification is consonant with the specification offered by rationality, we would not say that there persist "consonant dispositions." Rather, we would grant that any such causal influence is part of the habit, which indeed it is.

We are now veering into territory addressed in later chapters (e.g., the role of dispositions and the formative processes of becoming habituated). But our goal, to address the ramifications of an account of the distinction between dispositions and habits for the question of whether or not dispositions become habits, leads to the conclusion with the precise answer of no. A person's power that is disposed can become habituated, so the power is really the main point of continuity. Nevertheless, especially given Aquinas's position on the unicity of forms, the causal influence of dispositions can persist in various ways. So while it is not precise to say either that the disposition becomes the habit or that the disposition persists in the same way it existed while not a habit, aspects of the specification provided by sensory *causae transmutabiles* can continue to exert causal influence in the new habit. Having established the proper basis of the distinction between disposition and habit according to Aquinas, we turn to an examination of the ways that dispositions are attained.

NOTES

1. See the seminal essay by Pinckaers, "Virtue Is Not a Habit."
2. For recent examples of the use of *habitus* instead of "habit" to indicate this difference, see Miner, "Aquinas on *Habitus*." See also Breen, *Imagining an English Reading Public, 1150–1400*: "If the paradigmatic example of *habit* is drug use, especially in American vocabularies, the equivalent examples of *habitus* . . . are knowledge and virtue" (43). See also Austin, *Aquinas on Virtue*, 32–34.
3. For example, Miller claims that one contribution of the situationist critique is recognition of what he calls "surprising dispositions" in people that seem to threaten the existence of what are traditionally called virtues. See Miller, "Virtue Cultivation in Light of Situationism," 159. The distinction between habit and disposition articulated here and deployed later for attaining and growing in virtue would be a valuable resource in dialogue with situationism. This distinction would greatly augment popular insightful books on habit, such as: Clear, *Atomic Habits*, and Duhigg, *The Power of Habit*.
4. Recall there are four species of quality according to Aristotle's categories, namely: dispositions, capacities, passions, shape. Aquinas is claiming that the degree of stability, or the difficulty of change, is a variable within the species of disposition, not a variable between disposition and another species of quality. An extensive explanation of or defense of Aristotle's terminology is not requisite for this project.
5. ST I–II 49,2 ad 3.
6. For a helpful look at Aquinas's use of one member of a class (genus) of things to refer to all members of the class, usually the "lowest" member, see Whitmore, "Dispositions and Habits," 107n46. Whitmore treats Aquinas's class of angels in ST II–II 160,1 ad 1, where the class (angels) is named for the lowest member of that class (angels).
7. Some authors deploy technical designations for the sense of disposition as genus or species. See Decosimo, *Ethics as a Work of Charity*, 89, for the latter as S-disposition (S for species).
8. Presumably it could also be on the way "down" from being a habit, such that it is no longer a habit (see chap. 5).
9. For treatments of this topic, see Whitmore, "Dispositions and Habits," 91; Miner, "Aquinas on *Habitus*," 68–69; Kent, "Habits and Virtues," 118; Knobel, "Aquinas and the Pagan Virtues," 347–48; Decosimo, *Ethics as a Work of Charity*, 91.
10. Since my task here is not to create a comprehensive account of the distinction between habit and disposition throughout Aquinas's corpus, I rely primary on his two mature works, *Summa Theologiae* and *Disputed Questions on Virtue in General*. For treatment of the various texts on habits and dispositions across Aquinas's corpus, see Whitmore, "Dispositions and Habits," 120, as well as Knobel, "Aquinas and the Pagan Virtues." Knobel claims that Aquinas's early works do not distinguish habits and dispositions so clearly (346n27, citing *De malo.* 7,2 ad 4, and III *Sent* d. 23, q. 1, a. 1). Except where noted, English translations of Aquinas's *Disputed Questions on Evil* (cited as *De malo.*) are taken from Oesterle and Oesterle, *On Evil*. Passages from Aquinas's *Commentary on the Sentences* (cited as *Sent.*) are taken from https://isidore.co/aquinas/; except where noted, English quotations come from Aquinas, *On Love and Charity*.
11. Hence Aquinas says in this sense a disposition is related to habit as imperfect is related to perfect. On this sense of imperfect/perfect see also III Sent d. 23, q. 1, a. 1; *De malo.* 7,2

ad 2; and I–II 53,4 ad 1. Since Aquinas uses imperfect/perfect in varying ways, including to indicate natural and supernatural flourishing, to avoid confusion I generally avoid using these terms.

12. See Miner, "Aquinas on *Habitus*," 72; Whitmore, "Dispositions and Habits," 110n48, 111n53; and Decosimo, *Ethics as a Work of Charity*, 75–76, 88–90. Decosimo also uses the term "operative" for habits of the soul, reflecting Aquinas's claim in ST I–II 55,2 that human habits are operative since they are in the soul.
13. *De virt.* a. 1: "We require virtuous habits for three reasons. First, for uniformity in activity. For those things depending solely on activity are easily changed, unless they are given *stability* by some habitual inclination" ("*habitus virtutum ad tria indigemus. Primo ut sit uniformitas in sua operatione; ea enim quae ex sola operatione dependent, facile immutantur, nisi secundum aliquam inclinationem habitualem fuerint stabilita*") (author's translation, emphasis added).
14. ST I–II 49,1 ad 3.
15. ST I–II 49,2 ad 3. Recall the Latin for "have" is *habere*, so Aquinas reminds the reader of the etymological origin of *habitus*.
16. ST I–II 49,2 ad 3.
17. Decosimo, *Ethics as a Work of Charity*, 83.
18. Decosimo, 84.
19. Decosimo explains in what sense bodily dispositions are indeed related to the soul, though in a different way than what he calls "operative" (or what Whitmore calls "psychic") habits, or habits of the soul: "Thomas distinguishes between soul in its capacity as: a) body's form and b) rational power and principle of [presumably properly human] action. . . . Thomas stresses that bodily habits are not found in body simply but in body-by-reason-of-its-relation-to-the-soul" (*Ethics as a Work of Charity*, 84). Decosimo's analysis, focused mainly on the distinct ways body is related to soul, is affirmed here, though my focus is more on the distinct "souls" or "powers of the soul" as discussed in ST I 78,1.
20. Note in Aquinas's very first question on virtue in the *Summa Theologiae*, the very one where he claims virtues are operative and addresses the body and soul, he opens by asking whether *human* virtue is an operative habit. See ST I–II 55,2.
21. *De virt.* a. 8. Here nature is being distinguished from reason, though of course in important ways reason is "natural" to human nature.
22. *De virt.* a. 8. See also ST I–II 63,1: "All virtues are in us by nature, according to aptitude and inchoation, but not according to perfection." Aquinas consistently uses the terms imperfect and perfect to correlate with what here is called dispositions/habits (e.g., ST I–II 49,2 ad 3). There are, of course, other meanings of imperfect-perfect/t, perhaps most commonly the distinction between supernatural and natural happiness (e.g., ST I–II 65,2).
23. ST I–II 63,1. See also III *Sent.* q. 1, a. 2, qa. 1, ad 2: "Reason adds a mode of causing to the mode in which something is caused by another naturally. And it is according to this additional mode that reason is principle of the virtues."
24. In the tradition a classic description of a virtue is that it is the "highest reach" or "utmost limit" (*ultimum potentiae*) of a power. For Aquinas's reference to this claim as found in Aristotle and Augustine, see ST I–II 66,1 ad 2 (and obj. 2). See also *De virt.* a. 1 resp. ad 6, a. 4 ad 2, a. 9, a. 11 ad 15, and a. 13 ad 1.
25. *De virt. card.* a. 2. This translation is based on McInerny's, though *ratio* of habit is changed to character (not mark). Atkins's translation is used to correct McInerny's characterization

of the horse not being passively beaten, but banging into things. See ST I–II 58,4 ad 3, where the translation offered here is corroborated. See also II *Sent.* d. 36, a. 1.

26. These two examples are from Aquinas, at ST I–II 51,1.
27. Though Aquinas most frequently describes health as a bodily disposition, he does at times call it a habit, and once uses the rather equivocal "habitual disposition" (*habitualis dispositio*) (ST I–II 49,3 ad 3). For a more detailed examination of Aquinas's texts on health as a disposition or habit, see Whitmore, "Dispositions and Habits," 98–99.
28. ST I–II 50,1.
29. See Annas, *Intelligent Virtue*, 14, 20. For a similar attempt to distinguish what are here called dispositions from habits, see Vogler, *Reasonably Vicious*, 98–99, for her contrasting "norms" and "behavioral dispositions" (what is here akin to dispositions) from virtues and vices.
30. Annas, *Intelligent Virtue*, 95.
31. Russell, *Practical Intelligence and the Virtues*, 171.
32. Hursthouse, *On Virtue Ethics*, 106–7, 145.
33. See Annas, *Intelligent Virtue*, 102–4. Annas claims this "commitment to goodness" is found in virtues but not in vices, which forms the basis of her argument that virtues and vices differ as to their "internal structure" (104n6).
34. *De virt.* a. 8.
35. ST I–II 50,3 ad 2.
36. *De virt.* a. 7, citing *Nic. Eth.* 2.6.2. This phrasing is from ST I–II 56,3.
37. ST I–II 50,1; *De virt.* a. 4.
38. ST I–II 50,3 ad 3; ST I–II 56,5.
39. ST I–II 50,4; 56,3; *De virt.* aa. 6, 7.
40. ST I–II 50,5, 56,6; *De virt.* a. 5.
41. ST I–II 50,3, 56,4; *De virt.* a. 4.
42. *De virt.* a. 11 (Atkins): "A form is said to come into being not because it itself comes into being, but because something comes to be it."
43. ST I–II 49,2 ad 3.
44. Decosimo, *Ethics as a Work of Charity*, 90.
45. Miner, "Aquinas on *Habitus*," 69.
46. Miner, 68.
47. The assumption here is that both the previously held disposition and the new habit are aimed to good acts of temperance.
48. For a helpful introduction to this medieval debate, see Gilson, *The Christian Philosophy of St. Thomas Aquinas*, 194–95. For its relevance to virtue, see Kent, *Virtues of the Will*, 214–15.
49. See ST I 77, 4.
50. ST I 76,3.
51. ST I 76,3: "If, therefore, man were 'living' by one form, the vegetative soul, and 'animal' by another form, the sensitive soul, and 'man' by another form, the intellectual soul, it would follow that man is not absolutely one." Also: "Therefore of necessity by the same form a thing is animal and man; otherwise man would not really be the thing which is an animal, so that animal can be essentially predicated of man."
52. ST I 76,3.
53. How persistent these contrary dispositions need to become before they disqualify the person from having a habit depends on both their stability and the amenability of the (bodily) source of specification to participation in reason.

CHAPTER 3

BECOMING DISPOSED

Nature and Nurture

When reflecting on how individual persons become who they are, it is common to use the terms nature and nurture. At their most basic, these two terms refer to who people are from birth (nature) and who they become due to various influences and ways they act in their lives (nurture). But both terms are significantly more complicated than that. For instance, "nature" can refer to the human nature that is shared with other persons, which here we call level one ends toward which people are directed. But it can also refer to the particular characteristics that individual persons are born with but which are accurately understood as level two qualifications of their natures, since those characteristics are not essentially who the persons are but rather particular ways that level one ends are specified for them as individuals. We commonly use the term "natural temperament" to describe such characteristics. These are the focus of the beginning of this chapter. Additionally, though "nurture" describes ways that people are more or less stably formed at level two by various influences and ways people act in their lives, it turns out that there are different ways that these influences and activities shape them. To use familiar terminology, nurture, particularly formation from repeated and socially mediated activity, can lead to dispositions or to habits at level two. Aquinas calls this process "accustomization," and dispositions from accustomization are the focus of the second section. Thus this chapter focuses on two different types of dispositions before turning in the following chapter to habits in the proper sense of the term.

Recall Julia Annas's claims that "we cannot understand what virtue is without coming to understand how we acquire it" and that "understanding the process of ethical education is a part of virtue ethics."[1] Despite the mining of Aquinas's work in the recent resurgence of attention to virtue, there remain untapped resources. One such resource is his thought on formation in virtue, which really provides the beginnings of a Thomistic account of education. Another is the important role of a person's community for formation in virtue. We now delve deeper into Aquinas's thought on education and the important role of the community in the processes of acquiring virtue.

Throughout all of his treatments of virtue, Aquinas inquires as to the "causes" of virtue.[2] Given the various possible meanings of "cause," it will help to clarify exactly to which sense of cause Aquinas refers. As evidenced in recent work by Nicholas Austin, SJ, one can examine Aquinas's broader account of virtue through the classic Aristotelian four causes.[3] But we are not talking in this chapter about the material cause of virtue, concerning which human powers are stably specified. (Aquinas addresses this topic under the name "subject" of virtue; see chaps. 1 and 2.) Neither are we talking about the final cause of virtue. (The final cause of virtue is human flourishing, toward humanity's natural end, or including and beyond the natural end to the supernatural end; see chaps. 6 and 7.) Nor are we talking here of the formal cause of virtue. (The formal cause of habits and dispositions, i.e., the origin and content of the specification of their more particular end, is supplied by the senses or in a manner engaging a person's rationality, and the exact content of that specificity varies.) Our focus is the efficient cause of habits, namely, the process(es) whereby human powers amenable to habituation come to be more or less stably specified. In the language of "levels," we now explore how a person's powers (level one) have their ends made more particular through dispositions and habits (at level two) so as to contribute to her activity (level three). How does a person come to be disposed or habituated?

Aquinas consistently names several different efficient causes or processes whereby persons come to possess habits or dispositions. He identifies four such efficient causes.[4] On several occasions throughout his corpus Aquinas addresses this topic, and though they are found across the span of writings from his entire career, they are remarkably consistent. "One person is better disposed than another to attain the mean of virtue which is defined by right reason; and this, on account of either greater accustomization, or a better natural disposition, or a more discerning judgment of reason, or again a greater gift of grace."[5] These various (efficient) causes of habits or dispositions are able to be conceptually distinguished from one another. In reality, however, they generally operate in conjunction with one another in mutually reinforcing ways or in mutually impeding ways. Our focus in this chapter is on two of these four processes, namely, nature and accustomization, or as we often colloquially name them, nature and nurture. The two are appropriately treated together and distinct from acquired virtue and infused virtue since nature and custom cause dispositions whereas acquired virtues and infused virtues are habits. We will find that only dispositions, not habits, can be caused by nature and custom, and yet dispositions can continue to exert causal influence on properly human habits.

"HABITS" (DISPOSITIONS) CAUSED BY NATURE

In every treatment of the various efficient causes of virtues (or habits), Aquinas first asks whether they can exist in us by nature. He addresses the classic philosophical question of whether habits like virtue and knowledge are taught or come from within. His answer is both. But relevant for this project is his description of how this is so. He claims that virtues exist in us by potential and are brought to realization through interactions with our environments.[6] In doing so he once again situates virtues on level two, between the underdetermined ends supplied by nature (level one) on the one hand, and the activities that bring further specificity and connaturalize that aptitude (level three) on the other.[7]

Granting that a certain "aptitude" to virtue exists within people at what here is called level one, in what sense can nature be a cause of level two dispositions? After all, it would seem that any such orientation toward an end supplied by nature would place that "endedness" at level one.[8] Aquinas considers various ways that nature can cause a level two disposition. For example, he claims that there are species-wide habits, such as the first principles of speculative reasoning and the seeds of virtue (e.g., synderesis), both of which are habits in that they require interaction with the environment to be activated, even though they are specified in only one way.[9]

More interesting for an inquiry into growing in virtue is Aquinas's description of individual (rather than species-wide) natural dispositions toward certain activities. Aquinas is speaking here of what we might call natural temperament, that is, an individual's ends that are more specific than those of the species yet possessed from birth. This could include dispositions ranging from the obviously nonmoral, such as good (or bad) digestion or healthy (or pallid) complexion, to the morally important natural tendencies, such as a disposition to desire pleasures temperately (or intemperately) or to face dangers courageously (or cowardly).[10] Why are these dispositions at level two rather than at level one ends supplied by nature? Aquinas claims that in these cases the relevant human powers (e.g., digestion, pleasure-seeking) are underdetermined as to human persons in general and can be variously disposed, though in individual persons they are disposed by nature toward one way of actualization (we might say "natural temperament"). Hence these powers are able to be variously disposed, even if any individual person is by natural temperament disposed or not disposed to a specific way of actualizing a given power.

Though dispositions to health or good digestion are less important for this inquiry since these dispositions can never be properly human habits, Aquinas's description of natural dispositions toward activity that can be virtuous (e.g., meekness, chastity) is quite relevant for our inquiry. In what way are these rightly called virtues? And why are they in the end not called virtues in the proper sense? What do Aquinas's treatments of natural virtues tell us about the ongoing causal influence of dispositions caused by nature in the person who becomes habituated in the properly human sense? These questions warrant a closer look at so-called natural virtues.

Aquinas thinks all differences of "natural temperament" are due not to individual differences in the rational soul, but to "bodily" differences or, more properly, differences in the embodied pre-rational soul.[11] Yet such differences can impact activities of a person that can proceed from the rational soul, such as those of the moral and intellectual virtues. For instance, he claims that by natural temperament one person may be "more apt than another to understand well."[12] In addition to natural differences in intellectual activity, natural differences can also exist with regard to activities of the moral virtues, as Aquinas claims, "Some are disposed from their own bodily temperament to chastity or meekness or the like."[13] In sum,

> by reason of a disposition in the body, some are disposed either well or ill to certain virtues: because, to wit, certain sensitive powers are acts of certain parts of the body, according to the disposition of which these powers are helped or hindered in the exercise of their acts, and, in consequence, the rational powers also, which aforesaid sensitive powers assist. In this way, one man has a natural aptitude for knowledge, another for fortitude, another for temperance; and in these ways, both intellectual and moral virtues are in us by way of natural aptitude, inchoatively.[14]

Thus the level one natural potential of individual persons can be variously disposed at level two, not only by more obviously bodily habitual dispositions like beauty and health but also by dispositions toward activities of the moral and intellectual virtues. This matches colloquial discussion about natural temperament, where we might say that some people are naturally quick tempered, or prone to eating moderately, or quick at math, and so on.[15] For Aquinas this is the sense in which nature causes "habits."

All that said, Aquinas is quite clear in these passages that such "natural habits" possessed by individuals are not properly considered habits, even though they are specifications (possibly even stable ones) of underdetermined human capacities toward certain activities. Aquinas claims such an "inclination is a kind of beginning of virtue [*inchoatio virtutis*], but is not perfected virtue because for perfected virtue the governance of reason is needed."[16] What exactly is this "governance of reason" that dispositions caused by nature lack? Recall Aquinas's claim distinguishing dispositions from habits: "Intellectual and moral virtues are in us by way of a natural aptitude, inchoatively, but not perfectly, since nature is determined to one, while the perfection of these virtues does not depend on one particular mode of action, but on various modes, in respect of the various matters, which constitute the sphere of virtue's action, and according to various circumstances."[17] He summarizes this quite directly at the close of his disputed question treatment of nature as cause of virtue: "The rational power relates to opposites whereas nature is ordered to one. Obviously then the perfection of virtue is from reason not nature."[18] Recall also his vivid image involving a blind horse to describe a disposition to action that does not engage the person's rationality.[19] Therefore, "natural virtues" are properly described as dispositions not habits. On occasions when Aquinas refers to these as habits, he is using this term in a more extended manner, akin to the other ways he sometimes labels dispositions or habits as "virtues" even though they are not properly virtues.[20]

Though it can lead to confusion if not read carefully, Aquinas's occasional extended use of habit, including when the disposition does not have the *causa immobilis* of the rational human soul, does emphasize an important continuity between properly human habits and dispositions that occur from causes such as nature. Though natural dispositions are not properly habits, calling them such indicates that the causal influence of the natural dispositions does not cease even when that specification comes to be supplied by the person's rationality. Ideally, natural dispositions support and operate in conjunction with rationally specified habits, as when a person who is chaste by natural temperament attains the properly human habit of chastity.[21] Perhaps it also may not, however, in which case reason must overcome the natural habit, such as when a naturally mild person must go to battle. This point is actually a continuation of the examination of the unicity of forms. Aquinas claims natural "habits" are bodily dispositions or, more properly, sensory specifications attained not by repeated activity but as a result of natural bodily (including genetic) temperament. When a person attains a habit properly so-called, the rational soul specifies activity and takes up or "annexes" the sensory dispositions to the extent that they are relevant to the activity at hand.[22]

These natural dispositions can support the habit and be taken up in it or can run counter to the habit and need to be quelled. Either way, the properly human habit is hylomorphically united to the bodily sensory dispositions, since as Aquinas's position on the unity of forms debate shows, the person is essentially one, that is, as both rational and animal. The term "natural habits" helps emphasize that unity. We might say natural dispositions are constitutive of complete or perfect virtue but do not on their own wholly constitute it. (The exact manner of this ongoing causal influence of sensory dispositions is addressed later.)

An examination of natural "habits" reveals that a person can be disposed, from birth, at level two, with the specification of a more particular end supplied not by rationality but rather by (*causa transmutabilis*) sensory specification of that person's powers, in a manner that differs among individuals. Since specification is not supplied by the *causa immobilis* of the rational soul, such natural habits are actually dispositions, even if they are more stable. That is why Aquinas consistently distinguishes perfect habit (or perfect virtue) from dispositions caused by nature and custom. "An imperfect moral virtue, temperance for instance, or fortitude, is nothing but an inclination in us to do some kind of good deed, whether such inclination be in us by nature or by custom."[23] Nature and custom can provide specification (and at times stably so) to human potential, but that specification can occur in the absence of reason. We now turn to custom, which shares important characteristics in common with natural disposition.

CUSTOM DISPOSITIONS CAUSED BY ACCUSTOMIZATION

We now turn to an examination of one oft-neglected efficient cause of dispositions, dispositions that pervade all of our lives and can be quite powerful and stable. In many cases these are the dispositions colloquially referred to as habits, as in Servais Pinckaers's classic "Virtue Is Not a Habit." Yet there is a striking, near-total neglect in scholarship on Aquinas's thought on virtue of these dispositions and how they are formed. These dispositions are called customs. They are caused by a process called accustomization, though, as noted later, there is significant overlap between the process whereby custom dispositions are formed in a person and the process whereby habits are formed. Our primary focus is establishing the place of custom in virtue formation for Aquinas, and noting what changes in a human person who, through accustomization, comes to possess a (mere) disposition called custom. The first task is to substantiate from Aquinas's texts whether that person does indeed have a distinct sort of disposition called custom, which involves a distinct (efficient) cause whereby such customs are attained. The second task is to identify what precisely changes in a person who through accustomization comes to possess a custom disposition.

There are four extended treatments of the (efficient) causes of virtues (or habits) in Aquinas's corpus. Aquinas consistently considers three possible answers in the titles of his articles on the causes of virtue: by nature (*a natura*), from acts (*ex actibus*), or from infusion (of grace, *ex infusione*).[24] Yet, relying on certain passages within these articles, the current focus is on four processes whereby habits are caused.[25] The first and last of the three article titles clearly correspond to the first and last of the four causes, namely, by nature and from grace. The middle one, from Aquinas's three article titles, is "by actions" or "by repeated practice."[26] Why, then, address treatments on accustomization and on judgment of reason as two distinct efficient causes of habits, especially when they are both caused by repeated activity (rather than by nature or from infusion of grace)? Is this an "add on" to Aquinas's thought? Where do each of these fall in Aquinas's triplet? To anticipate the conclusion, while both of these can be treated together, in that their efficient cause is repeated action, they are best treated separately, since the types of repeated actions that form them and therefore the dispositions that are formed need to be distinguished. Recall that a custom formed from repeated activity is a (mere) disposition with a sensory specification of a person's powers (*causa transmutabilis*), whereas a habit formed from accustomization by judgments of reason is stably specified by her rational soul (*causa immobilis*). How is this conclusion substantiated through Aquinas's texts?

"Custom" is a tricky topic in general, and equally so in the thought of Aquinas. He recognizes two distinct meanings for custom.[27] One recent author translates the first meaning as "practice," that is, some sustained (repeated) communally mediated activity that presumably has intelligible purpose.[28] One might imagine some common repetitious practice such as saying please and thank you, holding doors, or saying "I love you" upon departing from a family member. These could also include religious practices, as when Catholics have a "custom" of blessing themselves with holy water upon entering a church. The second meaning is a "natural or quasi natural inclination to do some action," as is even found in (nonhuman) animals.[29] Thus while the first sense describes persistent communally mediated activity (level three), the second describes a disposition possessed by a particular individual (level two).

These two senses seem to correspond to our contemporary English usage. We speak of the customs of a people, such as Native American religious customs or Italian culinary customs. We also speak of custom as a disposition in an individual, as when we say, "He has a custom of eating late at night" or "She is accustomed to speaking before listening." In this latter sense, the custom is a quality in the person (level two) that comes about by, and inclines that person to do more of, some sort of activity (level three) in a certain way. The point for our purposes is that Aquinas uses the term custom to speak of a disposition to action, though of course such a disposition results from (and inclines toward participation in) persistent communal practices. In fact, at times Aquinas uses language regarding custom in the sense of a disposition that is strikingly similar to his language of habit. On repeated occasions across his corpus Aquinas claims that custom is "second nature."[30] As one contemporary scholar notes, "Both *habitus* and *consuetudo* are regularly described as a second nature that becomes virtually inalterable over time, and both can be used positively or negatively."[31]

In fact, one might rightly wonder, especially given the lack of a separate article on custom in his major treatments of the causes of virtue, whether or not Aquinas's account of custom is simply an account of the repeated activity that engenders a properly human habit. If that were the case, custom would refer to both the repeated activity (also called accustomization) and to the properly human habit that inclines the person to more such activity. There are reasons to hold this belief. The first is Aquinas's decision not to devote separate articles in his treatments of causes of habit to both repeated *acts by custom* and repeated *acts from a judgment of reason*. The second is Aquinas's frequent description of custom as "second nature."

That said, it is very clear that Aquinas does not regard all inclinations attained through repeated activity as "full-blown" habits. As previously noted, in his arguably clearest and most succinct text on various (efficient) causes of virtue, Aquinas lists: greater accustoming (*assuetudinem*), or a better natural disposition (*dispositionem naturae*), or a more discerning judgment of reason, or a greater gift of grace.[32] Here accustoming is distinguished from judgment of reason, a position that is reaffirmed in a parallel text on the equality of virtues and in another text on the connectivity of the virtues.[33] In the context of natural dispositions, Aquinas claims that there are imperfect virtues, which are nothing other than inclinations to do good deeds, such as those inclinations provided by nature or custom (*ex aliqua consuetudine*).[34] These imperfect virtues are marked by their inclining to only certain good acts but not to others, such that people who are only accustomed can be "prompt in doing deeds of liberality, but are not prompt in doing deeds of chastity."[35] These "imperfect virtues," as he calls them, are really dispositions, distinct from habits properly understood.

Therefore, Aquinas's use of custom (*consuetudo*) and by accustoming (*assuetudine*) has similarities to his use of disposition. Accustoming (as a practice) means simply the process of formation through repeated activity whereby a person attains a custom disposition or a habit, the latter only when stable specification is provided by rationality. When Aquinas uses custom to describe the disposition that is obtained, it is generally paralleled with dispositions from nature and depicted in distinction from properly human habits. Having established that Aquinas has a concept of custom that can be distinct from a habit, we can now examine what changes take place in a person who possesses a disposition by custom.

We may wonder what exactly is happening when a disposition is caused in a human person not by natural temperament but by repeated activity even while that repeated activity does not cause a properly human habit. In one key text Aquinas uses the example of animals. He claims that we can admit the existence of "habits" in animals, citing Augustine's reference to the process of accustoming in brutes: "By man's reason brutes are disposed by a sort of custom to do things in this or that way, so in this sense, to a certain extent, we can admit the existence of habits in dumb animals: wherefore Augustine says . . . 'We find the most untamed beasts, deterred by fear of pain, from that wherein they took the keenest pleasure; and when this has become a custom in them, we say that they are tame and gentle.'"[36] It is interesting that Aquinas uses (in his own voice) the term "habit" for this dynamic, while Augustine himself uses custom. Nonetheless, the fact that this is an example of an extended use of habit is indicated in the very next line, where Aquinas claims: "But the habit is incomplete, as to the use of the will, for they have not that power of using or of refraining, which seems to belong to the notion of habit: and therefore, properly speaking, there are no habits in animals."[37] There are stable dispositions in animals caused by repeated activity (as efficient cause), but such dispositions lack the use of will and therefore do not attain to the notion (*ratio*) of habit properly understood. In animals we commonly describe the cause of such dispositions, when supplied by human guidance, as "training." Given the lack of rationality in animals, the disposition (level two) has as a formal cause, the specification supplied by sensory connaturalization as *causa transmutabilis*.

At this point we might rightly ask whether this dynamic in animals is comparable to one that can occur in human persons. After all, since human persons possess rational powers, can they develop dispositions from repeated actions (as efficient cause) that are not properly human habits, since the specification (formal cause) of those habits is supplied without involving rationality? Yes, they most certainly can, as especially any parent or teacher of children knows.[38] It is this dynamic that is labeled here (mere) accustoming, and the dispositions formed are labeled customs. In another key text on this topic, Aquinas inquires as to whether the human person's sensory powers of apprehension can be seats of habits. Again, Aquinas uses the term habit initially broadly to say that there can be "habits" in such capacities. He deploys Aristotle, who also equates custom with "second nature": "In the interior sensitive powers of apprehension there are some habits. And this is made clear principally from what the Philosopher says (*De memoria* ii) that 'in remembering one thing after another, what is at work is custom, which is a second nature.' Now a habit of custom [*habitus consuetudinalis*] is nothing other than a condition [*habitudo*] acquired by custom [*per consuetudinem*], which like unto nature."[39] This may be surprising, given which human capacities can be habituated (i.e., not the exterior senses). Indeed, in the very next line Aquinas qualifies this extended use of "habits" by quoting Cicero to give a precise definition of virtue (and by extension habit): "Wherefore Tully says of virtue in his *Rhetoric* that 'it is a habit like a second nature in accord with reason.' Yet, in man, that which he acquires by custom in his memory and other sensitive powers of apprehension, is not a habit properly so called, but something annexed to the habits of the intellective faculty, as stated above."[40] This is perhaps the most explicit reference to the distinction between dispositions called customs and properly human habits in Aquinas's work, in his own voice and buttressed by Aristotle and Cicero.[41] "Accustoming" can lead to what seems like a habit, since human powers (level one) become stably specified and thus become second nature (level two). However, in the case of nonrational animals and at times with human animals, this change in (more or less) stable specification occurs through the powers of sensory apprehension—not the exterior senses but rather the interior senses ("memory and other sensory powers of apprehension"). When this occurs in human persons, due to the absence of specification by rationality, such "customs" are not habits in the proper sense.[42]

In sum, custom may be understood as the repeated activity that leads to a stable disposition (though not proper habit) toward specific activity. Aquinas uses custom to refer both to the repeated activity leading to the disposition (a process that can be called "accustoming") and to the disposition itself, even at times calling custom (in the sense of disposition) second nature. It is possible for a person to possess a custom, a disposition from repeated activity, that is not a habit in the proper sense, since the stable specification of the natural capacity's activity is supplied at level two by changes in the sensory facets of the person (as *causa transmutabilis*) without the involvement of that person's rationality (as *causa immobilis*).

The distinction between mere dispositions (customs) caused by repeated activity and proper habits caused by repeated activity suffers great neglect in contemporary moral theological scholarship on virtue in Aquinas. A possible reason for that neglect is that when the formative processes of repeated activity (accustoming) are functioning well, they lead not simply to "mere" custom but to proper habits. In other words, repeated (generally communally mediated) activity leads a person's habituate-able natural powers (level one) to be stably specified not only by "accustoming" of the person's senses (e.g., the interior senses such as memory, imagination, etc.) and corresponding sensory appetitive but also by the more stable rational specification of her powers. Though we can "get used to" (or become accustomed to) activities in a manner that does not engage our rationality, normally the process of repeated activity will entail stable specification of the sensory in a manner informed by her rationality such that the sensory "participates in reason." In the same way that a person's natural temperament is not complete virtue (or vice), even as virtue properly understood "includes" such innately provided sources of specification of her natural powers, so too is mere custom not complete virtue (or vice), even as virtue properly understood commonly includes the sensory changes that ensue from the dynamics of accustoming.

Since the social practices called customs commonly bring about dispositions called customs, but as part of the more complete process of formation of properly human habits, it is easy to neglect this distinct role for custom—or the possibility of it existing before or without a proper habit.[43] But as already noted, these often untapped resources in Aquinas's thought on habit formation are enormously useful for a Thomistic approach to education, as well as for focusing attention on the crucial role of social structures in formation. As for education, any parent or teacher of young children knows how important accustoming children to stable good activity is, even when that activity is not yet truly understood by the child, for developing virtues as the child comes to age. "Getting used to" eating well, being polite, paying attention to tasks, or standing fast in difficulties—accustomization like this provides fertile ground for the development of the true habits that are the virtues.

Since all of this formation happens in social context—be it in the family, the neighborhood, the country, or some other community—Aquinas's thought on how communal customs engender custom dispositions in people, especially but not only children, helps explain how communal practices mediated by social structures have an intelligibility that is impressed on people, for good or for bad. Social theorists in recent decades have become increasingly aware of the formative influenced of social structures. Some recent critical realists have attempted to explain the power of such social forces in a manner that does not eliminate personal agency.[44] Aquinas's work on how accustomization further specifies human endedness at the sensory level helps explain how people are viscerally formed by society for good and for bad, long before Pierre Bourdieu's now classic treatment of this dynamic in the context of class distinction.[45] Recognition of the impact of social structures on personal formation is well placed within the discussion here, whether they be part of sensory accustomization or rational habituation or ecclesial formation, or some combination of these.

This treatment of custom should make it clear that one context for growing in virtue is when a person's powers, disposed by custom (accustomed), are more stably specified by the *causa immobilis* of her rationality, so as to be qualified by a properly human habit rather than a (mere) disposition. The next task is to examine what characterizes properly human habits, whose stable specification is supplied by the *causa immobilis* of rationality.

NOTES

1. Annas, *Intelligent Virtue,* 21.
2. The four extended treatments of what Aquinas calls the "causes" of virtue in the sense addressed here are: *Sent.* l. 3 d. 33, q. 1, a. 2, qae. 1–4; ST I–II 51 (on habits in general); ST I–II 63 (on virtues); and *De virt.* aa. 8–10.
3. Austin, *Aquinas on Virtue,* 66–68.
4. Though there are four, they should not be confused with Aristotle's four causes (one of which is efficient cause); these rather constitute various efficient causes of virtue.
5. ST I–II 66,1. Though the translation used here is taken primarily from the English Dominicans, that use of "accustomization" is changed to "habituation" (*propter maiorem assuetudinem*). For a similar yet slightly different list of these four causes, see *De virt. card.* a. 3. There Aquinas similarly lists causes of virtue as natural disposition, judgment of reason, or gift of grace. The remaining cause he refers to as "greater exercise" (*propter maius exercitum*).
6. See *De virt.* a. 8 for the most extensive treatment of the influence of environment. Other treatments are found at III *Sent.* d. 33, q. 1, a. 2, qa. 1; ST I–II 51,1; and, ST I–II 63,1.
7. For Aquinas's repeated use of "aptitude" (*aptitudo*) to describe the way a person's nature is oriented toward habituation, see *De virt.* aa. 8–9, esp. a. 8 ad 8. See Knobel's treatment of aptitude in *Aquinas on the Infused Moral Virtues,* 25–33.
8. For Aquinas's description of how the "ends" of human activity are supplied by nature even as they require further perfection, see *De ver.* XIV.2: "Nothing can be directed to any end unless there pre-exists in it a certain proportion to the end, and it is from this that the desire of the end arises in it. This happens in so far as, in a certain sense, the end is made to exist inchoatively within it, because it desires nothing except in so far as it has some likeness of the end. This is why there is in human nature a certain initial participation of the good which is proportionate to that nature."

9. See *De virt.* a. 8 for Aquinas's example of a first principle of speculative reasoning, where "every whole is greater than its part," and the first of practical reasoning is "evil is to be avoided." See also ST I–II 63,1 for the "seeds of virtue," such as the will's appetite for the good according to reason.
10. These more obviously "moral" examples are from Thomas, ST I–II 63,1. See also ST I–II 51,1: "Some are disposed by their own bodily temperament to chastity or meekness or the like." For health-related examples see ST I–II 51,1. See note 21 in this chapter on Knobel's argument as to whether one can actually have a natural disposition to meekness or chastity.
11. See *De virt.* a. 8. Atkins translates *ex naturali complexione* as "natural temperament," which matches contemporary usage. (The English Dominicans do the same; see ST I–II 51,1.) McInerny uses "natural makeup."
12. ST I–II 51,1.
13. ST I–II 51,1. Aquinas at one point mentions the influence of heavenly bodies, which presumably is distinct from interior causes (*De virt.* a. 8). Though these terms might be foreign to us, they can be understood as akin to saying that an infant's health is influenced by (internal) genetic factors and (external) environmental influences, such as exposure to lead paint, cigarette smoke, or thalidomide.
14. ST I–II 63,1.
15. This is an obvious place to address what the natural sciences help explain about the different ways individuals are variously disposed to activities. See Sullivan, *Habits and Holiness*, 83–112.
16. See *De virt.* 8. See also ST I–II 63,1: "All virtues are in us by nature, according to aptitude and inchoation, but not according to perfection." Aquinas consistently uses the terms imperfect and perfect to correlate with what is here called dispositions/habits (e.g., ST I–II 49,2 ad 3, and ST I–II 65,1). There are, of course, other meanings of perfect and imperfect; perhaps the most common use of this distinction is between supernatural and natural happiness (e.g., ST I–II 65,2).
17. ST I–II 63,1. See also III *Sent.* q. 1, a. 2, qa. 1, ad 2: "Reason adds a mode of causing to the mode in which something is caused by another naturally. And it is according to this additional mode that reason is principle of the virtues."
18. *De virt.* a. 8.
19. *De card. virt.* a. 2. See also ST I–II 58, ad 3. For a shift to using a blind man in this metaphor, see III *Sent.* d. 36, a. 1.
20. For examples of calling "virtue," which he goes on in the same passage to say are not truly virtues, see *De virt. card.* a. 2; ST II–II 23,7; and ST I–II 65,1 and 65,2.
21. Knobel has questioned to what extent a natural disposition may incline one toward chaste or meek activities, since in their most proper sense rational specification is requisite. See Knobel, *Thomas Aquinas on the Infused Moral Virtues*, 34–35. She is technically correct that such natural dispositions are not "plastic" and thus the more specific ends they supply do not incline one toward action that is informed by other (including further) ends, as Aquinas's blind horse example indicates. In this sense one cannot have a bodily disposition toward truly meek or chaste acts since such acts require rational specification. However, not only does Aquinas describe such dispositions using names of virtues, but his doing so indicates how some natural dispositions incline one toward acts that more commonly approximate the acts of these virtues. This leads Aquinas to claim, within the very text where he describes the imperfection of such dispositions, that the person who acts out of such natural dispositions "does well" (*exercitetur bene operando*)

(ST I–II 65,1). This topic is closely related to the relationship between residual dispositions from acquired virtues and the infused virtues.

22. For this term "annexed" (*annexum*), see ST I–II 56,5.
23. ST I–II 65,1. Aquinas seems to use *inclinatio* in a manner comparable to *dispositio*. Here it names a disposition that is not a habit, though presumably at times it can be used like disposition as a genus term to include both habits and dispositions that are distinguished from habits.
24. Three of the four treatments of cause (excepting *De virt.*) contain four articles. Compare the topic of the fourth article in each of these: III *Sent* d. 33, q. 1, a. 2, qa. 4 is parallel to I–II 63,4, on whether infused virtues differ in species from acquired virtues; ST I–II 51,3 is on whether (acquired) habits can be caused by one act. These topics are related to the efficient cause of virtue but do not offer a distinct cause of virtue.
25. ST I–II 63,1; and *De virt. card.* a. 3.
26. Three of the four use *actibus* (*Sent.*; *De virt.*; and ST I–II 51). ST I–II 63 uses *assuetudine operum*. Definitions for *assuetudo* in "William Whittaker's Words" include custom, habit, and repeated practice, the latter of which is used here since it engenders both of the former two (see https://archives.nd.edu/words.html, accessed May 24, 2021). The relationship between *assuetudine* and *consuetudine* is addressed later.
27. See ST I–II 58,1, where he addresses custom in the context of the meaning of the Latin term *mos* (or the Greek term *ethos*).
28. See White, "Instinct and Custom," 601n82. There is a ready connection here to Alasdair MacIntyre's renowned concept of practice. See MacIntyre, *After Virtue*, 187. Such a connection is the first of many nods to the communal nature of habituation.
29. ST I–II 58,1.
30. See *De vert.* 24,10, citing Cicero as a source. On the subject of virtue see ST I–II 56,5, and repeated affirmations of the causes of virtue in *De virt.* aa. 8–10.
31. Breen, *Imagining an English Reading Public*, 46. Though custom dispositions can indeed be quite stable, calling them "virtually inalterable" is too strong.
32. ST I–II 66,1 (author's translation). The use of *assuetudinem* here rather than *consuetudinem* raises the question of how these two terms are related. Lacking comprehensive research, it seems the two terms are roughly synonymous. In fact, McInerny usually translates *assuetudine* in *De virt.* as "by custom" (a. 9, ad 21) or by "accustoming" (a. 9, obj. 22). He also uses "practice" (a. 8, obj. 18). Forms of *assuetudo* appear far less frequently in Aquinas's corpus (only a few dozen in reliably authored works) than forms of *consuetudo* appear (nearly two hundred times in the *Secunda pars* of the ST alone).
33. See, respectively, *De virt. card.* a. 3 and ST I–II 65,1.
34. ST I–II 65,1.
35. ST I–II 66,1.
36. ST I–II 50,3 ad 2. For more on this see White, "Instinct and Custom": "While insisting in the *Summa Theologiae* that brutes cannot, strictly speaking, acquire habits (because habit is a function of choice), he grants that reason can modify the dispositions found in animals inasmuch as human trainers can establish custom within them" (601).
37. ST I–II 50,3 ad 2.
38. As noted by White in "Instinct and Custom": "Custom is the component of human experience that humans and brutes have in common" (600).
39. ST I–II 56,5. This is the English Dominicans' translation, with certain changes, of "*in viribus sensitivis apprehensivis interius, ponuntur aliqui habitus. Quod patet ex hoc praecipue quod philosphus dicit, in libro de memoria, quod in memorando unum post aliquid, operatur*

consuetudo, quae est quasi quaedam natura, nihil autem est aliud habitus consuetudiunalis quam habitudo acquisita per consuetudinem, quae est in modum naturae." Note that, oddly, the term *habitudo* appears infrequently in Aquinas's thought on virtue. Though not infrequently used in Aquinas's corpus, it never appears in the *Summa Theologiae* treatise on habit and appears only four times (including this one) in the treatise on virtue. The term seems to be a more general term for a condition. Indeed, it is more commonly translated by the English Dominicans as "aptitude," though here they (wrongly) translate it as "habit."

40. ST I–II 56,5. English Dominicans' translation, with modification, of: *Ex consuetudine acquiritur*, from "acquired by use" to "acquired by custom."
41. It is puzzling why Kent fails to see the reasoning behind this distinction in Aquinas. She says: "Thomas' distinction between habit and custom seems rather strained—and, from the perspective of ancient philosophy, hopelessly misguided." See Kent, "Habits and Virtues," 120. Alternatively, Breen captures the distinction vividly by noting the etymological connections between the terms *consuetudo* and *habitus* on the one hand, and certain contemporary English words on the other hand, connections that have illuminating connotations. She highlights one English word whose origin is related to custom (*consuetudo*), namely "costume," is something that is put on but is not thoroughgoingly who one is. Yet an English word related to habit (*habitus*), namely, "habit," in the sense of one worn by a member of a religious order, indicates a more thoroughgoing transformation of the person. See Breen, *Imagining an English Reading Public*, 49. The use of such metaphors to indicate the thoroughness of the transformation by habit are unavoidable in scholarship on habit. Particularly common are metaphors of "depth." For example, see Hursthouse, *On Virtue Ethics*, 156; and Russell, *Practical Intelligence and the Virtues*, 375. Importantly for this project, these metaphors indicate the possibility of growth.
42. To make this point crystal clear, Aquinas goes on to reiterate that habits are not found in the sensory apprehensive powers, but they are preparations (*preparatoriae*) for virtues in the rational powers (ST I–II 56,5). For more on the way that the sensory apprehensive capacities "are in a certain sense" said to be habituated, but not properly so, see ST I–II 50,3 ad 3. There he says: "In the interior sensitive powers of apprehension are able to be posited certain habits [*aliqui habitus*], according to which man has facility of memory, thought [*cogitativus*], or imagination: wherefore also the Philosopher says . . . that 'custom' [*consuetudo*] conduces much to a good memory." It is noteworthy, especially for a treatment of the habituation of the passions, that Aquinas links the amenability of the interior senses, including the crucial cogitative power, to accustoming. For another treatment of this see Titus, "Moral Development and Making All Things New in Christ," 244.
43. With reference to social practices, Aquinas's neglected thought on custom is an excellent occasion to address social forces operative in the formation of virtue. Indeed, roughly half of the references to custom in the *Summa Theologiae* are made in the contexts (not of virtue but) of law and justice. For a helpful examination of custom in the context of law and formation of citizens in virtue, see Keys, "Aquinas's Two Pedagogies," 523, where she treats ST I–II 95,1 (compare I–II 97,3). See also Murphy, "Consent, Custom and the Common Good."
44. For an introduction to critical realism as an approach to the relationship between personal agency and social structure, see Finn, *Moral Agency within Social Structures and Culture*. A fine example of such an approach in action is Smith, *What Is a Person*. See

also Daly, *The Structures of Virtue and Vice,* which brings critical realism and virtue into dialogue.

45. See Bourdieu, *Distinction,* where he argues that class stratification occurs in societies not simply through varied accumulation of economic resources but through instillation (especially in children) of class-specific aesthetics and "taste."

CHAPTER 4

ATTAINING PROPERLY HUMAN HABITS

Acquired Virtues

We now turn to the third of Aquinas's four causes of habit or disposition, namely, repeated acts that entail judgments of reason. This is an enormous jump from the previous two causes, nature and custom, which engender mere dispositions. Repeated acts that entail judgments of reason entail the *causa immobilis* of stable rational specification that is characteristic of the properly human habits called acquired virtues.[1] The significance of the difference between dispositions and habits can be seen in the contrast between terms like "knack" and "full-blown" habits. This difference is so important that one contemporary Thomist describes dispositions as not even "on the same plane" as habits.[2] While this may be a bit overstated, it is certainly the case that the *causa immobilis* of stable rational specification at level two makes an extraordinary difference, not only "within" the habit but also "across" habits and for a person's life as a whole. Examining how acquired virtue as a properly human habit is attained, as well as the ramifications of its stable rational specification, is our task in this chapter.

The first section of this chapter examines the process by which a human power, amenable to habituation, becomes qualified through repeated activity—both why repeated activity is required for these acquired virtues and what distinguishes these virtues from custom dispositions that are caused by repeated activity. While stable rational specification of a level two end characterizes a virtue, a virtue in the "fullest sense" of the term both involves a person's rationality and makes a person good. This leads to the necessity of repeated action and has ramifications for how virtues are enumerated. The second section investigates the difference that rational specification makes "within" virtue, focusing on how the stable rational specification of ends supplied by habits can be particular enough to aid but not impede practical reasoning in level three activity. It will be evident that rational specification does this while leaving "room for growth" in virtue. Next is a turn to the impact of rational specification "across" virtues and the connectivity of the virtues. The final section addresses a person's life as a whole through the oft-neglected topic of the "last end." By the end of the chapter it will be clear how a person can have room for growth, not only in the possession of individual virtues, but also in the extent to which her virtues are connected and there is coherence in her life as a whole, which points toward the ensuing chapter on growth in acquired virtue.

PROPERLY HUMAN HABITS: ACQUIRED VIRTUES CAUSED BY REPEATED ACTS

Though it may be a truism that "doing something over and over again causes a habit," Aquinas offers an account of how and why this happens. Recall that human powers moved and specified solely from the outside (e.g., the exterior senses) or inclined only to one act (e.g., the nutritive powers) are not disposed or habituated. Powers can be disposed or habituated if they both move and are moved, if they are underdetermined in the specificity of their acts, and if they are able to be specified well or poorly. Reflective of the moved mover condition, we must examine how a person's own movements can make her inclined toward specific activities.

Habituation-amenable human powers are oriented toward underdetermined ends and their activities fulfill them in specific ways. When an underdetermined power (level one) is specifically actualized many times through activity (level three), Aquinas claims a disposition (level two) toward such a specific way of doing the activity "settles on" the power.[3] These specific activities become "connatural" to the underdetermined power.[4] The power, now characterized by a quality, thus becomes inclined "by its own movement."[5] Whether as a habit or disposition, the form abides (more or less stably) in its possessor and inclines the individual toward a more specific end instead of the end supplied by nature. The result is "second nature." Therefore an agent's own acts can cause these habits or dispositions.

This process holds true not only for properly human habits, but also for dispositions, where specification of ends comes from sensory accustomization. What distinguishes the former from the latter is addressed later. First we must ask: Why is repeated action necessary for the formation of both custom dispositions and habits? For Aquinas, the answer has everything to do with the involvement of both "appetite" and "apprehension" in dispositions and habits, as well as the fact that moral actions concern contingent matters. First consider contingency.

Aquinas suggests that "in intellectual matters" it is possible for "one powerful demonstration to cause [the virtue of] knowledge [*scientiae*] in us."[6] However, "because things to be done [i.e., practical actions] are contingent and probable, one act does not suffice to cause virtue but many are required."[7] Whereas the intellectual virtues, such as knowledge, wisdom, and understanding, concern necessary matters and can be attained immediately by qualifying the speculative intellect, habits of the practical intellect, including both skills and acquired virtues, concern contingent matters and can be attained only through repeated action.[8]

Yet the contingent nature of moral action is not the only reason why repeated acts are necessary for attaining acquired virtue and dispositions. Repeated activity is necessary whenever the object, that is, the more particular level two end, is supplied by the powers of apprehension—as the specification of an underdetermined power always is (reason, in the case of habits)—and with the necessary involvement of the appetite. The speculative intellectual virtues not only concern necessary matters but their objects are also specified by reason alone. Aquinas distinguishes skills from acquired virtue by noting that although skills concern contingent matters, reason alone specifies their objects.[9] Thus a person can possess intellectual virtues and skills without the involvement of the appetite in the particularization of the level two end. The involvement of the appetite not only necessitates repeated action to attain a virtue; Aquinas also claims it is *only* virtues that involve both appetite and apprehension in the specification of the ends or objects of the habit that are virtues "in the fullest sense."[10] What does it mean for the appetite to be involved in this way, and why is that so important?

In Aquinas's terms, apprehension is a person's cognitive ability, whether it be sensory or rational (the latter of which, of course, includes the senses in this life). Through apprehension a person grasps how things are; apprehension is ordered to the truth. Appetite is the person's source of movement, not (just) physical movement but pursuit of ends. Through appetite a person seeks fulfillment; appetite is ordered to the good.[11] So Aquinas's claim that the appetite must be involved is simply another way of saying that "virtue makes its possessor good," a classic claim in virtue approaches to ethics that Aquinas takes as axiomatic.[12] It is through the appetite that a person is ordered to the good as such.[13]

Yet what does it mean to say the appetite is involved in the very particularization of a habit's (or disposition's) level two end? Consider two ways the rational appetite (the will) may be involved with rational apprehension (reason) in the human person.[14] On the one hand, skills and intellectual virtues do not "exist in, or depend on" the appetite for the specification of their particular end. A person may subsequently will to use her intellectual skill or virtue, and even will to use it well or poorly. But she "has" (Latin *habere,* origin of habit) these virtues, these stable particularizations of the speculative or practical intellect's ends, regardless of whether or not the appetite is involved subsequently. On the other hand, certain virtues "exist in, or depend on" the appetite to even be "had" and to be possessed in the specific way that they are.[15] This is obviously true of the virtues of the appetite, whether those be the sensory appetite or the rational appetite (the will). Yet it is also true of certain intellectual virtues that, while qualifying intellectual apprehension (reason) rather than appetite, they nonetheless rely on the involvement of the appetite to be specified. Aquinas says they "follow" the will; we might say they only come to be "had" with the involvement of the will. He gives two examples.

Prudence inclines a person (more specifically, inclines a person through her practical intellect) to choose well the means to ends supplied by the appetite. The particular (level two) end qualifying the prudent practical intellect depends on that good appetite. The virtue of faith inclines a person (more specifically, inclines the person through her speculative intellect) to believe truths about God. Aquinas details how all acts of belief, and certainly acts of belief in God in which faith consists, require the will to assent to something as true.[16] Thus the particular (level two) end that qualifies the faithful speculative intellect depends on that good will. In the cases of both prudence and faith, the habit's more particular (level two) end perfects the intellect but requires the appetite for the specification of its object.[17] In sum, virtues "in the fullest sense" involve both apprehension and appetite in the particularization of the end at level two.

Before a further examination of why and how repeated actions cause a (more or less stable) more specific (level two) end, the prior point about the conjunction of apprehension and appetite presents occasion to address how many virtues exist and on what basis can a list of virtues comprehensively cover the moral life. Contemporary philosopher Daniel Russell calls this the "enumeration problem."[18] The "problem" is how to sort through the myriad lists of virtues in contemporary and historical thought on virtue. Aquinas's approach derives from his point about the nexus of apprehension and appetite: he recognizes that intellectual habits like knowledge and wisdom and skill can rightly be called virtues. After all, in line with the definition of virtue presented earlier (see chapter 1), they are examples of habituation-amenable human powers having their underdetermined natural ends (level one) become more specific, and stably so, with specification (level two) engaging the person's rationality. However, Aquinas's treatment of the cause of virtue completes that account, since he claims that virtues in the fullest sense not only engage the person's rationality but also involve both apprehension and appetite in the specification of more particular ends. Hence this is an apt place to pause and note Aquinas's enumeration of the virtues, since his approach centers on these virtues in the fullest sense and whereby a person becomes good.

Aquinas organizes his analysis of individual virtues based on virtues "in the fullest sense." Though this does not include skills or (nearly all) virtues of the speculative intellect, it still includes a vast number of virtues. Aquinas approaches this enumeration problem through an account of general and particular virtues.[19] Though myriad lists of virtues may exist and differ from one another, Aquinas claims all particular virtues fall under general virtues and correspond to the powers of the human person that are rational (or able to participate in reason) and include the nexus of apprehension and appetite.[20] For general virtues Aquinas relies on the four cardinal virtues, a list having numerous Christian and non-Christian precedents.[21] The will as rational appetite is stably specified by justice. The sensitive appetite, as able to participate in reason, can be moved as concupiscible and irascible passions, and the sensory appetite is stably specified by temperance and fortitude, respectively. The practical intellect is stably specified by prudence toward acts of practical reasoning, which entail contributions from both appetite and apprehension. We can further categorize under the four cardinal virtues any virtue concerning some activity accessible to unaided human reason and making its possessor good.[22] While contemporary moralists at times feature the cardinal virtues in their work, they are less willing than Aquinas to ground them in a robust anthropology.[23]

What has any of this to do with the need for repeated acts in order to attain a virtue? The very features that characterize acquired "virtues in the fullest sense" necessitate repeated action. This is due to the contingent nature of moral action, and especially the necessary involvement of the appetite (inclined to "many things"), that repeated activity is required for the attainment of acquired virtue. Aquinas's most vivid description of this "fullest sense" involves water and stone: "One act does not suffice to cause virtue but many are required. And though these many are not simultaneous, they still cause a habit, because the first act causes some disposition and the second act, finding the matter disposed, disposes it even more, and third yet more and thus the ultimate act acting on the strength of all the preceding [acts] completes the generation of virtue, like the many drops that hollow the stone."[24] This vivid image suggests two points. First, initial acts further and further "dispose" a person until eventually the generation of the habit (here, virtue) is "completed." Aquinas thus indicates that repeated acts can cause dispositions, but at some point a person "crosses the line" from possessing a disposition to possessing a habit. (What constitutes crossing the line to possess a habit rather than simply possessing a disposition is addressed later.) A second point is that repeated actions are a necessity due to the involvement of the appetite.

Dispositions and habits caused by human activity require repeated acts because the specification supplied by apprehension must be impressed on the appetitive powers (or, in the case of prudence, impressed on the practical intellect in conjunction with the appetitive powers). Aquinas describes it this way:

> Habit is caused by act, because a passive power is moved by an active principle. But in order that some quality be caused in that which is passive the active principle must entirely overcome the passive. Whence we see that because fire cannot at once overcome the combustible, it does not enkindle at once; but it gradually expels contrary dispositions, so that by overcoming it entirely, it may impress its likeness on it. Now it is clear that the active principle which is reason, cannot entirely overcome the appetitive power in one act: because the appetitive power is inclined variously [*diversimode*], and to many things [*ad multa*]; while the reason judges in a single act, what should be willed in regard to various aspects and circumstances. Wherefore the appetitive power is not thereby entirely overcome, so as to be inclined like nature to the same thing, in the majority of cases; which inclination belongs to the habit of virtue. Therefore a habit of virtue cannot be caused by one act, but only by many.[25]

When habits are caused by acts in a habituation-amenable human power, repeated acts are necessary because the appetite is inclined toward "many things." This dynamic occurs in dispositions where specification is supplied by sensory apprehension being impressed on sensory appetite.[26] Yet Aquinas here addresses properly human habits, where reason "impresses its likeness" on the appetitive powers.[27] In both cases an underdetermined appetite (to "many things") is impressed upon by a person's cognitive apprehension so as to be supplied with a more specific (level two) end. We are now ready to more clearly identify what differentiates a habit from a disposition in light of this comparable dynamic.

In his most extended treatment of how virtues are caused by acts, Aquinas addresses the continuity yet difference between dispositions and true habits that are formed by repeated acts.

> When reason repeatedly inclines the appetitive power to some one thing, a disposition is implanted in it by which it is inclined to the thing to which it has become accustomed. It is this implanted disposition that is the habit of virtue. Rightly considered, therefore, the virtue of the appetitive part is nothing other than a disposition or form which is sealed and impressed on it by reason. Because of this, no matter how strong a disposition to something there may be in the appetitive power, it will only be a virtue if it is the result of reason. That is why reason is put into the definition of virtue.[28]

Here Aquinas uses "disposition" in its broader genus sense, since he notes that such a disposition is only a true habit (virtue) if it is reason that is "impressed on it." Even if there is stability, a virtue (as opposed to mere disposition) results only if the cognitive apprehension impressed on the appetite is supplied by reason. A person could also conceivably possess merely a disposition, even with rationality supplying the specification, even if on the way toward stability (as suggested by those initial drops on the stone) before the "generation of virtue" is completed. After all, it is the repetition that supplies stability, by impressing on the appetite the more particular end of the (level two) habit. Here we have reiteration of what qualifies a habit distinct from a disposition, namely, stability and specification supplied by reason.

Granting the necessity of repeated action to form both dispositions and habits, what distinguishes habits from mere dispositions (both at level two)? By now the clear answer is stability and rational specification. But what exactly do we mean by the latter term? In the first articles of the *Prima Secundae,* Aquinas addresses what distinguishes properly human acts (level three) from the acts of a human person. Properly human acts proceed from reason and will, he says, giving the person, as created in the *imago Dei,* dominion over them.[29] Aquinas describes what it means for properly human acts to proceed from reason and will. All activity proceeds toward an end, but in properly human activities the agent grasps the end: "When a person acts on his own toward an end, he knows the end" as an act of reason.[30] Furthermore, a properly human act "pertains to the will" since it "terminates at that which the will intends as the end."[31] Therefore, "the end is not extrinsic to the human act."[32]

Custom, as we might commonly call upbringing or societal influence, can cause dispositions to complex and socially mediated action toward ends. So, what distinguishes properly human action at what we refer to here as level three, and thus habituation rather than mere accustomization at level two? Properly human habits are caused by repeated acts that are properly human, that is, when the agent grasps the end with reason and intends it with the will.

In ensuing *Prima Secundae* articles about the "last end," Aquinas says that grasping and intending a goal includes not only the end itself but the end as directed toward further and in relation to other ends.[33] He intends the same in claiming that the stable specification of action in a properly human sense accounts for "various modes, in respect of the various matters, which constitute the sphere of virtue's action, and according to various circumstances."[34] Repeated properly human action at level three engenders a habit at level two for which the object is attuned to various ends and circumstances in a manner that is lacking in a disposition caused only by nature or custom. Human habits are thus enormously "plastic," unfortunately for bad (in the case of vices) as well as for good, due to this attunement to various ends. The plasticity at the level of habit (level two) is further increased by the various ways it can be acted upon in practical decision-making (level three), in a manner attuned to various circumstances yet also influenced by the connaturality of the object of the level two habit.

This is precisely what it means to say specification is supplied by practical reasoning. Individuals grasp their properly human habits' objects from the first-person perspective, such that the habit's purpose is understood by reason and intended by will. Indeed, the person grasps and intends not only the habit's end but also further ends the habit serves. The person also grasps the end in relation to other ends according to their relative importance.

It is this facet that distinguishes properly human habits.[35] After all, excellent upbringing and/or societal influence can dispose a person through custom to activities for which the individual is culturally and situationally attuned; education, in fact, relies on the process to give children's acts their specificity—hopefully for good, but also possibly for bad. Accustomization can supply a high degree of specificity in a person's activity but not in the same way as a properly human habit. It is only to the extent that the person grasps an act's end, as well as its relation to other ends, that level three activity and ultimately level two habit becomes fully human, perfectly voluntary, and truly her own.[36]

We have now established what distinguishes a habit from a disposition and what distinguishes habituation, properly understood, from (mere) accustomization: repeated actions are required to cause both a disposition arising from custom and a habit arising from habituation, due both to the contingency of moral matters and to the involvement of both apprehension and appetite in the specification of the habit's more particular end, such that a virtue makes its possessor good. Yet the acquired virtues have particular ends (level two) that are understood and willed rationally and grasped as ends in relation to other ends, including further ends. Thus habits are more truly "one's own" than are dispositions. We now turn to examine three ramifications of this account of acquired virtue: the challenges raised by practical reasoning "within" a habit; the ramifications "across" habits; and the ramifications for a person's life as a whole or as "last end."

PRACTICAL RATIONALITY WITHIN VIRTUE: INFORMING PRACTICAL REASONING, WITH ROOM FOR GROWTH

How does the possession of stable rationally specified ends (i.e., habits) influence practical reasoning that issues forth in particular actions? Every human power contains an inchoate end of its activity, lest there would be nothing to "get the ball rolling," so to speak, in human action.[37] This is simply another way of stating that human powers capable of being habituated are already inclined to something, albeit in an underdetermined way. Aquinas calls the general principles, or level one ends, the seeds of virtue.[38] At the other end of the spectrum are the particular actions, at level three, which are instantiated in concrete circumstances and which fulfill a person's powers. Habits are neither requisite for nor necessarily cause particular actions. If habits were requisite for all actions, they could not be acquired in the first place, since it is just this repetition that engenders a stable, more particular end and connaturalizes the powers toward more specific activities. Though habits incline toward more particular ends than are supplied by Aquinas's seeds of virtue, they neither necessitate action (since a person can fail to act on a habit, as evidenced when a habit changes) nor specify actions sufficiently for instantiation in every circumstance.[39] Level two habits are therefore neither requisite for nor a replacement for level three practical reasoning (the deliberation and choice leading to particular actions).

So how do habits influence level three activity? Aquinas tells us they enable habituation-amenable human powers to act with stability, promptness through specification, and pleasure or rest. Angela Knobel augments this answer in describing how level two habits supply "particular principles" to the human powers and guide their activity. Rather than precise actions for exact situations, Knobel says habits supply "appetitive inclinations" toward certain sorts of activity.[40] The inclinations move an agent toward more specific actions than do Aquinas's seeds, but they do not obviate practical reasoning. For example, whereas a person's will is naturally oriented to her overall good as a member of the human community, the general virtue of justice inclines the person to give everyone individually their due; the justice-governed particular virtues incline a person to seek conformity between speech and reality (truthfulness) and recognition of benefactors (gratitude). Whereas her concupiscible appetite, or desirous part, is naturally inclined toward sensual pleasures in a manner informed by reason, the general virtue of temperance inclines a person to moderate pleasure, and the temperance-governed particular virtues incline a person to enjoy alcohol to enhance social interactions (sobriety) or engage in sexual acts in the context of exclusive, permanent, procreative love (chastity). In each case, deliberation and choice is required to instantiate each virtue in specific situations.[41] The ends or principles provided by the virtue aids that deliberation and choice.[42] In this way habituation adds to but does not obviate practically reasoned actions.

There is a challenging balance to maintain here. If habits serve the role Aquinas describes—promptness, consistency, and pleasure/rest—their ends must be more specific than what human nature alone supplies. But in order to apply to the diverse situations humans face and to preserve a role for deliberation and choice, the habit-supplied end(s) cannot be overly specific. Habits must therefore advance the deliberation process without being either so general as to be obvious and unhelpful or so specific as to obviate deliberation and choice and mislead in unforeseen circumstances. Knobel describes this dynamic and offers examples of such particular principles in Aquinas's works.[43] In her recent work on virtue Jean Porter is quite emphatic that habits always have as their objects particular acts.[44] We might call these particular objects the "paradigmatic acts" of habits. For example, a person does not become temperate simply by desiring pleasures well; rather, she becomes temperate (with regard to food) by having a stable inclination toward and satisfaction in a well-balanced meal of various food groups. Or she becomes intemperate by possessing an inclination toward and satisfaction in foods with high amounts of salt and fat and sugar. Whether fast food or frozen pizza or a home-cooked meal or some healthy item on a restaurant menu, in all these cases the habit supplies more specific ends and yet requires further deliberation and choice.

While these appetitive inclinations may seem helpfully specific and more obviously show how people are formed, this account of the specificity of the objects of habits, their paradigmatic acts, does not come without challenges. One challenge is the possibility that the more specific end supplied by the habit might be *too* specific, so as to actually impede virtuous activity on occasion. Let's call this the "ham and eggs problem" and assume ham and eggs is a healthy breakfast.[45] Being inclined to eat ham and eggs each morning is therefore an inclination toward activity that is constitutive of human fulfillment and thus is virtuous.[46] Do occasions arise when eating ham and eggs would not be virtuous? One example is during religious fasting. Consider also occasions where national rationing might make eating breakfast an immoral act, or when a scheduled medical procedure might make eating ham and eggs bad for the individual. On these occasions an inclination toward ham and eggs would not be toward an activity constitutive of human flourishing, though we know that a virtue is supposed to be a habit that makes one good and with which no one can make bad use.

Some Thomists, in response to this "problem" in the case of temperance, suggest this virtue simply quells the sensory appetite so as not to disrupt reason. For them, temperance does not supply particular ends.[47] Indeed, Aquinas clearly and repeatedly claims that the moral virtues enable us to obey reason promptly.[48] But do the moral virtues assist us with practical reasoning? Do they supply ends or rather simply keep the appetite out of the way? Knobel argues that they do supply ends, using the account of particular principles taken mainly from Aquinas's inquiry as to whether prudence can exist without the moral virtues.[49] I endorse this position, and fortify it with an account of how the movements of the sensitive appetite called passions operate.

Since a passion is a movement of the sensory appetite, by definition the specification of that movement (i.e., an activity) is supplied by the sensory powers. Therefore any account of a passion whereby it is made virtuous simply by being (nonspecifically) quelled to await specification by reason is not a Thomistic account of passion. When we engage the world through our senses, we respond with our passions. The response can participate in reason to the extent that any object's sensory apprehension is governed by reason. Consider fast food french fries and assume they are unhealthy. Without ceasing to apprehend the fries in a sensory manner—their scent, their salty taste, and so forth—the agent apprehends the fries' specific characteristics in relation to broader attributes—the weight gain they cause, the digestive pain they inflict, and so on. Some of our learning with regard to fries happens solely by sensory accustomization. One might recoil at fries without rationally associating them with impending indigestion because the interior sensory powers have already made the association based on prior experience.[50] This accustomization disposes the individual to apprehend french fries as unhealthy through the senses alone. But a person can also have a reflective, rational grasp of fries' unhealthiness, recognizing the end of eating them as well as further ends to which they lead and how they are related. Here the rational apprehension of the object informs its sensory apprehension. The movements of the sense appetites are not merely quelled so that reason can supply the apprehensions; rather, as Aquinas puts it, the sensory apprehensions are informed by "various modes, in respect of the various matters . . . and according to various circumstances."[51] Nondisruption of reason may occur, but it is not due to the absence of sensory appetite specification until it can be supplied by reason. It is the appetite's spontaneous response toward action specified by sensory apprehension as informed by reason. The notion that the sense appetite is well habituated only when it does not respond until reason supplies its specification, a position Porter derisively labels the "good dog" approach to passions, not only deprives the person of well-formed passions contributing to action but also relies on the passions functioning counter to Aquinas's understanding of sense appetite.[52]

This brief foray into the recent debate among Thomistic moralists as to the "spontaneity" of the passions is warranted for an exploration of how properly human habits are stably specified by rationality.[53] If habits supply particular principles that specify the general ends supplied by nature, how can they do so while both advancing the actualization of those powers in a stable way and yet avoiding precluding the ongoing role for practical reasoning? One erroneous response to the challenge is as follows: out of legitimate concern that the particular principles that habit supplies—not leading a person away from virtuous activity in certain situations—the content of our level two dispositions must be something like "whatever reason supplies." The approach eliminates the role of habits as perfecting human activity by supplying more particular ends and enabling a person to act promptly, consistently, and with pleasure. Indeed, the whatever-reason-supplies account offers such little specificity that all virtue is reduced to prudence (a topic addressed later in the context of the connectivity of the virtues).

What of the opposite error in response to the challenge, namely, the over-specification of moral virtues so that on occasion they incline individuals to activity not constitutive of flourishing? Three things should be said on this. First, consider again the ham-and-eggs problem. Eating ham and eggs every morning is indeed excessively specific, and at times the habit almost certainly would impede human flourishing.[54] As Aquinas would say, the disposition from nature or custom is "ordered to one" act.[55] To be a habit rather than a custom—and a person could indeed become accustomed to ham and eggs each morning and disposed to it in a merely sensory manner—the stable specification would be engendered by the specific act of eating ham and eggs every morning. But abstracted from the act are less precise but still particular characteristics (e.g., amount of food, types of food groups, relation to a need for calories) that might render it good. Though this occurs only in and through objects as particular as ham and eggs, a properly human habit would not be directed simply toward a sensory object like ham and eggs.[56] It would be ordered to an object with regard for various modes, circumstances, and so forth, but one that still requires further specification in a concrete action.

This is why practical reasoning "within" a habit, so to speak, as the source of additional specification, is so important. Thus the ham and eggs argument attacks a straw man account of habit that is more akin to custom.

Before turning to the second response to the challenge of overspecification, note that both of the preceding arguments of the whatever-reason-supplies position (namely, that well-habituated passion is simply being quelled and that a habit toward something like ham and eggs is overly specific) share a commonality. Both offer an account of movements of the sense appetite (passion) in which the specification of the movement supplied by sensory apprehension cannot itself be informed by reason. Now, of course, the specification cannot be reason itself, lest the movement would be one of intellectual appetite or will. But nor does the underspecification approach have an adequate account of how the sensory apprehension can be changed by (i.e., governed by, participate in) reason, even as it remains sensory.[57] Lacking such an account, the passions cannot participate in reason in a manner whereby the (formal) causal influence of reason is constitutive of the passion itself *qua* passion. Reason either supplies the specification (in which case it is no longer a passion in the Thomistic sense) or quells or redirects a passion (whose specificity arises in a manner not influenced by reason). In both cases the passions are only disposed by custom or nature, with simple sensory specification. They are not truly habituated such that their sensory specification participates in the rational specification. The ultimate result of this account of passion is that the sense appetite cannot truly be habituated, or be considered a "subject" (material cause) of virtue.[58] Whatever the merits of this position, and there have been robust accounts of it in the Western moral tradition, at the very least it is not Aquinas's (or Aristotle's) position.[59]

The second response to possible overspecification in even properly human habits is that it can happen. Knobel suggests properly human habituation toward natural ends can impede the infused virtues' later activity toward supernatural ends.[60] This claim is true, and is addressed later with regard to the infused virtues. On the natural level we can understand that if the particular principles supplied by level two habits are more specific than the ends supplied by nature, such that they aid the actualization of human powers in precise activities, the principles on occasion may not be fitting for the actualization of the power in a manner most constitutive of flourishing. We have seen this already, in the case of dispositions endowed by nature and custom in Aquinas's blind horse example.[61] Though natural meekness or chastity might commonly lead to observably good acts, occasions may arise in which that disposition impedes good activity. Therefore, meekness and chastity are dispositions, not properly human habits. Indeed, the reason properly human habits are rationally specified is precisely to attend to various modes and circumstances. Yet can even such rational specification be at times too specific?

It is true that the particularization supplied by practical reasoning cannot anticipate every possible new situation. Elijah Millgram has addressed the topic through his "super Talmud" thought exercise. Millgram's *Practical Induction* offers an inductive account of practical reasoning and refutes instrumentalism (which assumes a person's desires are given and supply the ends of action, to which practical reasoning only determines the means). Whether Millgram's attack on Humean instrumentalism also implicates Aquinas, since Aquinas clearly thinks practical reasoning relies on "given" ends in some sense, is a fair question but beyond the scope of this book.[62] Millgram offers an account of how human practical reasoning, including the ends toward which a person acts, develops from experiences of interaction with the world. Though his focus is not on habit, his claim is that practical reasoning is incapable of possessing a set of principles that would neatly dictate the best course of action in every new situation. He imagines the possession of a "super Talmud," or book of practical wisdom, that contains guidance for every possible situation.[63] He claims that even the possession of such an imagined resource would nevertheless still require ongoing "practical induction" both to assess contingent situations that are unable to be fully anticipated and to assess those situations coherently from the perspective of the agent's variety of ends. In referencing particular principles, Millgram's work may address habits more than explicitly recognized. Regardless, if his claim is true about the novelty of future situations precluding the possibility that *practical reasoning* alone can ever be so fully formed as to anticipate every occasion, it is certainly true of the objects of habits, which are one step further from the particularity of specific situations.

As helpful as Millgram's work is, it turns out that Aquinas also treated this issue. While Millgram claims practical reasoning necessarily faces novel situations, Aquinas similarly claims it concerns contingent matters. This leads Aquinas to claim, contra the Stoics, that even after one possesses a virtue, virtue can be possessed to a greater or lesser degree. Addressing the objection that Aristotle's description of a virtue as the "highest reach of a power" (*ultimum potentiae*) necessitates that virtue is a maximum and thus no virtue can be more or less, Aquinas responds that the "reach" attained by a virtue can indeed be "more or less," since that toward which it reaches is not indivisible.[64] Even when rationally specified, there is still "room for further growth," if you will, in the possession of a virtue. He claims the Stoics denied this and that they were wrong:

> One man is better disposed than another to attain to the mean of virtue which is defined by right reason; and this, on account of either greater habituation, or a better natural disposition, or a more discerning judgment of reason, or again a greater gift of grace. . . . And here the Stoics erred, for they held that no man should be deemed virtuous, unless he were, in the highest degree, disposed to virtue. Because the nature of virtue does not require that man should reach the mean of right reason as though it were an indivisible point, as the Stoics thought; but it is enough that he should approach the mean, as stated in Ethic. ii, 6. Moreover, one same indivisible mark is reached more nearly and more readily by one than by another: as may be seen when several archers aim at a fixed target.[65]

Here Aquinas also depicts the four distinct processes by which a person may obtain a disposition or habit. He claims that not only habits but also dispositions can more or less approximate right reason even without rational specification, as in the case of nature and custom. But when right reason specifies a virtue, a person truly possesses the virtue in the properly human sense, even if the virtue is not followed at its highest degree. Though "room for growth" in virtue is not limited to further attunement to the measure of right reason, this is surely one reason why there is room for growth.

An agent's specification of particular level two principles can be complex and amenable to further growth, even when caused by merely sensory accustomization from societal context. However, the rational specification that is characteristic of habituation enables a person not only to grasp and take on ends more fully but also to have the particularized ends more finely attuned to various modes and circumstances. The difference is so great that Aquinas says dispositions are ordered to only one act and can impede a person in a manner akin to a blind horse, neither of which he claims about properly human habits.[66]

That said, even properly human habits are amenable to further growth, in part due to further attunement to additional modes and circumstances, given that practical matters are contingent. In other words, the specification of even properly human habits requires ongoing attunement.[67] This is precisely why properly human habits do not determine or necessitate activity, but rather inform it through particularized ends. Attainment of virtue is not a "one and done" phenomenon but requires ongoing active attunement. At this point we have reached the need to attend to how such growth occurs "within" a virtue, the topic for the next chapter.

Rational specification, characteristic of a habit, can minimize the frequency of situations where a habit inclines us to act in a manner not constitutive of human flourishing, even if it does not eliminate these occasions altogether. This is not an indictment of properly human habits. After all, our natural inclinations (e.g., to eat) can move us toward activity that is not fitting on particular occasions. But it does provide occasion to address another way that a person's rational powers are needed to ensure that activity proceeding from a habit is most conducive to human flourishing. This third response to the problem of overspecification concerns the importance of practical reasoning, not simply "within" each properly human virtue but "across" all properly human virtues. This is the classic topic of the connectivity of the virtues, which is both the third response to the challenge posed by possible overspecification supplied by the particular principles of second nature habits and as a topic important enough to warrant its own discussion.

PRACTICAL RATIONALITY ACROSS VIRTUES: CONNECTIVITY OF THE VIRTUES

Rationality within properly human habits supplies stable specification. Even within a stably specified human power, both rational apprehension and appetite are required to attain virtue in the fullest sense. Therefore, it is no surprise that there is connectivity between, or "across," properly human virtues, particularly virtues that qualify apprehensive powers (e.g., intellectual virtues like prudence) or appetitive powers (e.g., moral virtues).

Classical ethicists nearly universally affirm the connectivity of the virtues, a position that can be most basically summarized as "one cannot have any one virtue without possessing all virtues."[68] Contemporary moralists, on the other hand, almost univocally deny this position.[69] It is well beyond the scope of this project to offer a comprehensive account of the connectivity of virtues in Aquinas's thought or beyond, let alone the various different ways this classical position has been articulated or the possible responses to various contemporary objections to the plausibility of this position.[70] Yet a brief account of Aquinas's thought on the connectivity of the virtues is offered here, for two reasons: the very rationality that characterizes a properly human habit ("within" a virtue) also renders the different virtues connected with each other ("across" virtues), and the specificity of the particular principles supplied by habits can at times impede rather than contribute to good action. A grasp of the connectivity of the virtues offers a valuable resource in understanding how the more particular ends of human habits can incline a person toward human flourishing.

Before offering the two reasons in support of the connectivity of the virtues, it should be noted that while Aquinas does acknowledge that virtues need not be connected, unconnected virtue is imperfect: it is an "inclination to do some act which is in general good to do, whether such inclination be in us by nature or by accustomization."[71] Aquinas therefore refers not to properly human habits but to dispositions obtained by nature and/or accustomization. For example, he says individuals who are affable yet not chaste display dispositions caused by nature or custom. Thus when "virtues" are not connected, they remain dispositions. This is an indication that the specification supplied by right reason is not simply requisite "within" a properly human virtue; that role, of practical reasoning, stretches "across" virtues. The very condition that renders a quality a properly human virtue is the one that renders the virtues connected.

Aquinas's first argument for the connectivity of properly human virtues relies on the way we understand the four cardinal virtues, namely that discretion belongs to prudence, rectitude to justice, moderation to temperance, strength of mind to fortitude, and so on.[72] Citing Gregory the Great, Aquinas says such an understanding means we can have no strength of mind without moderation, no rectitude without discretion, and so forth. For example, if an individual's temperance fails, the individual cannot bravely resist temptation. One cannot give others their due in justice without sound discretion as to what they are due.

But Aquinas does not stop there.[73] He ascribes to Aristotle his second argument in support of the virtues' connectivity, suggesting we might envision the connectivity "according to the matters," that is, the virtues' material causes or subjects. Aquinas references the apprehensive and appetitive powers as informed by human reason. He claims the moral virtues—which qualify the appetite—require prudence, since they provide more particular ends than those provided by nature. But the moral virtue's possessor must then make choices among its ends.[74] Prudence allows practical reasoning, or making choices, to be done well. Conversely, prudence is right reasoning about things to be done, or choosing the correct acts, to reach an end. For prudent right reasoning, Aquinas says, "the starting point is the end of the thing to be done, to which a person is rightly inclined by moral virtue."[75] Therefore, if moral virtues qualify the reason-informed appetite to supply the ends of good acts, and if prudence qualifies the apprehensive power of practical reasoning to deliberate, choose, and act well toward those ends, the virtues are connected and agents cannot truly have one without the other.

This argument, which relies on a distinction between particularized ends as supplied by virtues and practical reasoning that implements such principles into action, fits in with the overall argument here, despite the fact that we are now relating "across" virtues rather than "within" a virtue. Virtues supply particular ends, ends represented by (and commonly attained by the performance of) actions, actions that are attuned to various modes and circumstances since they are human acts specified by practical reasoning. Such particular ends of the virtues do not replace but rather inform and aid practical reasoning. This seems to be exactly the dynamic Aquinas describes in the connectivity of the virtues: when the particular ends supplied by moral virtues are concretely instantiated through practical reasoning, the latter being done well habitually indicates prudence.

Prudence plays a distinctive role in Aquinas's vision of ends and means. It is itself a habit, supplying particular level two ends as a stable specification of human practical reasoning akin to the way a moral virtue functions. Yet it also represents the qualification of the practical reasoning that instantiates level three acts proceeding from the ends supplied by level two moral virtues. Is this Thomistic vision of prudence coherent? Some confusion arises when speaking of the virtues, especially prudence, as agents themselves. In the following quotation from Aquinas, the most common English translation is the following: "Right choice requires not only the inclination to a due end, which inclination is the direct outcome of moral virtue, but also correct choice of things conducive to the end, which choice is made by prudence, that counsels, judges, and commands in those things that are directed to the end."[76] But in the Latin text Aquinas neither says that "choice is made by prudence" nor posits prudence as the subject of the verbs "counsels, judges, and commands." The person, not prudence, is the agent. Alfred Freddoso's translation is more accurate: "But what is sufficient for a correct choice is not only an inclination toward a fitting end, which comes directly through the habit of a moral virtue, but also one's directly choosing a means to that end, which comes through prudence and which involves deliberation, judgment, and command with respect to the means to an end."[77] It is "through" prudence that a person makes a right choice, and prudence "involves" deliberation, judgment, and command. But prudence neither makes choices nor commands means: prudence is only a habit qualifying and supplying particular ends for a person's practical reasoning. In other words, prudence *qua* habit supplies the ends that then require instantiation in concrete action.

This suggests the second response as to the coherence of Aquinas's account of prudence, and it is a common claim in the literature.[78] Ends can exist at a variety of levels, some immediate and some more remote. The corresponding means to those various ends therefore vary in proximity. Indeed, what may be decided as a means to a further end becomes an end to which means are required. Prudence qualifies practical decision-making at all those levels, and thus its activity, that is, determining the means to serve particular ends through choices, exists at varying levels. In short, while it may seem that prudence is being referenced equivocally—sometimes qualifying as a virtue and thus supplying particular ends (level two) and sometimes qualifying as practical reasoning in choosing means to ends supplied by moral virtues (level three)—both are in fact the case.

The stable specification of properly human habits, as supplied by practical reasoning and not simply by the senses, not only "qualifies" an inclination to be a properly human virtue but also necessarily entails connectivity across virtues. Connectivity is not just an added feature of properly human habits; it is, rather, an inherent condition. David Decosimo describes the phenomenon: "Stability and unity [i.e., connectivity] mutually implicate one another and are inextricably related, inhering in virtue's *ratio*. . . . 'Connected moral virtue,' then, is no perfected subset within the habit of virtue, any more than 'person having attained age of reason' is of 'morally responsible human.' Nor is unity an independent addition that turns imperfect virtue perfect. Unity, *difficile mobile, recte ratione*, true virtue—these rise and fall together."[79]

Specification by right reasoning and connectivity are therefore inherent features of virtues and, as Decosimo says, they "rise and fall" together.[80] We know that rational specification does not preclude further growth "within" virtue. Similarly, connectivity is not solely a binary feature. In other words, though one can possess connected virtues or not (and if there is not connectivity, there is not virtue), one can also possess more or less connected virtue. At some point level two ends become sufficiently specified by reason, and therefore sufficiently connected, to be virtues. Just as the Stoics were wrong to assume that a person possesses a virtue only if it is possessed perfectly, it is equally wrong to assume that virtues are connected only if perfectly so. Examination of how growth in connectivity occurs is the task for a later discussion. For now we get a first glance of how practical reasoning "opens up," if you will, a person's habit beyond the limits of the habit itself to other habits, a topic further addressed later in the chapter. Consider now our third response to the ham and eggs problem.

Habits for which acts are specified by practical reasoning are not typically as narrowly construed as eating ham and eggs for breakfast every day. The habits are not mere sensory dispositions. However, even practical reasoning's stable specification need not and cannot anticipate every possible situation encountered by a human power. Thus, further practical reasoning must instantiate the ends supplied by properly human habits, or virtues. The condition is not a deficiency in human habituation and reasoning, but rather a maintenance of the balance between, on the one hand, stability, promptness, and pleasure inherent in acting in a manner constitutive of flourishing, and, on the other hand, openness to contingent situations and circumstances.[81]

So, habits supply particular ends that can themselves be revised and attuned to individual and communal flourishing, not only from practical reasoning within a habit but also across habits. Prudence enables a person to engage effectively in practical reasoning regarding the ends of moral virtues. And practical reasoning attunes ongoing activity to the person's various modes and circumstances. This repeated activity then reinforces and/or refines the habit and its particular ends. Just as habits inform practical reasoning, practical reasoning informs or attunes prudence and the moral virtues. Jean Porter has described this as a balance between "domain-specific rationality" and an "ideal of general reasonableness."[82] By the former she means that possessing a virtue inclines one, in some "domain" of activity, toward a more particularized end than what is supplied by nature. The object of such a virtue is not merely "doing what is reasonable," but rather some paradigmatic action in the relevant domain. By the latter she means that such paradigmatic action must be attuned to activity in other domains. This is why practical reasoning is so important for properly human habits, not only within but also across virtue. To complete this broadening trajectory and attend to how virtues are specified by an "ideal of general reasonableness" that attends to a person's "life as a whole," we now turn to the relationship between practical reasoning and last end.

PRACTICAL REASONING AND LIFE AS A WHOLE: THE LAST END

I claimed earlier that the connectivity of the virtues is universally affirmed in classical ethics and yet nearly universally denied in contemporary moral philosophy. Perhaps unsurprisingly, given how closely it is related, something similar can be said about the "last end."[83] The last end was taken for granted in classical ethics and yet plays nothing close to a comparable role in contemporary thought on virtue, at least not explicitly. Yet while today the last end is more commonly neglected rather than denied, it plays a greater role in contemporary thought on virtue than easily recognized. Indeed, another claim here is that, similar to Decosimo's argument that connectivity is inextricably related to possessing properly human virtue, possessing a last end and acting in a manner related to it is an inherent feature of properly human action. A survey of some recent dismissals of the classical notion of the last end and an account of the last end in Aquinas's thought that is not susceptible to such criticisms will make it clear why it is the case that possessing a last end is an inherent feature of being a practical reasoner.

The Last End in Recent Scholarship on Virtue

In her recent book on practical reasoning, Candace Vogler claims: "There is no longer philosophical agreement that individuals *have* last ends in the sense of final destinations toward which their doings tend in general."[84] This is an understatement! In one sense it is and always has been obviously true that people disagree as to what constitutes the last end of a particular life. The relative place of pleasure, virtue, and/or external goods in human flourishing was *the* focus of debate in ancient ethics. Aquinas notes in his discussion of the last end that people disagree as to whether the last end is pleasure, money, or something else.[85] Yet Vogler references not merely disagreement as to the "content" of the last end, but rather the very existence of a last end for persons, and how it might function within the practical reasoner. Why is this question commonly dismissed in contemporary moral philosophy?

Consider two such explicit dismissals. In her hugely influential *On Virtue Ethics,* Rosalind Hursthouse dismisses what she calls the "Platonic fantasy." This is the error of assuming that some sort of "grand end theory" equivalent to "an explicit, comprehensive, and substantial vision of the good" is requisite for the possession of virtue.[86] Daniel Russell likewise decries such a view as a "blueprint view," with "phronesis beginning with a correct and comprehensive blueprint of the human good, and choosing actions that realize this blueprint."[87] Hursthouse and Russell both aptly summarize the problems with this view.[88] First, it is "elitist" to expect from ordinary people high level and comprehensive philosophical acumen. Second, it is "deductive" to assert that in order to make practical decisions, a "comprehensive and substantial vision of the good" is required from which to deduce such decisions.

If the possession of a "last end," and its impact on practical reasoning, occurs in the manner described by Russell, Hursthouse, and others from whom they draw, it is rightly dismissed. Yet it is a classic straw man objection to an untenable account of the last end. Even Hursthouse and Russell seem to recognize this. Hursthouse claims: "If one is sufficiently cautious it is (just) possible to follow Aristotle in such things"—namely, the claim that the virtuous person possesses "a correct conception of *eudaimonia*, and thereby a grasp of acting well in accordance with the virtues"—"without making that mistake," the mistake being the Platonic fantasy of ascribing to the virtuous person "ludicrously, an explicit comprehensive and substantive vision of the good."[89] Russell rejects the blueprint view but then queries: "Even though phronesis is not about implementing some grand scheme of *eudaimonia* in particular circumstances, might it nonetheless be the case that a *phronimos* needs to *have* a conception of the good life as a whole in order for phronesis to function properly?"[90] Indeed, some conception of "the good life as a whole" is necessary for any practical reasoning and a fitting conclusion to this subject.[91]

A Thomistic Account of the Last End as an Activity

The first thing to say about the last end is that it is basically a claim about a person's life "as a whole."[92] It is an affirmation of unity in the myriad activities of a person's life. As Julia Annas says:

> All schools in the ancient world agreed that even before we can reason about our lives we have an instinctive tendency to think of our lives as wholes. . . . [W]e do not typically find arguments to show that it is rational to think of one's life as a whole, *to see one's activity as given shape by a single final end*. This is taken to be what we do anyway; at least we all do it instinctively, and the more reflective do it in a reflective way. We do not all do it well, of course."[93]

Porter consistently uses the phrases "the overall point and shape of one's life" as well as "one's life as a whole."[94] As some thinkers describe it, the claim that each person has a last end is thus an affirmation of coherence in a person's life to some degree.

Note that the affirmation of a last end is not a claim about the unity of a life from an observer's perspective; it is a claim about the person's perspective, or what might be called "the perspective of the acting person."[95] It is one thing to claim that a person's life can be regarded as a unified whole from an observer's perspective. Certainly that perspective can inform, even correct, the acting person's point of view. But, as Annas puts it, "essential to virtue [is] the global grasp of the agent's good unified from the agent's perspective."[96]

Second, the final end is related to various activities, even "giving shape" to them. Annas notes that a standard definition of the last end in ancient ethics is the "ultimate object of desire."[97] It is ultimate, or last, not as the final part of a sequence but rather as the "final good [that] unifies and organizes all my other aims and goods."[98] "It puts a stop to our desires by including and organizing into a whole the ends of smaller-scale desires."[99] It does so by being the "goal toward which our whole life and all our actions are oriented."[100] Jean Porter supports this by saying that part of "reflecting on the overall shape of a human life" is "to try and place the satisfaction of these basic desires and needs into the context of one's overall sense of a desirable or ideal human life."[101] Thus the last end is an affirmation of the unity of a human person's life, from her perspective as an acting person, in a manner that informs all of her activities.

Aquinas presents such a vision of the last end in the first question of the *Secunda secundae*, affirming that people have a last end, that each person has one such end, and that each person does all for the sake of it.[102] It is telling that Aquinas's "mini-treatise" on the last end follows immediately upon his account of human action as end-directed.[103] As Aquinas notes there, end-directed activity is far from unique to human persons. Activity toward ends that are constitutive of flourishing is endemic to all living creatures, even if the activity in fact fails to attain its end. What distinguishes a properly human action, as Aquinas describes in his famous distinction between a "human act" and an "act of a human," is that the end is grasped by rational apprehension (reason) and intended with rational appetite (will). Though Aquinas claims there are many voluntary actions of a person that are not properly human (e.g., scratching one's beard), in properly human action the end is known and willed. Those who have reason move themselves toward ends and are said to have dominion (i.e., free will) over their acts.[104]

Yet what does Aquinas's description of properly human action toward an end have to do with the *last end*? The very same features of a properly human action that render it free also relate it to the last end.[105] Properly human action entails acting rationally, that is, choosing particulars with an understanding of their place in a larger context, ultimately "the whole." To reference Aquinas's earlier quote, it is to act "in respect of the various matters, which constitute the sphere of virtue's action, and according to various circumstances."[106] Thus in discussing bravery, Annas claims that "the properly brave person grasps how acting bravely, while done for its own sake, also forms part of her overall good in her life as a whole; indeed understanding this is part of what it is to grasp what bravery is."[107] Central to human practical reasoning is the desire to not only act for an end but to do so in the context of how that particular end fits into further ends. What it means to choose particular actions *rationally* is simply to act in the context of a grasp of the universal, the overall point and shape of a person's life. In other words, practical reasoning simply *is* making choices with regard to particulars in the context of the whole.

Porter addresses this movement toward coherence by describing how children grow in practical reasoning. "The virtue of practical wisdom . . . is nothing other than a developed capacity to judge in accordance with one's *overall* aims and to choose a particular action accordingly."[108] Further, "practical reason . . . functions in such a way to bring order to diverse aims and considerations."[109] It entails "consideration of one's life as a whole, [and] the proper place for discrete goods within such a life."[110] There is something inherently holistic about action according to reason.[111] This is precisely what is meant in the claim that for the ancients, virtues "all reflect *his* considered conception of his overall good."[112] Therefore the Thomistic argument that all acts are for the sake of a final end is actually a corollary of the claim that human action is for an end as grasped by practical intellect. Porter summarizes this idea:

> The claim that every person necessarily directs all of her actions toward a final end may seem implausible at first, but on Aquinas' view this claim is a necessary implication of the view that a human person acts voluntarily, that is to say, in pursuit of some end. If the agent did not have a final end in view, her pursuit of intermediate ends would have no rationale or point—which is tantamount to saying that her behavior would not be sufficiently rational to count as [truly human] action at all.[113]

As Annas puts it starkly, "my life is not just a series of, so to say, one damned end after another."[114]

Understood in this manner, the last end is more of a feature of contemporary accounts of virtue than explicitly recognized. The assumption that possessing a last end and acting toward it necessarily entails a fully determinate and coherent account of all of a person's activities makes it seem impossible to contemporary philosophers. Annas claims a common mistake today that leads to dismissal of the last end is an assumption that it is "something given in a determinate way."[115] She goes on to offer a corrective as to both the level of determinacy and the active process of such ordering: "The final end, then, is the indeterminate notion of what I am aiming at in my life as a whole. And the role of ethical thinking is to get us to think more determinately about it, to do a better and more intelligently ordered job of what we are already doing anyway."[116] The last end cannot, of course, be wholly indeterminate, lest it be useless in supplying any coherence. But Annas is surely correct that it is not fully determinate. And not only the goal of "ethical thinking" (assuming this is more formal) but also the goal of any everyday practical deliberation, is to act in an increasingly unified manner. As Christine Korsgaard describes it, "The function of deliberation is not merely to determine how you will act, but also to unify you. . . . [Y]our movement will not be a [properly human] action unless it is attributable to you—to you as a whole or a unified being—rather than merely to something in you."[117] It should be clear at this point that the last end is not simply a fixed goal "out there" but also an ongoing activity of bringing coherence to our lives.[118] Due to the contingent nature of practical action, it is an activity that will never be complete in this life.

An important ramification of this claim is that there is room for growth in the coherence of a person's activities toward the last end. Just as the claim that the virtues are connected admits of the possibility in further growth in virtue, and thus increased connectivity, so too can activities be more or less coherently ordered to a person's last end, even while the person already possesses a last end. Millgram describes well such a continuum of coherence:

> At one extreme, someone in whom action is triggered by whatever impulse happens to come over him, without any regard to other concerns or interests he may have, is a mere collection of reflexes rather than a cohesive acting self. At the other, the thoughtful deliberator whose every decision is appropriately informed by the full range of considerations available to him is the *phronimos*, . . . [an] ideal of practical intelligence, unified agency, and virtue. . . . Between the extremes of infancy and wisdom lies the modicum of coherence that we demand of responsible adults.[119]

These contemporary depictions of what happens in practical reasoning are indeed accounts of how each human person has a last end and how a person orders all of her activities toward that last end. It is an active, ongoing process that admits of room for growth, the topic of the following chapter. But first some attention to the "content" of the last end is warranted.

The Last End as What Life Is "All About"

It is common in virtue-based approaches to morality to treat happiness as both something "out there" to be attained and the human activity of attaining it.[120] For instance, after his opening question in the *Summa Theologiae* I–II on acting for ends and the last end, Aquinas poses a question on what out there is sought as our happiness (I–II 2) and then a question on the manner of attaining happiness (I–II 3). The same may be said for the last end, which is both something "out there" to be attained and an activity. Moralists who neglect or dismiss the last end tend to regard it solely in the former sense (and assume the latter sense is constituted by mere deduction from an excessively complete account of it). One main purpose of the previous section is to emphasize that acting for the sake of the last end is an ongoing, active process capable of growth. We might even call it the verbal "last end-ing."[121] In the same way that happiness is an activity, "last end-ing" is an ongoing activity for the practical reasoner.

This raises a topic for virtue-based approaches to morality common to both classical ethics and contemporary moral philosophy: if happiness and the last end are properly understood as human activities, and virtues are those habits that stably incline a person toward such activities, rendering virtue *necessary* for happiness, is virtue also *sufficient* for happiness? Does any outcome or state of affairs (i.e., results) need to be attained for a person to be truly happy, to attain a last end?

The answer may seem to be an obvious yes, but that was not at all obvious to certain classical approaches to virtue, especially among the Stoics.[122] Even Aristotle, who contra the Stoics represents an "unstable view" of happiness, whereby happiness requires both virtue and certain outcomes or states of affairs, is read today as closer to the Stoics than one might expect.[123] In contemporary treatments of virtue this classical issue is always addressed, and many leading figures who are influential on this study signal their proclivity toward the Stoic equation of happiness and virtuous activity.[124] There are persuasive reasons to adopt the Stoic position in a manner that does not dismiss the importance of a person's friendships, family relationships, engagement with worldly concerns, and so forth.[125] And surely this position is all the more attractive for contemporary moral philosophy, since it seems to obviate any "metaphysics of value" account of what out there is to be sought as the highest good.[126]

That said, it was not Aquinas's (nor Aristotle's) answer. They considered the standard candidates for what life could be "all about" to include pleasure, money, power, fame, friendship, and the communal good, or (in Aquinas's case) the uncreated God. When directed toward any of these as last end, a person not only prioritizes that end above others but also allows that last end to inform how the myriad other activities in a person's life are accomplished. Aquinas regards the common good to constitute natural human flourishing, a true good even if humanity is ultimately ordered to the more perfect last end of supernatural happiness in union with the uncreated God and others in God.[127] He offers arguments on both why the common candidates (pleasure, money, fame, etc.) cannot constitute true happiness and why only the uncreated God can fully do so.[128]

There is a multitude of issues raised by a recognition that happiness, the last end, is not wholly constituted by human activity. For instance, consider the classic question of how a variety of goods are united with regard to a person's last end.[129] Another worthy inquiry is the extent to which what Alasdair MacIntyre calls the "dominant account" of happiness today, namely, the subjective state of "feeling good—enjoying life and wanting it to be maintained," is comparable to the common enemy of the Stoics and the Aristotelians in antiquity, namely, the Epicurean focus on pleasure.[130] There is the question of whether or not various common candidates for the last end (e.g., money, pleasure) reduce ultimately, as Augustine thought, to the prideful self as last end such that a person must choose either God or herself as her final end. Finally, there is the question from a Christian perspective of whether or not it is possible for a non-Christian to have true but imperfect natural human flourishing as a last end, particularly given the effects of human sinfulness. Clearly these various important questions as to the "content" of the last end cannot be addressed in any detail here. But three points are appropriate about the "content" of the last end that will serve the upcoming treatment of growth in acquired virtue.

First, regardless of what serves as a person's last end, there remains in this life ample opportunity for that last end to provide increasing (or decreasing) coherence to the person's life. This may explain why thinkers like Annas describe the last end as an "indeterminate" notion. Even when specified (e.g., as God, or money), the necessarily contingent nature of human practical action means that "last end-ing" is an ongoing activity of practical decision-making and that a person can act toward her last end to a greater or lesser degree. How Aquinas claims both that she does all she does for the sake of her last end and that it is possible to act in a manner that is not coherent with her life as a whole, is a topic for a later discussion, since it is one arena where we find room for growth.

Second, from the perspective of the acting person, she can hold as her last end something like pleasure or money, and that last end can provide coherence to her activity. Yet, since according to Aristotle and Aquinas such candidates ultimately fail to constitute the true last end of human happiness, neither can they supply the level of coherence of a true last end or the complete fulfillment of human desires that are possible by acting in accordance with reason or the truthful grasp of the way things are. This is the step that modern moral philosophy eschews, since it is assumed that some metaphysical account of the good is needed to support such a claim. Contemporary moralists tend to rest content in claims that only virtue can provide the full coherence in a person's life.[131] Or they claim simply that the way we not only act but raise children indicates we believe virtue to be constitutive of happiness.[132] Others are willing to grant that the vicious life is not any less coherent than the virtuous one, insisting that theological claims are requisite for establishing true virtue.[133] Obviously Aquinas's argument about complete human fulfillment consisting in supernatural happiness gifted by God is granted here. Rather than rehearse those arguments or repeat Aquinas's and Aristotle's arguments in support of the idea that the common good (including virtuous activity) is constitutive of natural human flourishing, it is beneficial to simply point out that such arguments mean that a life of true virtue (natural or supernatural) is indeed inherently more coherent than a life of vice. Though a last end such as money or pleasure does indeed provide coherence to a person's life, such coherence cannot match that of true human flourishing—and thus nor can the vices be connected in the manner that the virtues are connected.

Third, formation in possessing and acting coherently toward a last end is a thoroughgoing social endeavor. In our families and in society, particularly as children but really throughout our lives, social forces offer de facto claims about what life is or should be "all about." Though we rightly speak of an individual possessing a last end, that possession is far from an individualistic endeavor. Communities help form people as to their last ends, not simply by encouraging them to view their lives as wholes but also by supplying candidates for what unifies such lives. Children are raised with language and activities that convey the centrality of entertainment, or duty toward one's country, or supremacy of money, or the sovereignty of the living God. Today we are particularly aware of the pervasive role of social forces in shaping what people's lives are all about, be it through Bourdieu's social theory of *habitus*, MacIntyre's analysis of the practices of modernity, or critical realism's account of social structures.[134] In short, a focus on an individual's practical reasoning and the possession of a last end should in no way occlude the crucially important social forces of formation. These forces are an important part of the account of growth in virtue, to which we now turn.

NOTES

1. Attention to how God's grace (the fourth of Aquinas's causes) can also supply a *causa immobilis* of habits in the proper sense of the term is addressed in chaps. 6 and 7.

2. See Miner, "Aquinas on *Habitus*," 69.
3. *De virt.* a. 9: "*Et firmatur in eis inclinatio determinata in illud*" (author's translation).
4. For a helpful treatment of connaturality, see Maritain, *The Range of Reason*, 22–29. Though well beyond the scope of this discussion, the connaturalization that occurs in the formation of dispositions and habits provide a helpful contribution to currently stalled debates in Catholic moral theology about the role of "experience."
5. *De virt.* a. 9 (author trans.): "*Cum multoties inclinantur, determinantur ad idem a proprio movente.*"
6. *De virt.* a. 9 ad 11.
7. *De virt.* a. 9 ad 11.
8. See ST I–II 57,1 and ST I–II 57,4 ad 2.
9. ST I–II 57,4. See also Aquinas, *Comm. Nic. Eth.* vi.5 (1172). There are important similarities between virtues and skills that have prompted recent moralists, perhaps most notably Julia Annas, to describe virtues as skills. See Annas, *Intelligent Virtue*, 16–51, where she delineates the conditions that make virtue akin to a skill, rather than a "knack" ("knack" seems to refer to what is called here a disposition from custom or nature) (20). Annas also addresses objections that her account is too intellectualist (28–32). It is not until later in her account, when describing the "commitment to goodness" characteristic of a virtue (109–11), that she deploys a resource comparable to Aquinas's skill/prudence distinction.
10. See *De virt.* a. 7 for how intellectual virtues and skills are virtues "in some sense" but not "in the fullest sense."
11. This claim about virtues applying to human powers oriented toward the true and the good is worded in Aquinas's Aristotelian anthropology, but he makes a point that is not reliant on that terminology. For a comparable account of virtue at the nexus of cognition and affect, consider recent authors who deploy a CAPS (cognitive affective processing system) approach to personality. See Snow, *Virtues as Social Intelligence*, 12–13, 19–34, 117–18. See also Russell, *Practical Intelligence and the Virtues*, 242, 261–62, 323–31, where he speaks of both cognitive and affective elements and construal and responsiveness.
12. For Aquinas's affirmation of this claim, see ST I–II 55, esp. 1 and 3. See also *De virt.* aa. 2, 6–7. In this latter article Aquinas cites Aristotle's *Nicomachean Ethics* ii.6. This also means that vices make their possessor bad in a manner that the lack of skill or speculative virtues do not.
13. *De virt.* a. 7.
14. What follows is dependent upon *De virt.* a. 7. See also ST I–II 56,3.
15. In these cases Aquinas claims reason and will "involve each other" ("*intellectus et voluntas se invicem circumeunt*") in the very specification of activity (*De virt.* a. 7).
16. See ST II–II 2,1.
17. See *De virt.* a. 7: "Habits which are in the speculative [faith] or practical [prudence] intellect *insofar as intellect follows will* more truly have the notion of virtue, since by them a man is made not only capable or cognizant of acting well, but willing" to act (emphasis added).
18. For a contemporary philosophical account of the enumeration problem, see Russell, *Practical Intelligence and the Virtues*, 145–54.
19. For an analysis of Aquinas's use of general/particular virtues, along with attention to Aquinas's immediate predecessors, Philip the Chancellor and Albert the Great, see Houser, *The Cardinal Virtues*.

20. ST I–II 61,1 61,2.
21. The four cardinal virtues are found in Scripture (Wis. 8:7) as well as in the writings of Christian (e.g., Augustine, Ambrose) and non-Christian (Plato, Cicero) thinkers alike. Though reference to the four cardinal virtues are found consistently in the Western moral tradition, Aquinas's defense of the list as corresponding to morally significant powers of the person is not found in those more distant precedents, and indeed relies on succeeding anthropological developments, including regarding the will as a distinct power. For a classic account of the development of the "will" in Western thought, one where Augustine features most prominently, see Dihle, *The Theory of the Will in Classical Antiquity*.
22. See ST I–II 61,2 and 61,3 and *De virt. card.* a. 1. This schema is deployed in the *Secunda secundae*. In the *Secunda secundae* they are complemented by the three theological virtues, which have as their object not matters accessible to unaided reason but God's very Self. They qualify a person's will (charity and hope) and the speculative intellect (faith), though in the latter case needing involvement of the will. The theological virtues are addressed in chaps. 6 and 7. For Aquinas's explanation of how "human" (rather than superhuman) virtues, i.e., the cardinal virtues, can be treated distinctly before the graced virtues, see ST I–II 61,1 ad 2.
23. For a contemporary moralist who does adopt a general/particular approach to enumeration, or what he calls "cardinality," see Russell, *Practical Intelligence and the Virtues*, 155–58, 196–208. Despite his appeal to "cardinality," Russell's refusal to base the cardinal virtues in anything close to an anthropology leaves him floundering to offer any list, at times saying, "It falls to each particular virtue theorist to say *which* virtues are cardinal," and on the same page, "It would be a mistake to suppose that identifying and individuating virtues is *entirely* down to the discretion of the theorist" (158) (emphases in original). For an example of another contemporary who references the cardinal virtues as possibly having some basis in human nature but who dares go no further in supporting the claim, see Annas, *Intelligent Virtue*: "It is extremely plausible that there is a basis in human nature for at least some central virtues" (98), after she had just referenced the cardinal virtues. Like Russell, Annas references Christopher Peterson and Martin Seligman's influential list, which also nearly approximates the cardinal virtues. See Peterson and Seligman, *Character Strengths and Virtues*.
24. *De virt.* a. 9 ad 11. Author adjustment of McInerny translation, rendering *in virtute* "on the strength of" rather than the confusing "in virtue of."
25. ST I–II 51,3.
26. For a description of the impression of sensory apprehension on the appetite, see ST I–II 56,5.
27. See also *De virt.* a. 9: "Because the appetitive power concerns one thing or another, it does not tend to one object unless it is determined to do so by reason" ("*Quia igitur vis appetitiva se habet ad utrumlibet; non tendit in unum nisi secundum quod a ratione determinatur in illud*") (author's translation).
28. *De virt.* a. 9. Here Aquinas uses "disposition" in the genus sense, since he is explaining how a habit is formed rather than distinguishing habit from disposition.
29. ST I–II 1,1, Prologue.
30. ST I–II 1,2 ad 1.
31. ST I–II 1,3 ad 2 and 1,3, respectively. For more on end-directed activity, on the link of appetite and apprehension, and on the "becoming one's own" of action, see Porter, *Nature as Reason*, 195–203.

32. ST I–II 1,3 ad 1.
33. See ST I–II 1,4–1,6. Aquinas's account of the last end, and its relation to properly human activity, is addressed later.
34. ST I–II 63,1. See also *Sent.* l. 3 q. 1 a. 2 qa. 1 ad 2. See also ST I–II 51,3: "Reason judges in a single act, what should be willed in regard to various aspects and circumstances." This phrase serves as a marker for action and indeed the objects of habits that are specified by practical reasoning. For comparable descriptions in recent moral philosophy, see Annas for a similar phrase: "Practical intelligence gets things right in very diverse circumstances" (*Intelligent Virtue*, 95). See also Russell: "Virtues in the strict sense . . . involve practical reasoning, since virtue in the strict sense involves integration and balance of diverse demands" (*Practical Intelligence and the Virtues*, 171); and "Every virtue is a form of responsiveness to practical reasons within its sphere of concern, where these reasons are situated within a broader range of other practical concerns" (371). Vogler describes "end-based" activity as "grounded in an appeal to our private [*sic*: own?] ends, desires, plans, projects, character traits, or what have you" (*Reasonably Vicious*, 102).
35. This is obviously a high standard of distinctively human action that is variously achieved. Recent debate among moral philosophers has also focused on whether moralists like Julia Annas, who regard virtue as a skill, demand for the possession of virtue too high a degree of "articulacy," namely, the "role of reason-giving." Annas requires that the virtuous person not only do good acts for good reasons (and stably so) but also gives reasons for such action on demand. For an account of virtue as skill that addresses Annas's high standard of articulacy, see Stichter, "Virtue as a Skill," 60–66.
36. This notion of action as truly one's own is commonly described in recent moral philosophy as "for its own sake." For an influential treatment of what it means to do an act "for its own sake," see Hursthouse, *On Virtue Ethics*, 126. See also Annas, *Intelligent Virtue*, 41–51, for treatment of right action and virtue and recognition of differences among virtue ethicists on this topic (51n39).
37. Recall *De ver*. XIV.2: "Nothing can be directed to any end unless there pre-exists in it a certain proportion to the end, and it is from this that the desire of the end arises in it. This happens in so far as, in a certain sense, the end is made to exist inchoatively within it, because it desires nothing except in so far as it has some likeness of the end. This is why there is in human nature a certain initial participation of the good which is proportionate to that nature." Knobel offers a helpful treatment of this passage in *Aquinas and the Infused Moral Virtues*, 25.
38. For a helpful treatment of the seeds of virtue, see Knobel, *Aquinas and the Infused Moral Virtues*, 25–35. Knobel claims there is development in Aquinas's work regarding his use of seeds: "Aquinas uses 'seed' to refer indiscriminately to *all* components of man's natural aptitude for virtue. In later texts, however, he consistently reserves the term "seed" for our natural habitual knowledge of the principles of the natural law" (chap 1, n39). Both seem true, since surely all human powers have seeds, if by that is meant some existence of the end of the power's activity in the power itself. Knobel recognizes as much in citing *De ver*. XIV.2 (25–28). However, if referencing properly human acts and habits, these must spring from first principles of practical reason, including as those that inform sense appetite. For another treatment of this issue, see Titus, "Moral Development and Making All Things New in Christ," 242.
39. This topic, where the impact of a habit on action supplies a particular end, understandably raises the question of whether action out of a habit can truly be considered free. For a helpful recent treatment of the causal impact of a habit on action while guarding the

possibility of responsibility and change, see Russell, *Practical Intelligence and the Virtues*, 388–92. For such an analysis focusing on Aquinas, see Jensen, *Sin*, 238–84.

40. Knobel, *Aquinas and the Infused Moral Virtues*, 37–39.
41. See Porter on this point: "The ideals of particular virtues are themselves indeterminate, and stand in need of further specification" (*Nature as Reason*, 226); for reference to this further specification of virtues (level two) in activity (level three) with reference to natural law: "The virtues provide mediating principles between a basic teleological conception of human nature and the properly moral norms of the natural law" (177–78).
42. For the claim that habituation aids rather than precludes reasoning, see Annas: "Rather than the rest of the mind being shut off from patterns of routine and proceeding independently, the ability, though a habituated one, is constantly informed by the way the person is thinking. . . . The practical mastery is at the service of conscious thought, not at odds with it" (*Intelligent Virtue*, 14).
43. Knobel, *Aquinas and the Infused Moral Virtues*, 45–46.
44. See Porter, *Perfection of Desire*, 41, 66, 70. Porter commonly cites ST I–II 49,3 and ST I–II 54,2 to support her claim.
45. The ham-and-eggs example is inspired by Butera's treatment of temperance and breakfast in "On Reason's Control of the Passions," 143–44, 149.
46. For a helpful treatment of good activity as constitutive of happiness/fulfillment, see McCabe, *The Good Life*, 5–6.
47. See the accounts of the passions' participation in reason as offered by Butera, "On Reason's Control of the Passions"; and Kahm, *Aquinas on Emotion's Participation in Reason*.
48. See, e.g., ST I–II 68,3, as well as Knobel, *Aquinas and the Infused Moral Virtues*, 42.
49. See ST I–II 58,4, which is addressed in Knobel, *Aquinas and the Infused Moral Virtues*, 43–47.
50. Note that in this case, despite the seeming accuracy of the sensory disposition, we still have only a disposition, not a habit, because that inclination is supplied only by the senses. Such associations can of course happen to incline a person to healthy or unhealthy acts. In either case they are not yet "moral," since there is no participation in reason. See ST I–II 24,3 ad 1. The possibility of what Aquinas calls "the interior senses" operating without influence by reason or in a manner informed by reason has prompted much recent discussion on the cogitative power (see note 53).
51. ST I–II 63,1. Note that Aquinas's claim, that the human cogitative power is the interior sense that is both firmly sensory and yet also able to be informed by reason, has led to many recent studies of this power. See De Haan, "Moral Perception and the Function of the *Vis Cogitativa*," and "Thomistic Hylomorphism, Self-Determination, Neuroplasticity, and Grace." See also Uffenheimer-Lippens, "Rationalized Passion and Passionate Reality. In Thomistic psychology, the cogitative power (i.e., the human version of the estimative power in animals) is the nexus of the sensory and rational. For a recent critique of the claim that it serves this role, focused on DeHaan's work, see Kahm, *Aquinas on Emotion's Participation in Reason*, 256n44.
52. See Porter, *Perfection of Desire*, 57. She is referring to Korsgaard, *Self Constitution*, 147. In *Nature as Reason* Porter makes a comparable point when she claims, "If the virtues were sheerly dispositions to act in accordance with reason, they would render the passions otiose" (192).
53. For a helpful overview of this debate, despite my disagreement with his position, see Kahm, *Aquinas on Emotion's Participation in Reason*, 24–25. Other important

contributions include Butera, "On Reason's Control of the Passions"; Jensen, "Virtuous Deliberation and the Passions"; Gondreau, "The Passions and the Moral Life"; Titus, "Passions in Christ"; Cates, *Aquinas on the Emotions*; and Lombardo, *The Logic of Desire*. Note the importance of distinguishing between how the habituated sense appetite (level two) can participate in reason and how a particular movement of the sense appetite (level three) can participation in reason (e.g., Knobel, *Aquinas and the Infused Moral Virtues*, 42–43, and Kahm, *Aquinas on Emotion's Participation in Reason*, 261).

54. Butera does not specify the breakfast at this level of particularity but seems to assume it by suggesting how it can mislead. Kahm does offer such a level of specificity (*Aquinas on Emotion's Participation in Reason*, 246).
55. *De virt.* a. 8.
56. Those familiar with recent scholarship on natural law may see a point of contact with Porter's claim that more general precepts of natural law are grasped only in and through particular conventional activity. She describes this as a Ciceronian account of natural law as distinct from an Aristotelian one (see *Nature as Reason*, 266–67.) There is a parallel where the particular ends of habits (level two) develop in and through more specific activity (level three).
57. The most extensive treatment of this issue by one such proponent is in Kahm, *Aquinas on Emotion's Participation in Reason*. Kahm does provide such an account, but problematically asserts the object of the habit is simply the "act of prudence": "The habit, in an appetitive way, also inclines to an action like the one that caused it. Habits are forms, and all forms qua forms incline to something. I will argue that these habits incline to virtuous acts, and that means that they incline to the act of prudence, namely, the prudential command. In other words, they are inclined toward participating in reason" (257).
58. For Aquinas's claim that the sensitive appetite can be a "seat" or "subject" of virtue, see I–II 50,3 and 56,4, as well as *De virt.* a. 4.
59. For a classic discussion of Aquinas's differences from Bonaventure on this topic, see Chenu. Miner helpfully corrects Chenu by noting that it is, properly speaking, the sensitive appetite, not its movements (called passions), that is the "seat" of virtue for Aquinas. See Miner, *Thomas Aquinas on the Passions*, 288–89. For differences between Aristotle and the Stoics on this topic, see Annas *The Morality of Happiness*, 53–66. For broader historical overviews, see Sorabji, *Emotion and Peace of Mind;* and Knuuttila, *Emotions in Ancient and Medieval Philosophy*.
60. Knobel, *Aquinas and the Infused Moral Virtues*, 234–36.
61. ST I–II 58,4 ad 3.
62. For a robust account of Thomistic practical reasoning as being instrumental (in the sense of "calculative") without being susceptible to critiques of Humean practical reasoning, see Vogler, *Reasonably Vicious*. Though, as noted earlier, many contemporary moral philosophers recognize some "givens" in practical reasoning—and despite an allergy to speaking of "nature"—Millgram speaks less of such givens. Though also see his admission that practical reasoning must start with some sort of personal identity (48–49). While his account of practical deduction is deployed here to demonstrate a similarity with the account of habit and practical reasoning, Millgram's account is not endorsed in all aspects. Something similar may be said of the (importantly different) account of "self-constitution" offered by Korsgaard in *Self Constitution*.
63. Millgram, *Practical Induction*, 70.
64. ST I–II 66,1 ad 2.
65. ST I–II 66,1.

66. This difference, made by practical reasoning as *causa immobilis,* is so significant that Miner describes habits as not "on the same plane" as dispositions (Miner, "Aquinas on *Habitus,*" 69).
67. For this claim, that possession of virtue requires ongoing attunement (which is addressed in the next chapter as well), see MacIntyre, *Ethics in the Conflicts of Modernity,* 54–55, 231.
68. See Annas, *Morality of Happiness,* 73.
69. See Porter, "The Unity of the Virtues and the Ambiguity of Goodness," 138. For an extensive contemporary treatment of the connectivity of the virtues, and an endorsement of a certain version of it (though not one supported here), see Russell, *Practical Intelligence and the Virtues,* 335–73.
70. For an outstanding study of just these issues, see Kim, "Thomas Aquinas on the Connection of the Virtues." The term "connectivity of the virtues" is used as an umbrella term to include various accounts of their connectivity, be it the "reciprocity" of the virtues—whereby various virtues remain distinct even while interconnected (as depicted by Thomas and Aristotle)—or the "unity" of the virtues—whereby various virtues are in fact reduced into one (as depicted by the Stoics and arguably by Augustine). For this point, see also Annas, *Morality of Happiness,* 76; and Russell, *Practical Intelligence and the Virtues,* 335n1. Kim's work is not only enormously helpful in depicting various accounts of connectivity but also in responding to various contemporary objections to the connectivity of the virtues. Certain of his claims regarding the latter are relevant, including a proper understanding of virtues as the "highest reach" of a power and a recognition of the distinction between dispositions and habits. For an article-length version of his research see "Progress in the Good."
71. ST I–II 65,1: "*Aliqua inclinatio in nobis existens ad opus aliquod de genere bonorum faciendum, sive talis inclinatio sit in nobis a natura, sive ex assuetudine*" (author's translation).
72. This account is based on ST I–II 65,1. See also *De virt. card.* a. 2. Note that though "perfect" in 65,1 refers to connected, "perfect" in 65,2 refers to the supernatural end of such virtue. While it is the case that infused supernatural virtue is always connected, these two senses of perfect are not accurately grafted onto one another. In other words, virtue can be perfect in a connected sense (65,1) without being perfect in the sense of being directed toward one's supernatural end (65,2). See *De virt. card.* a. 2 and ST II–II 23,7. Osborne argues to the contrary in "Perfect and Imperfect Virtues in Aquinas." For a rebuttal of Osborne on this point, see Decosimo, *Ethics as a Work of Charity.*
73. Nor should he. Though this appeal to experience has prima facie credibility, so too does a contrary appeal to experience that posits those who seem to be virtuous in one way yet vicious in another. Furthermore, this initial argument for connectivity does not adequately distinguish Aquinas's reciprocity of the virtues position from a unity of the virtues position, such as that of the Stoics who reduce all virtue to one (prudence).
74. In addition to ST I–II 65,1 and *De virt. card.* a. 2, see also ST I–II 58,4, where in ad 3 Aquinas again references the blind horse. Here Aquinas also claims the moral virtues require understanding, since this latter intellectual virtue enables a person to know self-evident principles not only in speculative but also in practical matters. The fact that in practical matters the principles are self-evident makes understanding (and also *synderesis*) a distinctive sort of habit. For a recent treatment of understanding, see Knobel, "Intellectual Virtue."
75. ST I–II 65,1. See also *De virt. card.* a. 2 and ST I–II 58,5.
76. I–II 65,1: "*Ad rectam autem electionem non solum sufficit inclinatio in debitum finem, quod est directe per habitum virtutis moralis; sed etiam quod aliquis directe eligat ea quae sunt ad*

finem, quod fit per prudentiam, quae est consiliativa et iudicativa et praeceptiva eorum quae sunt ad finem."

77. See Freddoso's translation at https://www3.nd.edu/~afreddos/summa-translation/Part%201-2/st1-2-ques65.pdf.
78. There is an extensive literature on whether an Aristotelian or a Thomistic account of prudence concerns ends or simply means. For a helpful overview of the relevant issues and texts in both thinkers, see Bradley, *Aquinas on the Twofold Human Good*, 204–19.
79. Decosimo, *Ethics as a Work of Charity*, 156 (emphasis in original).
80. For a comparable claim in recent moral philosophy, see Russell, *Practical Intelligence and the Virtues,* where he notes the centrality of prudence for connectivity: "Simply put, then, where there is connectivity there must be 'phronesis'" (205).
81. Expecting to dissolve completely the latter would be akin to a desire for omniscience and omnipotence, which is not to say that humanity has not persistently striven for exactly that from nearly the beginning, as recounted in Gen. 3.
82. Porter, *Perfection of Desire*, 70.
83. Aquinas calls this the "*finis ultimus*." *Ultimus* is variously translated as "last" or "final" or "ultimate." *Finis* is variously translated as "end" or "goal" or "purpose."
84. See Vogler, *Reasonably Vicious*, 41 (emphasis in original). Vogler makes a case that it is only appeal to the last end, understood in a theological sense, that can differentiate the virtuous from vicious life (34–42). This claim is not endorsed here due to Aquinas's affirmation of true virtue that is nonetheless not oriented toward the supernatural. See ST I–II 65,2; and ST II–II 23,7, as well as *De virt. card.* a. 2.
85. ST I–II 1,7–8.
86. See Hursthouse, *On Virtue Ethics*, 136–37. Hursthouse relies on Sarah Broadie for the quoted terms, found in *Ethics with Aristotle,* 198.
87. Russell, *Practical Intelligence and the Virtues*, 27. Russell refers to John McDowell, as does Hursthouse, on the use of the term "blueprint." For McDowell's use of that term see McDowell, "Deliberation and Moral Development in Aristotle," 25–26.
88. See Hursthouse, *On Virtue Ethics*, 138–39; and Russell, *Practical Intelligence and the Virtues*, 28.
89. Hursthouse, *On Virtue Ethics*, 139, again citing Broadie, *Ethics with Aristotle*, 198.
90. Russell, *Practical Intelligence and the Virtues*, 29.
91. For recognition of this in Russell, see *Practical Intelligence and the Virtues*: "Phronesis is a grasp of the reasons there are for the virtues, and therefore how the virtues do fit into one's life as a whole" (206).
92. For this basic account of the last end, I rely mainly on Julia Annas and Jean Porter, augmented by others as necessary.
93. Annas, *Morality of Happiness*, 39 (emphasis added). For an example of such an assumption in a contemporary moralist, see Annas, *Intelligent Virtue*: "The important assumption here clearly is that practical intelligence itself is unified over the person's life" (87).
94. Porter, *Nature as Reason*, 201. See also Porter, *The Perfection of Desire*, where she speaks of how an "individual desires and pursues her overall perfection as a creature of a certain kind," as well as the "full development and expression of the agent's capacities, integrated into one satisfying and praiseworthy life" (52). See also Pinckaers, who claims that it is due to one's last end that "our actions are no longer isolated; finality draws them into a dynamic whole" (*Sources of Christian Ethics*, 12).
95. Pope John Paul II, *Veritatis splendor*, 78.

96. Annas, *Morality of Happiness*, 83. See also Porter, *Nature as Reason*, 197–98.
97. Annas, *Morality of Happiness*, 35.
98. Annas, 38.
99. Annas, 40.
100. Pinckaers, *Sources of Christian Ethics*, 12. Pinckaers also claims: "Our final end need not be viewed as a kind of finish line, bringing our action to a full stop. It is more like an outcome, perfecting our actions and bringing our capacities to full performance" (12).
101. Porter, *Nature as Reason*, 201–2.
102. ST I–II 1,4–6.
103. ST I–II 1,1–3.
104. For a similar contemporary account using "critical distance" rather than dominion, see Russell, *Practical Intelligence and the Virtues*, 388–92.
105. This is why it is not uncommon for analyses of end-directed human activity to turn to freedom, as evidenced in recent treatments on critical distance in Russell, *Practical Intelligence and the Virtues*, 388–92, and Jensen, *Sin*, 238–84.
106. ST I–II 63,1.
107. Annas, *Morality of Happiness*, 75. See also MacDonald, "Ultimate Ends in Practical Reasoning," 55. For a helpful and influential treatment of a comparable account of action using language "for its own sake," see Hursthouse, *On Virtue Ethics*, 126–31. For such an account of action "for its own sake" that explicitly counters incommensurability theorists, see Jensen, *Sin*, 41–60.
108. Porter, *Nature as Reason*, 199 (emphasis added). See also Porter, "Why Are the Habits Necessary?," 131.
109. Porter, *Nature as Reason*, 202. See also MacDonald, "Ultimate Ends in Practical Reasoning," 55.
110. Porter, *Nature as Reason*, 201.
111. MacIntyre makes a similar point in *Ethics in the Conflicts of Modernity*, when he says: "The final end must be such that we are to aim at it in the course of aiming at the achievement of our other ends" (228). In a sort of mini-treatise on the last end he goes on to say: "The good that is our final end constitutes our lives as wholes, as unities. So in acting for the sake of achieving some particular good, we also act for the sake of achieving our final end, and it is this that, if we act rightly, gives our lives a directedness toward that end" (229).
112. Annas, *Morality of Happiness*, 78 (emphasis in original).
113. Porter, *Nature as Reason*, 209. See a similar claim in Russell, *Practical Intelligence and the Virtues*: "Phronesis is a grasp of the reasons there are for the virtues, and therefore how the virtues do fit into one's life as a whole" (206).
114. Annas, *Morality of Happiness*, 31.
115. Annas, *Intelligent Virtue*, 123.
116. Annas, 123.
117. Korsgaard, *Self Constitution*, 125–26. Korsgaard goes on to say: "The work of practical deliberation is reunification, reconstitution, and the function of the principles that govern deliberation—the principles of practical reason—is the unification of the self" (126).
118. For more on this distinction as an interpretation of Aquinas's ST I–II 1,7–8, see Mattison, "A New Look at the Last End."
119. Millgram, *Practical Induction*, 53. Millgram calls the *phronomis* an "unattainable" ideal (which is omitted in this quote). If he means that attaining *phronesis* is unattainable, I disagree with that claim. But he more likely means it is unattainable that a person can be

characterized by perfectly complete virtue, a claim that is true of this life and affirmed even by Aquinas (see chap. 7).

120. See Aristotle, *Nicomachean Ethics* i.7, and Aquinas, *Summa Theologiae* I–II 1,8. See also Pinckaers, "Aquinas's Pursuit of Beatitude."
121. For a detailed account of this view of the last end, and why it is legitimate to claim that Aquinas holds such a view, see Mattison, "A New Look at the Last End."
122. On this issue see Annas, *Morality of Happiness*, 388–411.
123. See Irwin, "Stoic and Aristotelian Conceptions of Happiness." For the language of Aristotle's account of happiness as "unstable," see Annas, *Morality of Happiness*, 364–84.
124. For instance, though at times distancing herself from Stoic claims (*Intelligent Virtue*, 65), more frequently Annas signals explicitly or implicitly her accord with Stoic commitments on happiness (168n19; 92–93, 129–30, respectively). See also Korsgaard for signals of Stoic commitments (*Self-Constitution*, 24–25, 43, 123, 139, 209).
125. See, for example, Korsgaard, *Self-Constitution*, 43, 162.
126. For a helpful overview of this scholarship, see Hursthouse, *On Virtue Ethics*, 163–91.
127. See ST I–II 65,2; and ST II–II 23,7. See also *De virt. card.* a. 2.
128. For the former, see ST I–II 2, especially 2,4, on why humanity's ultimate happiness cannot consist in any external goods. For the latter, see I–II 2,8. For a contemporary philosophical account of why nothing finite can serve as humanity's complete happiness, see MacIntyre, *Ethics and the Conflicts of Modernity*, 230.
129. For now-classic treatments of whether happiness for Aristotle is a dominant or an inclusive end, see Hardie, "The Final Good in Aristotle's Ethics"; and Ackerill, "Aristotle on Eudaimonia." For a comparable analysis focusing on Aquinas, see Jensen, *Sin*.
130. MacIntyre, *Ethics and the Conflicts of Modernity*, 195. Note that despite common misconceptions, the Epicureans were not radical hedonists in search of intense and immediate pleasure, but rather focused more on the absence of pain and stable tranquility. A classic account of this debate is found in Cicero, *On Moral Ends*. See the excellent treatment of this in Annas, *Morality of Happiness*, 334–50.
131. See Hursthouse, *On Virtue Ethics*, 239–65, for an example of such an approach to "objectivity" in the context of virtue, including reference to her "Neurathian" approach (263). See also Russell, *Practical Intelligence and the Virtues*, 390.
132. See Hursthouse, *On Virtue Ethics*, 174–77. See also Anna, *Intelligent Virtue*, 146–47.
133. See Vogler, *Reasonably Vicious*, 40–42, 110.
134. On *habitus* see Bourdieu, *Outline of a Theory of Practice*, 72–95; MacIntyre, *Ethics in the Conflicts of Modernity*; and Finn, *Moral Agency within Social Structures and Culture*. Perhaps most interestingly for this project, given his reference to temperament and social role (akin to custom) and his recognition that Aquinas's account needs to be augmented by more recent research, is MacIntyre's claim: "Education into the virtues consists in key part in making those so educated aware in detail of the possibilities of error and of the errors to which each of them will be particularly inclined, because of temperament or social role or whatever. Here the traditional insights of Aristotelian Thomism need to be enriched by more recent findings" (191). MacIntyre goes on to cite social psychological work on distortion bias.

CHAPTER 5

GROWING IN ACQUIRED VIRTUE

Crossing the Line and Various Ways of Growing

There is a sense in which this chapter's text (along with that of chapter 7) provides the *telos* of growth in virtue: the dynamic processes whereby a person can grow further in virtue once attained. Yet the conceptual work needed for the account offered here has already been established: the crucial distinction between disposition and habit and the related sensory and rational source of specification of the end at the level of disposition or habit. Also closely related are the processes whereby dispositions and habits are attained, including natural temperament, custom, and properly human activity. The fact that dispositions and habits are second nature qualifications "in between" nature and activity, if you will, is a potent explanatory tool to use in the explanation of changes in habits. Finally, the properly human activity of "last end-ing" supplies an account of how a person can grow (or regress) in the coherence of her activities unified toward that last end. We begin with a basic account of the formation of habit in the human person, or how a person's natural powers become qualified by dispositions or habits through social processes of accustomization and habituation (in a manner attentive to individual-level natural dispositions) so as to be inclined toward activity that is prompt, consistent, and pleasant. This basic account raises certain questions that are then addressed, including the related question of whether or not, and if so, how, the sensory powers continue to exert causal influence "within," so to speak, a habit. The next section examines several questions pertaining to when a person "crosses the line" from possessing a disposition to possessing a habit. The final section explores what happens to a person's powers when a habit is lost.

BEGINNINGS OF A THOMISTIC ACCOUNT OF EDUCATION

Although Thomas Aquinas is not commonly thought of in the context of education or child development, he does indeed supply key resources for these subjects. Our task is to put them together into a basic account of development. It is not the formal process of schooling, though what is described here hopefully occurs in schools. Nor is it the acquisition of intellectual virtues and skills that occurs through both formal schooling and other learning. Rather, "education" is something more like formation: the attainment of qualities, be they dispositions or properly human habits, that qualify a person (or more properly her powers) and incline her toward activity that is prompt, consistent, and pleasant in a manner that makes her (and not simply her activity) good.

We turn first to literary scholar Katharine Breen, whose recent work explores the topic of habit as it relates to formation and education in the Middle Ages.[1] Her work is referenced in a recent essay on habit.[2] Her insightful account is useful in part because there is so little available in Thomistic moral theology about growing in virtue.[3] Breen draws on Aquinas's work and the work of other medievals. She has a clear grasp of distinctions between natural dispositions, dispositions from custom, and properly human habits, as well as the distinct yet ideally complementary role for each in the endeavor of education, or formation. Furthermore, though she acknowledges Aquinas's claim that properly human habits require rational specification of their ends, Breen describes the attainment of such habits in a rather inductive manner that is related to natural dispositions (which she calls *mores*) and customs (*consuetudines*).

Breen describes the (medieval and thus presumably male) process of education in a manner that aptly depicts the attainment of properly human *habitus* in relation to *mores* and *consuetudines*: "Even though virtuous *habitus* are by definition rational, they do not derive directly from abstract principles. Instead they are developed by carefully encouraging young boys' good *mores* until they establish good *consuetudines*. Later, once they are of age to exercise their rational powers and systematically relate them to their actions, these customs will gradually become *habitus*."[4] As any parent, teacher, or person who has spent time helping to form children knows, this is generally the path to properly human habits. Children have all sorts of natural dynamisms (level one) toward activities, including socialization, learning, play, eating, and so on. These natural dynamisms are not supplied by formation; they are presupposed. Of course there are always individual dispositions (level two) in how children are naturally inclined toward activities. Different children can be more subdued, more curious, less adventurous, prone to finicky eating, and so on. The good parent or teacher, attentive to how individual children are variously disposed, channels those natural dynamisms toward regular practices (customs in Aquinas's first sense) to help children treat others considerately, eat and drink well, listen to trusted authorities, persevere in difficult situations, and so on. Good formation (whether it occurs at home, in school, on the sports field, etc.) helps children "get used to" or become accustomed to certain practices such that they become second nature (or customs, in Aquinas's second sense). Aquinas describes this dynamic with reference to custom (displaying a touch of late twentieth-century power of positive reinforcement) in his commentary on *Nicomachean Ethics*: "Proper instruction for youths [enables them to] become accustomed to take pleasure in good works and be grieved in evil works. Therefore, teachers of youth compliment those who do good deeds and reprove those who do evil."[5] Child raising and education is in large part a process of accustoming, especially in younger years. When done well it is attuned to the individual temperament of the child.

Breen displays an awareness of how natural dynamisms are oriented toward activities, that there are natural dispositions toward doing those activities in distinct ways, and most importantly, that a child is accustomed in a social context such that certain ways of acting become second nature to her. Any time Aquinas discusses dispositions supplied by nature or custom as distinct from habits whose specification is supplied by practical reasoning, this formation in social context, particularly but not only in childhood, is in play.[6]

With reference to more technical language, what is being supplied in this rather straightforward account of formation? Although the child possesses by nature inchoate ends or principles guiding her activity, acting toward those ends is made more consistent, prompt, and pleasant when these natural dynamisms are qualified by more particular principles or ends. The child can be accustomed so that she has paradigmatic acts for how she eats, talks to adults, faces difficulty, and so on. Being so qualified does not guarantee activity, as there might be other factors in a situation that intervene; in other words, possessing a disposition (level two) between one's natural dynamisms (level one) and one's activities (level three) does not determine nor necessitate activity. But impressing on the child's dynamisms specified ways of acting serves as a disposition toward acting in that manner. The particular principles or ends supplied by qualities (habits or dispositions) are "midway" between the person's nature and activity.

Note that while the person's rationality is not necessarily engaged at this point, the specified activity can be rather complex, in large part due to its social mediation. Comparable to how (nonlinguistic) animals can be disposed toward complicated activity (e.g., beavers building dams), a human person can be accustomed in ways that are remarkably complex.[7] Think of how small children can be accustomed to long prayers with difficult vocabulary, or to fluid athletic or artistic activity, or to complicated (video) game playing. Certainly at some early age, which admittedly may be difficult to determine exactly and which may differ between children, the source of specification is not the *causa immobilis* of human rationality because a younger child is unable to undertake the end-directed activity in a manner whereby its specification is influenced by modes and circumstances that reflect the end's relation to other and further ends. This is what it means to lack rational specification. Nonetheless, the specification supplied by accustoming can be quite complex and the disposition can be quite stable.

How to describe the attainment of habits, that is, stable rational specification of one's habituation-amenable powers? An account should recognize not only the important difference between properly human habit and disposition (from nature or custom) but also the continuity between both the processes of attainment and the qualities attained. Turning back to Breen, she claims: "It is not unusual for writers to suggest that a good *consuetudo* is a kind of substrate from which a good *habitus* can develop."[8] She goes on to say, with reference to Aristotle, that "habits . . . build on the good *consuetudines* that are acquired in youth."[9]

While recognizing this continuity in process of attainment, Breen also indicates an awareness of the difference made by rational specification in properly human habit: "Though the good actions prompted by *consuetudo* may not be discernably different from the virtuous actions of full-blown *habitus*, they reflect different internal states. The habitual action is virtuous because it combines the stability of second nature with the order of right reason."[10] Thus even if the actions done from custom and those done from "full-blown" habit may be observably the same (and they also, of course, might not be), what distinguishes them? Breen claims that once children are able to "exercise their rational powers," they are able to "systematically relate" their actions rationally, employing the "order of right reason." To use the language of the previous chapter, actions that had been done voluntarily out of second nature are now understood and more fully taken on as one's own, both as to their own purposes and as to their relationship to further ends and the variety of activities in the person's life, including one's life as a whole.

It is obvious that acquiring "full-blown *habitus*" that engage a person's rationality occurs as part of development from childhood, since rationality is not able to be exercised in early childhood. But this more complex account of formation also explains how certain stable dispositions toward activity in an adult life might be custom rather than habit. In his classic article "Learning to Be Good," on Aristotle's account of attaining habits, M. F. Burnyeat claims that "for a long time moral development must be a less than fully rational process," most obviously in children. Yet the possession of custom dispositions is also quite possible in adults who are able to exercise their rationality.[11] Burnyeat claims being (merely) accustomed to act well does not mean there is no thought or intentionality involved. The specification supplied by the disposition is certainly end-directed, and might be rather complex. However, "if a piece of reasoning does not relate to one's conception of the good, Aristotle does not count it deliberation, nor its outcome choice."[12] The more particular specification supplied by the disposition simply does not give way to, nor is shaped by, other considerations. Burnyeat describes specification provided by custom as "pockets of thought in us which can remain relatively unaffected by our overall view of things."[13] Alternatively, in the "fully developed man of virtue and practical reason[,] they have become integrated with, indeed they have become infused and corrected by, his reasoned scheme of values."[14] Reminiscent of the discussion on reason "across" virtues and last ending, Burnyeat claims that in virtues there is not only rational specification but also an ongoing revision of specific activity in light of various other ends.

The process of attaining a true habit through repeated action whereby reason is impressed on the appetite was previously examined. Before proceeding to address changes in the person who already possesses virtue, it is worth pausing to address a comment made by Breen. She claims that "once [children] are of age to exercise their rational powers and systematically relate them to their actions, these customs will gradually become *habitus*."[15] Is it true that dispositions from custom (or from nature, for that matter) "become" habits? The answer is no.

Habits (or dispositions, in this case) are not nature; they are "second" nature. They are qualities, not substantial forms. And the qualification, or the (more or less stable) specification of the ends of that power by a particular principle, can change (from vice to virtue, e.g., or from disposition to habit). Yet what persists in the process of formation is the person, or more precisely, the person's natural powers. Recall Aquinas's claim that "a form is said to come into being not because it itself comes into being but because something comes to be it: namely when a subject is brought from capacity to actualization."[16] Breen might have spoken more precisely had she said that one's powers qualified by custom become *qualified by* habit, rather than that a custom *becomes* a habit. To recall a previous example, a child does not become an adult as much as a person who was a child becomes a person who is an adult.[17] Thus, properly speaking, dispositions do not become habits, nor do vices become virtues. Rather, people who are disposed—or, more properly, people's powers that are disposed—become habituated, or those who are vicious become virtuous.

So far we have a rather straightforward and rudimentary account of habit formation, especially in, but not limited to, children. Yet, though straightforward, this raises challenging questions. For instance, how do the sensory powers continue to exert causal influence "within," so to speak, a habit? Or do they not? How does a person cross the line so as to possess a properly human habit rather than simply possessing a disposition from nature or custom? In this process of crossing is there room for further growth? Finally, what happens when a habit is lost? These are precisely the questions that govern the ensuing sections.

THE RATIONAL AND SENSORY WITHIN THE UNIFIED PERSON

Even if the disposition from custom (or nature) does not *become* a habit, what happens with the change to the *person* and to that sensory connaturalization of the person's powers that occurred in the disposition? Does that change persist once the person becomes qualified by a habit? Breen speaks of a disposition from custom being a "substrate from which" good habits develop.[18] This language is helpful in that it alludes to facets of the prior existing custom that persist in the attainment of the habit. Though helpful in requiring some account of the relationship between nonrational and rational specification, it should not be taken as a claim that the sensory (bodily) dispositions of the person persist in a parallel manner "underneath," so to speak, the rationally specified habits. After all, it is the same unified human power, with both its rational and sensory aspects, that is qualified by the properly human habit. Once again we return to the relevance of Aquinas's position in the plurality of forms debate, where he affirmed the unity of the human person's sensory and rational "souls." Given that Aquinas claims the human person's sensory soul is not separate from the person's rational soul but rather the sensory is "contained" by or included in the person's rational soul that serves the source of unity, it is reasonable to assume this same understanding of the relationship between rational and sensory within a habit.[19]

What is the ongoing role of sensory connaturalization in relation to the rational specification of the ends of those powers, on the way toward or after the attainment of a habit? How can we acknowledge the distinct causal influences of these different sources of qualifications of powers and yet also affirm their unity within the rational person? It is certainly the case for Aquinas that the sensory aspects of human powers constitute part of properly human virtue to the extent that they participate in reason. Ideally this happens when sensory apprehensions participate in reason, even as they remain sensory, and thus they engender movements of the sensitive appetite that are rightly labeled properly human even as they are not reduced to the rational only, since they offer "something of their own."[20] When this occurs, the sensory powers and their contributions to the specification of human activity do not persist alongside or unconnected to the specification supplied by the rational powers. They offer something of their own that participates in one's rationality, and as such can rightly be called "seats" or subjects of properly human virtue.[21]

But, of course, in the case of acquired virtue this does not happen right away. Recall Aquinas's analogy of fire consuming its combustible to explain how contrary sensory dispositions are gradually expelled: "Whence we see that because fire cannot at once overcome the combustible, it does not enkindle at once; but it gradually expels contrary dispositions, so that by overcoming it entirely, it may impress its likeness on it."[22] What Aquinas describes here occurs on the way toward attaining a properly human habit. Even though there may be sensory connaturalization of the person's powers such that there are dispositions from nature or custom, at some point reason is impressed on these powers sufficiently such that they participate in reason and the person possesses a properly human habit.

Yet even when a person possesses an acquired virtue, she can still experience passions inclining her to bad acts. "Passions inclining to evil are not completely taken away by either acquired or infused virtue."[23] Now her sensory appetite "naturally obeys reason" and thus any disposition to such contrary movements can be diminished or even removed.[24] Indeed, the very same activity that engenders an acquired virtue (i.e., properly human good activity) is what enables her to increase in virtue.[25] Much of the work of growth toward or in virtue is precisely the impressing of (right) reason on the sensory appetites. In the case of acquired virtue, contrary sensory movements must be sufficiently expelled in order to attain such virtue.

Yet it is also clear that prior sensory dispositions from nature or accustomization continue to exert causal influence on a person who becomes habituated in the properly human sense. This is not limited to the more obvious case of sudden movements of passion, which occur even in a person who possesses virtue.[26] It can occur from residual sensory specification from prior dispositions. A virtuous person may do acts of one virtue more promptly than acts of another virtue due to that person's natural dispositions.[27] Aquinas makes this point particularly directly in another passage that lists the four processes to attain dispositions and habits: "As to the perfection or quantity of virtue insofar as it exists in a subject, there can be inequality even in the same species of virtue when one of those having the virtue is better related than others to the things pertaining to that virtue; and this because of a better natural disposition, or greater exercise, or a better judgment of reason, or a gift of grace."[28] The causal influence of dispositions from nature and custom, though they can be lessened or even removed, may persist in a person even after the possession of a virtue. Perhaps it is now more clear what prompted many medievals to affirm a plurality of forms in the human person! Even in the person who is virtuous, various causal influences may persist and may do so not in unison with one another.[29]

Yet Aquinas insists on a unicity of forms. Note that the previous references are to the persisting causal influence of dispositions from nature or custom. The bodily or sensory aspects of human powers are changed by such dispositions and can continue to exert causal influence due to that change, most obviously in the absence of stable specification by rational powers but also even when the latter occurs. Yet when properly human activity (at level three) engenders a properly human habit (level two), the person's power as a whole is qualified by that habit. To be stably specified by one's rationality is to possess a more particular end of one's habituation-amenable power, and thus to act consistently with regard to that power's activity. Any changes in the sensory (bodily) aspects of that power that emanate from nature or custom may exert causal influence but cannot alone stably incline a person toward activity that differs from activity as specified by the person's rationality; otherwise the person would not possess a properly human habit. Furthermore, what rational specification *means* is that a person is inclined toward activity in a manner attentive to various modes, circumstances, and so on. Sensory causal influences are part of those various circumstances. They are no longer the formal qualification of the person's power since that is supplied by the properly human habit. These causal influences can be described as "contrary dispositions" in the sense that specification differs from what is supplied by rationality. More precisely, Aquinas at times calls them *relictae* or "residual dispositions."[30]

Thus, Aquinas acknowledges the distinct causal influences of rational and sensory connaturalization in disposing a person toward activity. Ideally the sensory participates fully in reason. When it does, it still offers "something of its own." But even the virtuous person can experience the causal influence of residual sensory dispositions in a manner not reflective of the stable specification of the *causa immobilis* of one's rationality. Nonetheless, Aquinas affirms the fundamental unity of the sensory and the rational aspects of the human person, all under the authority of the rational soul. That unity is not simply stipulated; it also is a goal to be achieved in greater or lesser degrees. A human life entails a journey toward the impressing of reason upon the person's sensory powers. Once this occurs sufficiently, a person becomes habituated, for good or bad. Even then, the impressing of reason on the sensory aspects of the person's powers, especially as they are residually disposed by nature or custom, is an ongoing activity, indeed the activity of a lifetime.

Before addressing issues related to "crossing the line" from disposition to habit, several further points on the relationship between the sensory and rational are in order. First, it may seem that the goal of aligning the rational and sensory powers in the unified person is simply a matter of quelling bad sensory movements or bad sensory dispositions obtained from nature or custom. Yet the ultimate goal is not a quelling or a subduing but rather a forming. This recalls the argument against accounts of virtuous passion that render them simply as subdued so as to not disrupt reason.

Second, the habituation of the sensory dimension of a human power amenable to properly human habituation can be de-forming, as can occur in the formation of a vice. Perhaps a person possesses good dispositions from nature or accustoming. Such dispositions might incline the person toward (generically) good actions, but they would not be properly human habits. To become habituated the person's powers would have to be stably specified by one's rationality. One could imagine that a person could be habituated to become consumerist, racist, or sexually promiscuous, particularly in a corrupt society. Though it is commonly the case that dispositions from nature or custom incline a person toward bad action and need to be overcome, it could also be the case that good dispositions from nature or custom can be overcome by vicious habituation.[31]

Third, virtuous habituation requires impressing of reason even on *good* dispositions from nature or custom. Aquinas gives examples of people who are disposed by nature or custom to be meek or chaste.[32] He claims that people who are disposed from birth to good acts can use such dispositions harmfully, since they can act without discretion.[33] Even good dispositions formed by accustomization in a communal context, which can be rather complex and observably far more closely approximate properly human virtues, need to be rationally specified in order to become habits. Lack of specification by the *causa immobilis* of a person's rationality means that even observably good action is not attuned to various modes, circumstances, or "bringing many things together."[34] Without specification by rationality, the disposition may frequently incline toward observably good acts, but even then attainment of virtue will mean attunement of the particular ends (i.e., paradigmatic acts) of the disposition to reflect a person's various ends and overall view of things. This can render, say, a naturally meek person to more readily rise up in anger against injustice. Or it may render her restraint from rising up inappropriately a meekness that is a properly human habit rather than merely one that is dispositional. In either case, the causal influence of the disposition can persist even as it is transformed in its specification by the *causa immobilis* of her rationality.

Fourth, though a full treatment of continence is far beyond the scope of this project, the relationship between the rational and sensory provides occasion to address the pertinence of this topic to continence.[35] Continence is the condition of a person who has sensory desires toward bad activity yet who willfully chooses not to act on such desires. It is important to distinguish acting continently, as when a person contains wayward desires in choosing to act well, from the state of continence, whereby a person persistently acts well in having to overcome persistent wayward desires. Aquinas's comments on the presence of wayward desires in even the virtuous person's life suggests that acting continently will be part of any virtuous life. Yet, as to the state of continence, Aquinas denies that it is a virtue, even though it is obviously good to act continently, granting the presence of such wayward desires.[36] We might say that the continent person is not stably disposed to good activity (level two) though is able to make good choices by force of will (level three). Note that the latter occurs at the level of activity, not quality (disposition or habit). Indeed, it is precisely the lack of stable specification of a person's sensory desires, which are able to participate in reason, that precludes continence from being a habit in the properly human sense.

As noted earlier, the presence of bad desires in a person who resists them is not alone sufficient to disqualify a person from possessing a habit (in this example, temperance). Such desires occur even in people who possess the acquired virtues. So acting continently is compatible with acquired virtue. Yet if one's desires are more or less stably disposed badly (rather than on occasion moved badly), this generally precludes the possession of temperance. This once again reflects Aquinas's position on the unicity of forms, since the sensory desires that are able to be stably specified by rationality are not so specified, either because the person is not consistent in choosing the good or the person is consistently choosing the good but the sensory desires have not yet been stably specified in a manner reflective of those consistent good choices.

This raises the question of whether or not acquired virtue is ever compatible with persistent bad desires. The answer is no, assuming that the bad desires reflect that what can participate in reason is not doing so, or is not yet stably doing so. However, this rationale raises the possibility that the persistence of contrary sensory (bodily) dispositions is compatible with even acquired virtue if (and only if) the bad sensory desires are unable to be specified by the rational powers, due to some obdurate natural or accustomized disposition, *and* nevertheless the person's rational powers are stably specified rather than destabilized by the contrary sensory disposition.[37] One could imagine certain phobias from birth, the lingering effects of an eating disorder that must be overcome, or even the residual effects of accustomized alcoholism, each of which could conceivably result in sensory dispositions not amenable to rational specification and yet which do not destabilize the habit. As Aquinas notes, normally sensory dispositions can be lessened and even removed by habituation. But, just as dispositions from nature or custom can persist without displacing the stable specification of the rational powers, presumably contrary desires can coexist with acquired virtue if their presence is neither a reflection of nor the cause of failure of stable specification by the *causa immobilis* of rationality.[38]

"CROSSING THE LINE" FROM DISPOSITION TO HABIT: GROWTH BEFORE AND AFTER VIRTUE

At this point some attention must be paid to the challenging question of exactly when a person attains a properly human habit, such as a virtue. David Decosimo labels this "the problem of the heap."[39] At what point are there enough leaves to constitute a "heap," rather than just a few gathered leaves? It may be easy to observe that two leaves do not constitute a heap, and similarly that thousands of leaves do. But when does the bunch become a heap? This is a challenging enough subject with a grouping of discrete items such as leaves. It is even more difficult with less easily quantifiable things. When does a second language speaker become fluent? When do two people become friends? More relevantly, when does a child become an adult, or a person attain the "age of reason"?

It seems impossible to determine the exact moment of these changes. Daniel Russell describes such concepts using the term *satis*, from the Latin for "enough," as in, "When is one fluent enough to be fluent?" or "When is one reasonable enough to have attained the age of reason?" Russell claims virtue is just such a concept.[40] A person need not be maximally virtuous to be virtuous. She just needs to be virtuous enough. Just as a fluent speaker may speak in error, or a rational person may exhibit a failure of reason, a virtuous person need not be maximally virtuous. This is another way of reinforcing the earlier point that, contra the Stoics, a person need not be perfectly virtuous in order to possess a virtue. A benefit of such an approach to virtue is that there is "room for growth," not only on the way toward attaining virtue but even after attaining it. Indeed, such growth in virtue is a lifelong endeavor.

A challenge with viewing virtue as a *satis* concept is determining at what exact point a person attains a virtue. This problem leads Russell to claim that virtue is a "vague" *satis* concept. In other words, there is no exact point, or "boundary," at which she changes from not being virtuous to being virtuous. However, this does not seem to necessarily follow. It may be difficult to determine at what point she crosses the line to being virtuous, and in fact so difficult that it need not be precisely delineated. Yet that does not mean the person is not always one or the other.[41] Indeed, if a person were between the two states, presumably that would entail identifying the characteristics of that intermediate state and engender additional difficulties in determining when she entered and exited that "in-between state" on the path toward (or away from) virtue.[42]

However, even if it is not possible to identify the exact moment for such a change, we can identify the features that characterize such changes. When does a person with a disposition have a habit? As noted earlier, when the specification of the power's end is supplied by the *causa immobilis* of one's rationality, and stably so. Note that while much focus here has been on specification of activity shifting from the sensory to the rational (with the sensory participating in and "contained in" the rational), even when specification is supplied by the rational powers it must also be stable to be a properly human habit.[43] When this is caused by successive acts, at some point there is a breakthrough from disposition to habit. Aquinas illustrates this point with the now familiar metaphor of water hollowing out stone:

> Hence, in things to be done, because activities of the soul are not efficacious as are demonstrations, because things to be done are contingent and probable, one act does not suffice to cause virtue but many are required. And though these many are not simultaneous, they still cause a habit, because the first act causes some disposition and the second act, finding the matter disposed, disposes it even more, and third yet more and thus the ultimate act acting on the strength of the preceding completes the generation of virtue, like the many drops that hollow the stone.[44]

At some point (call it the "ultimate act") the line is crossed, and this is caused not just by the immediate act but also by the strength of the preceding acts.

What constitutes crossing the line is enough involvement of rationality to supply a *causa immobilis,* and enough stability (within the virtue and across virtues) for activity to be consistent, prompt, and pleasant. In fact, Aquinas adduces pleasure as a marker of the attainment of virtue.[45] Admittedly, pleasure is also a *satis* concept. (When is something pleasurable enough to be pleasant?) And, as will be seen in an examination of infused virtue, more precisely the marker is that "rest" of which sensory pleasure is generally a sign. Nevertheless, along with stability and attunement to other ends in life, pleasure is a helpful indicator that the line to attain virtue has been crossed.

Additionally, Aquinas claims that when this line is crossed, all the virtues are caused in a person simultaneously.[46] Though this claim pertains particularly to connectivity across virtues, it also indicates what Decosimo calls the "bright line" distinguishing disposition from habit.[47] Indeed, this is precisely why connectivity is not an additional characteristic of a habit, but inherent to attainment of a habit.[48]

The claim that there is a line crossed at which a person possesses a virtue, and indeed that crossing means possession of all the virtues, has led many to assume that attaining any one virtue requires that a person possess that virtue perfectly. With reference to connectivity, the claim that a person must have all the virtues if they have any is taken to mean that a person must be fully virtuous to have any virtue. Though often framed as an issue regarding the connectivity of the virtues, it is also an issue for determining when a person crosses the line to possess a specific virtue. This question was briefly addressed with regard to Aristotle's description of virtue as the "highest reach of a power." His description may seem to indicate that a person possesses a virtue only when it is possessed perfectly, without any possibility of further growth.[49] Even the previous quote can suggest as much, as when Aquinas speaks of the "ultimate act acting in virtue of all the preceding acts completes the generation of virtue." This could be read as saying that the ultimate act not only completes generation of the virtue but concludes all growth in that virtue. Though that is a possible *prima facie* read of Aristotle's phrase, and a feasible position on what is needed to "cross the line" to possess a virtue, this is not the only feasible position. In fact, Aquinas addresses it directly and repudiates it.

In his most important texts on growth in virtue, Aquinas adduces the Stoics as having "taught that no one has a virtue unless he has it to the maximum."[50] There are indeed certain forms that do not admit of "more or less." For instance, the number two. You cannot add to the number two to make it "more two."[51] The Stoic position might be more intelligible if virtue were like a mathematical proof: you may be closer or further from a successful proof (and the Stoics did indeed believe in progress before attaining virtue), but you either prove a theorem or do not, and once you prove it, you cannot prove it "more." Aquinas rejects this position with regard to virtue.[52] Since virtuous activity concerns contingent matters, its target is not an "indivisible point." And thus it can be attained to greater or lesser degree:

> The Stoics erred, for they held that no man should be deemed virtuous, unless he were, in the highest degree, disposed to virtue. Because the nature of virtue does not require that man should reach the mean of right reason as though it were an indivisible point, as the Stoics thought; but it is enough that he should approach the mean, as stated in Ethic. ii, 6. Moreover, one same indivisible mark is reached more nearly and more readily by one than by another: as may be seen when several archers aim at a fixed target.[53]

What makes one person able to attain the mark of virtue "more nearly and more readily" than another? The ongoing causal influence of nature and custom—as well as of course greater proper human habituation or grace—results in people attaining the mean of virtue "more nearly and more readily" than others, even once virtue is possessed.[54] But the idea for now is that a person need not attain virtue completely in order to possess it at all. There is room for further growth.

In some ways the Stoic position is conceptually easier. Claiming that attaining virtue requires that it be perfect avoids the problem of having to determine when a person crosses the line, being virtuous enough to have attained virtue. Part of any "line crossing" assessment concerns the particular activity at hand (e.g., what sorts of imperfect eating hit the mark closely enough to be virtuous, even if there is room for growth?). Another part is less the specific description of the activity (as important as that is) as it is the stability offered by the person's rationality. At some point the paradigmatic activities to which a person has been disposed by nature and custom can be grasped as to their purposes and their relation to other activities in life as a whole. Or, if the paradigmatic acts need to be changed to better align with the various ends in a person's life, then repeated properly human acts can do just that. This attunement to various modes and circumstances, and the pursuit of them in relation to the whole so as to make the person good (if the habits are good), means that she has crossed the line to possessing a habit. Aquinas's rejection of the Stoic position is not offered as an attempt to make virtue attainable for more people, or to more closely match the common human experience of the possibility of ongoing growth even after a person possesses virtue, true though both of those may be. His argument instead is based on the claim that virtue is toward the mean, and in contingent matters the mean that is sought may be more or less nearly attained.

This latter point suggests perhaps the most important way that growth toward and especially within habit occurs. For obvious reasons, given the developmental perspective and attention to how habits are preceded by dispositions from nature and custom, the thrust of this idea so far has been on how sensory and rational connaturalization relate to one another and are brought into greater and greater conformity. This could wrongly suggest that the sole or even the primary way that growth toward or within virtue occurs is through the impressing of reason on the sensory. As important as that is, it is not the whole of attainment of or growth in virtue.

Even when stable specification is supplied by one's rationality, the main way that ongoing growth in a habit occurs is through refinement of the more particular end (the paradigmatic act) that constitutes the object of the habit, by properly human activity that equals or surpasses the goodness of the specification of the existing habit. Aquinas describes it this way: "If the intensity of the act correspond in proportion to the intensity of the habit, or even surpass it, every such act either increases the habit or disposes to an increase thereof."[55] The most common term he deploys in describing growth in habit is *intensio*. It is a difficult term to translate into English, and the word most commonly used (intensity) has too much emotional connotation.[56] Better would be intensification, or even extension, as in, toward the goal (or "into the end"). If an act intensifies a power by helping it better attain its goal—and with properly human activity, that is, by better attunement to various modes, circumstances, and a person's overall view of things—then this refined object is impressed on the appetite, extending the reach of the power to attain its goal or end. Even after she crosses the line to attain a habit, ongoing growth occurs not only through the further lessening or elimination of contrary dispositions in the sensory powers but also through the paradigmatic act more closely approximating the mean through ongoing revision in light of those same modes, circumstances, and so on.

This is, of course, simply naming the way that acquired virtues are formed: by repeated activity. Acquired virtues are attained, and grow, not simply by the repeated acts that constitute mere sensory accustomization but through repeated properly human acts: "Human virtue directed to the good which is defined according to the rule of human reason can be caused by human acts: inasmuch as such acts proceed from reason, by whose power and rule the aforesaid good is established."[57] Despite the commonality of repeated activity, Aquinas distinguishes between acts with a "more discerning judgment of reason" and mere accustomization.[58] The repeated acts of properly human habits are specified with an awareness of how the act relates to other modes, circumstances, and the like. Yet that specification is not a one-time event, needing repeated acts simply to be impressed on appetite. Especially since habits concern contingent matters that can approximate the mean more or less closely, such repeated activity is constantly reaffirming—and also further attuning—the object of the habit. To use the language of earlier, this occurs "within" habits, since the object, or the more specific end, of a properly human habit is not set once and for all but presumably continually refined in a sort of "feedback loop" through ongoing properly human activity.[59] But it also occurs "across habits," since the refinement of the paradigmatic act of one habit occurs in relation to other and further ends and results in ongoing refinement and attunement of the objects of various habits in relation to one another. Once again we see the inherent connection between stable specification by rationality "within" a virtue and also "across" virtues. Furthermore, refinement of the object of a habit in relation to various habits (i.e., the connectivity of the virtues) is simply refinement with regard to a person's life as a whole. This activity of refinement by practical reasoning simply is last end-ing.

In fact, Aquinas's reasons for ongoing growth after attainment of virtue not only establish the *possibility* of such growth but establish the *necessity* of such ongoing growth.[60] First, since habits concern contingent matters, ongoing assessments of modes and circumstances are continually necessary. Second, Aquinas's account of increase in virtue suggests that a lack of growth (where growth is perhaps better understood less spatially as ongoing active reevaluation) leads to decrease in virtue, a topic to which we now turn.

LOSING ACQUIRED VIRTUE

The assumption so far is that a person crosses the line from disposition to habit when that person attains virtue. Though a line is crossed in attaining a bad habit, or vice, growth suggests improvement and movement from disposition to good habit. Furthermore, there is "room for growth" even after she attains virtue. "Growth" references a change in the habit, that middle level between the level one natural dynamisms qualified and the level three activity proceeding from habit, though with acquired virtue it is precisely the latter that makes growth in virtue possible. Perhaps this is obvious, but the possibility of growth also entails the possibility of decrease. A person's virtue can be less well or less stably specified, or even "cross the line" backward (as in the case of loss of virtue, though presumably the loss of a vice could be called growth, or moving "forward"), such that the virtuous habit is lost. In one sense an examination of losing a habit can be more brief, since it is simply the flipside of growing in virtue. But it also raises questions about whether a person who has possessed habits in the properly human sense can cease to be habituated, or if the person becomes otherwise habituated. Once again the disposition/habit disposition provides an indispensable resource.

Aquinas begins his treatment of loss of habit with a reminder that, *qua* second nature, habits are not nature and thus can be lost. "And so it is that while the nature of a thing cannot in any way be taken away from a thing, a habit is removed, though with difficulty."[61] The last point about difficulty is important, since the very stability that makes possession of virtue an asset to human activity also makes it difficult—though not impossible—to lose. Aquinas also reminds us that, properly speaking, the habit itself does not increase or decrease, but the person becomes more or less of that habit: "A habit, considered in itself, is a simple form. It is not thus that it is subject to decrease; but according to the different ways in which its subject participates in it. This is due to the fact that the subject's potentiality is indeterminate, through its being able to participate in a form in various ways."[62] Habits are accidents, not substantial forms or a person's nature, but rather a person's second nature. Using the example of color, Aquinas claims that "to be more or less white is not ascribed to whiteness but to a white thing."[63] Properly speaking, a person's temperance does not decrease, but the person becomes less temperate.

How does this occur, especially when the pertinent virtue had already been attained? Although in a sense it is the opposite of increasing a virtue, there are more ways to decrease than increase it. Most obviously, a person can act by a judgment of reason in a manner contrary to the virtue possessed: "A habit either of virtue or of vice, may be corrupted by a judgment of reason, whenever its motion is contrary to such vice or virtue, whether through ignorance, passion or deliberate choice."[64] In this case the specification of activity supplied by a judgment of reason is contrary to the virtue.

But Aquinas also claims a habit can decrease or be lost when a person simply fails to act on the virtue possessed, by omission, if you will: "When a man fails to make use of his virtuous habit in order to moderate his own passions or deeds, the necessary result is that many passions and deeds fail to observe the mode of virtue, by reason of the inclination of the sensitive appetite and of other external agencies."[65] In this case the specification of activity is supplied not by a different judgment of reason but rather by the sensory powers (though presumably not as participating in reason reflective of the habit possessed) or external sources.

Aquinas even claims it is possible for an act proceeding from a virtue to decrease that virtue: "Just as one who has a habit may fail to use it or may act contrary to it so may he happen to use the habit by performing an act that is not in proportion to the intensity of the habit."[66] Here we see in full bloom the ramifications of Aquinas's position, that further growth in virtue is possible when a person acts in a manner that is better attuned to various modes, circumstances, and an overall view of things. Conversely, activity that is still accurately called virtuous but is less well-attuned decreases the person's possession of virtue. In this latter case the person's virtue is still presumably possessed, though, having been less reasonably and less stably specified, it has not only decreased but is presumably more susceptible to loss by inaction or contrary action.

What might be the origin of activity that is counter to or even less well-attuned to the virtuous exercise of one's powers? Though the current focus is on acquired virtue, we are obviously talking about sin. A complete treatment of this topic would examine the distinct effects of original sin and actual sin, the internal and external causes of sin, and the various internal causes of sin (ignorance, malice, and sensitive appetite) as well as their relations to each other.[67] But the context here is on attainment of, growth in, and loss of acquired virtue, so the focus will remain on the causal influence of various movements, dispositions, and habits. One possibility is a principled repudiation of the prior habituation and affirmation of its contrary. (This can of course happen from virtue to vice or from vice to virtue.) Though such a repudiation is conceivable in the loss of a virtue, and perhaps is more common in the repudiation of a vice, such a manner of losing virtue is presumably less common.

Surely external influences can also prompt such activity. We might think of a corrupted society or community, or perhaps the bad influence of a peer group.[68] Furthermore, presumably movements of a person's own passions apply as well, whether they prompt the person to act contrary to a virtue, to not act at all, or to act in a virtuous manner but less well-attuned to various modes and circumstances. Though these may be fleeting, recall that the sensory powers may also exert a causal influence on someone possessing a virtue due to prior dispositions from nature or custom.[69] In any of these cases, the impressing of reason on the appetite takes time and repeated acts, as with growth in virtue.[70] The same is true when that impression by a person's rational powers is decreased or lost.

Whatever the source of a person's decrease in the possession of a virtue, the possibility of crossing the line backward so as to lose the virtue raises the question of how a person who loses a virtue is otherwise qualified, if at all. We began with a Thomistic account of formation from the perspective of development from childhood. In such a case it is easy to imagine a person possessing "mere" dispositions before attaining properly human habits. But what happens when a person who has attained properly human virtue, as specified by rationality, loses that virtue? Is the person's power completely unqualified? Can a person go back to being merely disposed? Or does the person immediately possess the contrary vice?

Aquinas claims that *any* action disposes a habituation-amenable power.[71] It could create a (presumably initially very unstable) disposition or strengthen or weaken an existing one. Therefore, once a habituation-amenable power is active, any action influences its qualification. It would thus never seem to be without any (even if a very weak) disposition. The question is, once a capacity is qualified by a habit (whether virtue or vice) due to stable specification by one's rationality, can it ever be *only* qualified by a disposition and not a habit properly understood?[72]

One possibility is that when a person ceases to possess an acquired virtue, the person immediately possesses a contrary vice. Since it is rationality that stably specifies any habit (virtue or vice) properly understood, judgments of reason contrary to virtue could engender a contrary habit. But the error here is assuming that the only requirement to possessing a habit (rather than a disposition) is the *causa immobilis* of rational specification. Yet both the *causa immobilis* and stability are required for possession of a habit. And while certain acquired (purely intellectual) habits can be possessed immediately without prior acts, Aquinas is insistent that many acts are needed with acquired virtue in the fullest sense in order for reason to impress its likeness on the appetite.[73] In the context of loss of virtue it seems unlikely even that rational powers specify a person's level three actions stably. But, even if they did, in some sort of wholesale repudiation of the person's previous life and all it entailed, combined with a full affirmation of an alternate overall view of things, even then the inherent "lagging" of the impressing of reason on the appetitive powers seems to preclude the possibility that a person who loses a virtue immediately has alternate (level two) habits stably specified by rationality.[74] One erroneous assumption in such an account is that a person, once habituated, can no longer *not* be habituated, that is, be merely disposed.

Another solution to this question is that a person's habituate-able capacities might cease to be qualified by a virtue, understood as a habit in the proper sense, and yet not be immediately stably specified by (contrary) practical reasoning, so as to be qualified right away by a vice understood as a habit in the proper sense. There could be an interim period (of varying lengths of time) before the specification of vice is stabilized or before the return to the virtue; this interim period occurs when the person is disposed but not habituated. Note the claim here is *not* that in such an interim period the person does not act out of practical reasoning, but rather that in such a period the qualification of the person's powers are not stably specified as habits at level two. If this were the case, how would the person's (level three) practical reasoning be operative?

I see two possibilities. Perhaps reasoning is confused and unstably vacillates between different goods. Or, perhaps reasoning is more coherent, but the appetitive powers "lag." Recall Aquinas's claim regarding the time and repeated acts needed to form acquired virtue: "Reason cannot entirely overcome the appetitive power in one act: because the appetitive power is inclined variously, and to many things; while the reason judges in a single act, which should be willed in regard to various aspects and circumstances."[75] Aquinas claims that reason "gradually expels contrary dispositions," eventually "overcoming it [the appetitive power] entirely" so as to "impress its likeness on it."[76] Presumably on the path toward growth in virtue those existing "contrary dispositions" could be caused by nature or custom. Yet surely they could also be caused by former habits, where the stable specification is provided by rationality as *causa immobilis* in a manner unified with sensory connaturalization, such that the latter is in accord with that virtue. But remove or change the *causa immobilis* and at the very least the corresponding sensory connaturalization, which previously existed as part of the habit properly understood as taken up or "included in" the person's rationality, remains residually connaturalized in a manner disjointed from practical reasoning until "impressed" by practical reasoning with new specificity (or returned to its former specificity). If a person's level three rational activity itself remains confused or uncertain, it will be all the longer until the capacities with those residual dispositions are requalified.

Therefore, in the case of acquired virtue, if we grant that virtue can be lost, then it is possible to possess dispositions to actions observably characteristic of the lost virtue even after the loss of stable specification provided by rationality, assuming a person's practical reasoning cannot immediately specify habituation-amenable powers in a contrary manner. In such a case, a person would be inclined to actions by a custom disposition rather than a habit properly understood.

The stakes are high in this loss of virtue. Aquinas claims that habits properly understood are necessary for a person's perfection. Since for Aquinas perfection or flourishing always entails activity, this means that a person's ability to act well is impeded by the loss of virtue. (Though impeded it is not precluded since one can regain the virtue.) Furthermore, the same *causa immobilis* of one's rationality "within" a virtue, which renders it a properly human habit, also entails connectivity "across" virtues. A person does not simply lose *a* virtue. The loss of one virtue means that the person has lost all virtues, even the acquired virtues.

In the same way that it may be difficult to observe when a person crosses the line from disposition by nature or custom *to* "full blown *habitus*," it can be equally difficult to observe when a person falls below the line and loses not only the one virtue but all of them. How could this not be obvious? Residual sensory dispositions to activities observably characteristic of the lost virtues persist. Furthermore, even without a habit stably specified by the *causa immobilis* of rationality, a person can indeed continue to act well in a properly human sense, lest it be impossible to regain the virtue.

What might this look like, more experientially? Again, there is a wide continuum of room for growth both below and above the "line" of possessing virtue(s), such that a person just below the line may be very well disposed to good activity. Nonetheless, there is a lack of a threshold level of coherence in the person's life, though perhaps not observably. To use a different analogy, it is conceivable that a thriving culture could accustom a person so well that the person's various activities attain a strong observable coherence, though this is perhaps difficult to imagine. Yet, even in such a case, the specification would come primarily from custom rather than the *causa immobilis* of rationality.

Something similar could occur in the person who has lost acquired virtue. In fact, it may be most appropriate to describe the person in such a situation as "lost." Deprived of the coherence supplied by rationality as *causa immobilis*, the person's life lacks robust coherence toward either a pernicious end or the natural good of human flourishing. It simply lacks coherence. How to explain any (even stable) dispositions toward seemingly good acts? It seems custom—the residual dispositions from past acts that no longer retain their former intelligibility (from the person's own rationality as *causa immobilis*) but do not (yet?) have intelligibility supplied by a new *causa immobilis*, such as the rationality relatively coherently inclined toward either some pernicious end or back toward natural human flourishing—fits the bill for explaining such stable action. In this case a person would not be performing such acts out of habit properly so-called, but rather out of the residual dispositions from nature and even the prior "accustomings" of the capacities of the lost habits.

Before turning to infused virtue, it will help to reaffirm certain key points from the account of growth in acquired virtue. The key distinction for this task is between disposition and habit. These two ways of being qualified are attained through various processes, including innate (individual-level) dispositions, accustomization, and repeated properly human activity. Ideally these all contribute harmoniously to the ultimate development, particularly through childhood, of "full-blown" habits. When they do, it is not that dispositions become habits, but rather that human powers amenable to habituation, which contain sensory and rational facets in the unified person, are stably specified with increasing coherence such that the *person* becomes habituated. The person is unified (under one rational soul), yet distinct causal influences are possible even when the sensory appetite participates in reason. These distinct causal influences are especially evident when there is a lack of harmony, as when a natural or accustomed sensory disposition must be held in check. But it is also true even when sensory dispositions are inclined toward observably good activity, since the specification supplied by rationality has a complexity and attunement that transcends what can be supplied by sensory connaturalization.[77] Though it is difficult, possibly impossible, to identify precisely when a person crosses the line so as to have her powers stably qualified by her rationality, whatever characterizes this specification can be described. Qualities becomes habits when they become stably specified according to "various modes in respect of the various matters which constitute the sphere of virtue's action, and according to various circumstances."[78] Given this account of rational specification "within" a habit, such specification occurs "across" habits such that possessing one virtue necessarily entails possessing the other virtues.

This account of attaining a virtue and the connectivity among virtues, however, does not mean that no further growth is possible once virtues are attained. Due to the complexity of specification regarding contingent matters, it is possible to continue to grow after one has attained a properly human virtue. This growth can occur not simply by ongoing harmonization of the sensory and rational facets of human powers by the former's increasing participation in reason but also by the ongoing attunement of the rational specification of one's powers through persistent activity. This account of virtue is dynamic and necessitates ongoing growth. In the absence of such ongoing growth, due to tepid activity proceeding from a virtue, inactivity, or, of course, activity contrary to the virtue, a virtue may be decreased or even lost. Though the virtues are lost all at once when one crosses the line backward, performance of comparable activity can remain, given sensory accustomization that was entailed in the formation of the previously acquired habit and that residually exerts causal influence until that sensory connaturalization can be otherwise impressed by reason. With this account of growth in acquired virtue in hand, we turn to infused virtue.

NOTES

1. Breen, *Imagining an English Reading Public.*
2. See Miner, "Aquinas on *Habitus*," 68–71.
3. Even the most rigorous of the recent works on Aquinas's works on virtue and/or habit do not offer any detailed account of growth in virtue. These include Decosimo, *Ethics as a Work of Charity*, Austin, *Aquinas on Virtue;* and Knobel, *Aquinas on the Infused Moral Virtues.* Of course, this is a function of their taking on other worthy tasks, though the consistent neglect of dynamics of growth is noteworthy. For some attention to such dynamics, in the context of Thomistic scholarship on virtue, see Porter's frequent references to raising children in *Nature as Reason* (e.g., 195–201) and *Perfection of Desire* (e.g., 117–22). Herdt is concerned with this topic throughout her magisterial *Putting on Virtue*, particularly the extent to which "semblances" of virtue are part of the process of growth toward virtue and/or occasions of hypocrisy (e.g., 24–25, 43–46, 80–82, 125–26). Herdt briefly touches on many topics that point toward the work offered here, including the possibility of ongoing growth in virtue (70); the difference between true habit and "getting used to" (66; compare 43); the importance of the last end (51, 76, 124); and even the gifts of the Holy Spirit (91). Her inquiry would be helpfully complemented by a Thomistic account of dispositions and habits and their various causes. In her treatment of Aquinas Herdt focuses on other important topics, such as the possibility of pagan virtue and the relationship between infused and acquired virtue. See also Sullivan, *Habits and Holiness*, whose last chapter explicitly addresses changes in habit, though Sullivan's focus is more on the sort of practical self-help techniques found in popular books, even as these reflect his account of habit from earlier chapters in his book. See especially Sullivan's treatment of Aquinas's account of knowledge of one's habits as well as very concrete steps for acquiring a habit. Nevertheless, the general lack of attention to the dynamics of growth in virtue is precisely the lacuna addressed here.
4. Breen, *Imagining an English Reading Public*, 48. Though Breen is examining the role of custom in medieval thought on habit in general, she relies on Aquinas in her argument, particularly ST I–II q. 56, a. 5.
5. Aquinas, *Commentary on Aristotle's "Nicomachean Ethics,"* 268.
6. For a recent account of the relationship between social structures and individual agency, deploying the concept of virtue, see Daly, *The Structures of Virtue and Vice.* For brief treatment of how Aquinas's sparse explicit treatment of the social forces involved in formation masks the wider amenability to the role of such forces in moral formation, see Titus, "Moral Development and Making All Things New in Christ," 239n20.
7. A relatively recent classic work on the continuity with yet difference between the end-oriented activity of nonlinguistic animals and rational animals is MacIntyre's *Dependent Rational Animals.*
8. Breen, *Imagining an English Reading Public*, 48. The "context" she references in Aquinas's thought is ST I–II q. 56, a. 5.
9. Breen, *Imagining an English Reading Public*, 64–65 (emphasis added).
10. Breen, *Imagining an English Reading Public*, 48.
11. Burnyeat references both "unreasoned evaluative responses with which his upbringing has endowed him" and "instinctive reactions," which seem to correlate well with dispositions from custom and nature, respectively. See Burnyeat, "Aristotle on Learning to be Good," 82. For a critical engagement with Burnyeat, see Curzer, *Aristotle and the Virtues*, 318–40.

12. Burnyeat, "Learning to be Good," 83. In addition to this reference to "one's conception of the good," Burnyeat references "one's overall view of the good," both of which are comparable to the last end.
13. Burnyeat, 80.
14. Burnyeat, 80. Despite his use of the term "infused," Burnyeat speaks of what Aquinas would call acquired virtue.
15. Breen, *Imagining an English Reading Public*, 48.
16. *De virt.* a. 11 (Atkins). Conversely, the loss of a virtue is a disqualification or, perhaps more likely, requalification.
17. Miner, "Aquinas on *Habitus*," 68.
18. Breen, *Imagining an English Reading Public*, 48.
19. For comparable claims about the relationship between the varying "levels" of a human person's powers, see Korsgaard, *Self-Constitution*, 98–99, and Hursthouse, *On Virtue Ethics*, 207–8.
20. ST I 81,3 ad 2.
21. See ST I–II 50 and 56, as well as *De virt.* a. 4. For a recent treatment of this point, see Porter, *Perfection of Desire*, 28–34.
22. ST I–II 51,3. Though Aquinas speaks of specification supplied by reason being impressed on appetite in general (including rational appetite), it certainly includes the sensory powers. See the quotations in the following two notes, from *De virt.* a. 10 ad 14 and a. 9 ad 21, for this claim made with explicit reference to the sensory powers.
23. *De virt.* 10 ad 14. Note that this is a question on infused virtue, and the objector makes a claim about the person with God's grace who continues to be disturbed by passions. Thus it is all the more noteworthy that Aquinas affirms this possibility in the case of both infused virtue and acquired virtue. Because Aquinas addresses differences in this dynamic between the person with acquired virtue and the person with infused virtue, people commonly think only the person with infused virtue experiences these (see ST I–II 65, 3 ad 2). This quote shows Aquinas thinks otherwise.
24. *De virt.* a. 9 ad 21.
25. ST I–II 53,2: habits "increase through the same cause as that which engenders them." See also *De virt.* a. 11 ad 13: "It should be said that just as the act coming forth from an agent can *cause* acquired virtue because of the impression of active powers on the passive, as was said above, so too it can *increase* it" (emphasis added).
26. A classic occasion to address this dynamic in the context of sin is the *fomes peccati*, which persist in this life and even in the life of one who possesses virtue. See ST I–II 74,3 ad 2. For detailed treatment of this topic see Johnson, "St. Thomas and the 'Law of Sin.'" Much discussion of the *fomes* occurs in the context of the passions in Christ. See ST III 15,2. See Lombardo, *The Logic of Desire*, 211–12; and Gondreau, *The Passions of Christ's Soul*, 350–64.
27. *De virt card.* a. 2 ad 1. See also ST I–II 52,1, where Aquinas mentions custom as well as nature.
28. *De virt card.* a. 3. In this passage the second cause is *vel propter maius exercitium* rather than *consuetudine* or *assuetudine*, as in ST I–II 66,1. Despite the use of *exercitium* here, and given the clear parallel of the passages, I take their meanings to be the same.
29. As noted in chap. 1, the possibility of contrary dispositions even in one with a habit is a potent resource for engaging the critiques of virtue by situationism. See Miller's discussion of "surprising dispositions," "Virtue Cultivation in Light of Situationism," 159.

30. See, for example, I–II 65,3 ad 2 and *De virt. card.* a. 2 ad 2. Here Aquinas uses the term *relictas*. See also the use of *reliquiae* in *De car.* a. 13.
31. Breen claims medievals most commonly contrasted good *habitus* from bad *consuetudines*, though she acknowledges customs can be good (*Imagining an English Reading Public*, 49). For treatment of what she calls "inverse akratics," see Hursthouse, *On Virtue Ethics*, 149–53.
32. ST I–II 51,1.
33. *De card virt.* a. 2. See also *Sent.* l. II d. 36 a. 1.
34. See *Sent* l. 3 d. 33 q. 1 a. 2 qa. 1 ad 3: *Quod homo propter hoc quod habet rationem, quae collativa est, se habet ad multas operationes.* John Bolin translates "*quae collativa est*" as "which brings many things together."
35. For helpful accounts of Aquinas on continence and incontinence, see Hoffman, "Aquinas on the Moral Progress of the Weak Willed"; and Kent, "Aquinas and Weakness of Will."
36. ST II–II 155,1.
37. Aquinas seems to envision something of this sort in ST II–II 155,4 ad 2, where he claims that the persistence of contrary dispositions caused by the body, not the soul, actually makes continence *more* meritorious than virtue.
38. For a similar claim in contemporary moral philosophy, see Hursthouse, *On Virtue Ethics*, 98. Hursthouse notes that overcoming contrary dispositions that "make [acting virtuously] hard" need not "show that his virtue is incomplete" and says the contrary dispositions do not necessarily spring from character (98n13). My claim is not that the "unreachable" persistent bodily causal influences do not impede the activities of the virtue. They do, indeed, much as a paralyzed limb impedes activity. Yet, comparable to the paralyzed limb, the impediment does not preclude the possibility of possessing virtue. Despite obvious and important differences (with paralyzed limbs or residual effects from accustomed alcoholism), this is a place to address the ways that disabilities both do and do not impede the possession of and activities of the virtues. For more on this discussion, see the work of Romero, such as "The Happiness of 'Those Who Lack the Use of Reason.'" See chap. 7 for more on how those unable to exercise their rationality (e.g., infants who are baptized) may nonetheless possess infused virtue.
39. See Decosimo, *Ethics as a Work of Charity*, 90.
40. See Russell, *Practical Intelligence and the Virtues*, 113–23.
41. Aquinas appears to say there is indeed a particular moment when one crosses the line, even if that line is difficult to identify. Textual evidence in support of this is found in his challenging claim that at some point a child "begins to have the use of reason" and thus can sin mortally. See ST I–II 89,6. For support of this claim in the secondary literature, see Hoffman, "Aquinas on Moral Progress," 136–37.
42. Russell acknowledges that virtue can indeed be a "boundary" (i.e., with a sharp delineating line) rather than a "vague" *satis* concept, though he claims it is vague (without any argument against the boundary view). See Russell, *Practical Intelligence and the Virtues*, 119n28.
43. Recall Aquinas's example of the beginner in virtue (or science) who possesses only a disposition to such (ST I–II 49,1 ad 3).
44. *De virt.* a. 9 ad 11.
45. See Aquinas, *Commentary on Aristotle's "Nicomachean Ethics,"* 265. Aquinas claims that habits are "second nature" and what is done according to nature is pleasant.
46. *De virt. card.* a. 2 ad 10. Though people commonly think this "virtues attained all at once" feature to be true only of infused virtue, it is indeed true of acquired virtue as well.

47. Decosimo, *Ethics as a Work of Charity*, 90.
48. Russell senses this connection in making a case for the connectivity of the virtues as a theoretical model of virtue, even if he also (disappointedly) claims that connectivity does not apply in a manner we can attribute to particular agents. He offers no argument in support of the "undeniable observation" that we cannot attribute connected virtue to any particular agent, and asserts the "undeniable claim that people develop . . . virtue in a piecemeal fashion" (*Practical Intelligence and the Virtues*, 372, 369, respectively).
49. Aquinas cites Aristotle's description of virtue (*virtus est ultimum potentiae*) by Aristotle (*On the Heavens*, 1) throughout his corpus: *De virt.* a. 1 obj. 6; *De virt.* a. 9 obj. 15; *De virt.* a. 11 ad 15; *De virt.* a. 13 obj. 1; *De virt. card.* a. 4; and ST I–II 66,1 obj. 2.
50. *De virt. card.* a. 3. See also ST I–II 52,1: "The Stoics . . . held that some habits are of themselves susceptible of more or less, for instance, the arts; and some are not, as the virtues." See also I–II 66,1.
51. *De virt. card.* a. 3. See also ST I–II 52,1.
52. As to Aristotle's description of virtue as the highest reach of a power, Aquinas claims: "It should be said that the notion of virtue does not consist in the superlative with respect to itself, but with respect to its object, because by virtue a man is ordered to the utmost of a power, which is to act well; hence, the Philosopher says in *Physics* 7 that virtue is the disposition of the perfected to the best. However, one can be more or less disposed to this optimum." *De virt.* a. 11 ad 15.
53. ST I–II 66,1. On this point about indivisibility, see also *De virt.* a. 13 ad 1, where Aquinas treats Aristotle's description of virtue as the highest reach of a power with this argument: "It should be said that the utmost of a power is taken from the utmost to which the power extends, and this is the most difficult, because it is most difficult to find the mean but easy to deviate from it. Thus, virtue is the utmost of a power because it lies in the mean."
54. See ST I–II 52,1: "Intensity and remission may be observed in habits and dispositions . . . , in respect of participation by the subject . . . according to a diverse aptitude arising either from nature, or from custom."
55. STI–II 52,3.
56. See esp. ST I–II 52,1–3 and *De virt.* a. 11. While most translations (e.g., English Dominicans, Freddoso) translate *intensio* as intensity, it is also translated as "intensive" (Atkins). Since intensity can connote passion or emotional accompaniment, which is clearly not Aquinas's intent here, other translations are preferable. He uses the term in two ways. First, as the opposite of remission of a habit, so on that score *intensio* may be translated as growth, or if a cognate is preferred, intensification. See especially ST I–II 52,1, though Aquinas at times uses *augeri* for growth or increase. (Note his connection of these terms, along with greater participation by the subject, at I–II 52,2: "*Augetur etiam nihilominus motus per intensionem, secundum participationem subiecti*"). Second, Aquinas speaks of growth occurring *per intensionem*, or *secundum intensionem* (see 52,3 for nominative and ablative forms). This usage is better understood not as emotional intensification but rather as in *intendere*, more fittingly "attaining the end sought." So a person's temperance grows *per intensionem* when its object more fittingly (with greater attunement to various modes, circumstances, and an overall view of things) attains the goals of eating. The Latin has a sense of tautness, or stretching, extending, aiming. Torrell uses "extension" which may best indicate this sense of growth (*Saint Thomas Aquinas 2: Spiritual Master*, 264).
57. ST I–II 63,2.

58. Recall also ST I–II 66,1, where Aquinas distinguishes repeated activity (accustomization) from the "more discerning judgment of reason." Aquinas uses the term "*assuetudine*" in both I–II 63,2 (on properly human repeated acts) and I–II 66,1 (on repeated acts distinguished from those entailing a more discerning judgment of reason). The Latin for "more discerning," *perspicacious*, is etymologically related to the English phrase "having greater perspective." See also *De virt. card.* a. 3 (which uses "*melius iudicium rationis*" rather than *perspicacious*).
59. Reference to "loops" to indicate the responsiveness of the specificity of a habit to one's apprehension of the environment is common in discussions of habits. For examples, see Sullivan, *Habits and Holiness*, 25–33. For a more popular example, see Clear, *Atomic Habits*, 49–51, 105–8.
60. For contemporary philosophical emphasis on the necessity of ongoing growth in habits, see Annas, *Intelligent Virtue*, where she addresses what she calls the "drive to aspire" that is inherent to virtue (25–26) as well as the virtuous person's "increasingly determinate" conception of happiness (161–62). See also MacIntyre, *Ethics in the Conflicts of Modernity*, which describes the necessity of ongoing assessment of the contingency of the practical life (191). MacIntyre claims that "we complete and perfect our lives by allowing them to remain incomplete" (231), not simply on a supernatural level but even on a natural one.
61. ST I–II 53,1 ad 1.
62. ST I–II 53,2 ad 1. In addition to increase or decrease by greater or lesser participation of the subject in the habit, Aquinas grants that habits can increase or decrease by extension toward a larger number of objects, as when a skill or knowledge applies to a greater number of things. But he claims that moral virtues, which are inherently connected to appetite and thus will (that is, habits in the proper sense), do not grow by extension because they extend to all things characteristic of their object. See ST I–II 66,1 as well as 52,1–2. This point, that growth in virtue occurs not through extension to more objects but rather through greater participation of the subject, is perhaps the main point made in the few available analyses of Aquinas on growth in virtue. See Miner, "Aquinas on *Habitus*," 78; Hoffman, "Aquinas on Moral Progress," 137; and Torrell, *Spiritual Master*, 354.
63. ST I–II 53,2 ad 3.
64. ST I–II 53,1.
65. ST I–II 53,3.
66. ST I–II 52,3. For a helpful treatment of the various senses in which an act that decreases a habit both can and cannot be precisely said to proceed from that habit, albeit with reference to the infused virtue charity, and whether or not charity, once possessed, can be lost, see *De car.* a. 12.
67. For a recent book that is a comparable to this one but with a focus on sin, plus necessary foray into topics like habit and last end, see Jensen, *Sin*. There he treats in great detail the internal causes on sin. The most relevant texts in Aquinas come from his so-called treatise on sin (ST I–II 71–89) as well as *De malo.*, particularly qq. 3–7.
68. For a detailed attention to social forces that make it difficult to be virtuous, and indeed prompt toward habituation of vice, see Daly, *The Structures of Virtue and Vice*.
69. Aquinas mentions nature and custom in precisely this context. See ST I–II 52,1.
70. ST I–II 51,3.
71. *De virt.* a. 9 ad 11.

72. Aquinas claims habits properly understood are necessary for a person's perfection. See ST I–II 49,4, as well as *De virt.* a. 1. Something is lacking if a human power amenable to habituation is "only" accustomed rather than habituated. I take Aquinas's claim on the "necessity" of habit to mean "necessary for full rational operation," not as literally necessary in the sense of unable to be without, since he clearly affirms the possibility of "imperfect" virtues. See Porter, "Why Are the Habits Necessary?," 113–15, 133.
73. ST I–II 51,3. See also I–II 53,3 ad 3: "The intellectual part of the soul, considered in itself, is above time, but the sensitive part is subject to time, and therefore in course of time it undergoes change as to the passions of the sensitive part, and also as to the powers of apprehension."
74. The claim that vices entail the stable specification of a person's capacities through practical reasoning that is vitiated, which Aquinas endorses, is not the same as the claim that sins of vices are connected, which Aquinas denies. See ST I–II 73,1.
75. ST I–II 51,3.
76. ST I–II 51,3.
77. See *De virt.* a. 8. See also ST I–II 63,1.
78. ST I–II 63,1.

CHAPTER 6

ATTAINING SUPERNATURAL HABITS

Infused Virtues

One of the great achievements of Aquinas's moral thought is the deployment of classical thought on virtue to the service of Christianity's account of the human person's journey toward supernatural happiness in a manner only possible through God's grace. This integration is not without significant challenges, and it has been criticized from a variety of angles as failing to achieve that desired synthesis. A comprehensive overview and evaluation of that endeavor is far beyond the scope of this project.[1] The immediate task here is to offer a Thomistic account of graced virtue for use in an analysis of growth in infused virtue. Grace is the last of Aquinas's four efficient causes of habits. The emphasis will be on the more technical aspects of infused virtues as habits, which will lead to an account of growth in graced virtue attentive to the embodied communal practices that serve as the venue for such formation.

A working hermeneutic is the Scholastic dictum that "grace perfects nature" and a robust account of properly human habits informs an understanding of the infused virtues. After all, the infused virtues are habits. While this discussion on infused virtue parallels the previous one on acquired virtue (see chapter 4), we will find the important ways the infused virtues differ significantly from acquired virtues. Indeed, if virtues are stable specifications of a person's habituation-amenable powers toward activities constitutive of flourishing, then infused virtues are radically different from the acquired ones, as they order the person toward a whole other order. Though there is important and oft-overlooked commonality between acquired and infused virtue, there is also radical difference. All of this will inform the ensuing account of gain of, growth in, and loss of infused virtue.

This chapter begins by offering an account of why the infused virtues are needed and in what ways infused virtues are truly habits, and thus similar to acquired habits. It helps to begin to identify and explicate their important differences from the acquired virtues. The next section addresses the difference grace makes "within" a virtue, including extended examination of the gifts of the Holy Spirit. I then examine the difference grace makes "across" virtues, with a focus on the connectivity of the infused virtues. The final section examines the last end and the claim that charity is the "form" of the virtues comes into focus.

INFUSED VIRTUES AS HABITS

We can begin this inquiry into infused virtue at the same starting point where we began inquiry into habit more generally. Why are infused habits needed? The first answer is that they provide what all habits provide, namely, stable specification of underdetermined human powers so that the person can attain the end to which she is ordered with promptness, stability, and pleasure. All of this goes without saying in Aquinas's account of infused virtue, for this is what all human habits supply. We can expect to find "given" yet inchoate or underdetermined ends possessed by a person and ordered toward activity. We can expect that infused virtues *qua* habits qualify habituation-amenable human powers and order those powers toward activity. These infused virtues will be characterized by both stability and specification of activity through the *causa immobilis* of the person's rational powers. Infused virtues will supply particular principles, or "appetitive inclinations" toward acts that are more specific than the inchoate ends in the person but nonetheless require instantiation through deliberation and choice. Infused virtues are virtues, and thus all of these characteristics apply.

Yet Aquinas's distinguishing answer as to why *infused* habits are needed is that, because they direct the person toward an end that far surpasses the capacity of unaided human powers, even rational powers, they can be attained only through God's grace:

> There are some habits by which man is disposed to an end which exceeds the proportion of human nature, namely, the ultimate and perfect happiness of man. . . . And since habits need to be in proportion with that to which man is disposed by them, therefore is it necessary that those habits, which dispose to this end, exceed the proportion of human nature. Wherefore such habits can never be in man except by Divine infusion, as is the case with all gratuitous virtues.[2]

In every treatment of the cause of virtues (or habits) in human persons, Aquinas claims that some virtues are infused in the person by God and this is so because the end to which they direct the human person is "happiness surpassing man's nature, and which man can obtain by the power of God alone, by a kind of participation of the Godhead. . . . Hence it is necessary for man to receive from God some additional principles, whereby he may be directed to supernatural happiness."[3] Since attainment of the supernatural end toward which the person is directed is only possible with God's grace, a person requires these principles of activity supplied by God's grace to direct her toward that end.[4] These are the infused virtues. Indeed, Aquinas makes it clear that any activity proceeding from such infused virtue is only possible with the assistance of God's grace.[5]

Aquinas repeatedly compares the human person's natural seeds of virtue (level one), acquired virtues (level two), and activities (level three), all of which are oriented toward the person's natural end, on the one hand, to God's grace, infused virtues, and graced activity, all oriented toward a person's supernatural end, on the other hand.[6] This point is commonly made in the form of a claim that as God provides on the natural level, so too does God provide on the supernatural level.

> It is not fitting that God should provide less for those He loves that they may acquire supernatural good, than for creatures whom He loves that they may acquire natural good. Now He so provides for natural creatures, that not merely does He move them to their natural acts, but He bestows upon them certain forms and powers, which are the principles of acts, in order that they may of themselves be inclined to these movements, and thus the movements whereby they are moved by God become natural and easy to creatures, according to Wis. 8:1: "She . . . orders all things sweetly." Much more therefore does He infuse into such as He moves towards the acquisition of supernatural good, certain forms or supernatural qualities, whereby they may be moved by Him sweetly and promptly to acquire eternal good; and thus the gift of grace is a quality.[7]

Thus Aquinas affirms this commonality between the natural and supernatural: not simply in that it is God who provides in both cases but also in the parallels of the manner by which the human person is provided.

Before continuing to note what and how God provides, note that the claim that God provides on the natural level is not a claim that God provides acquired virtues in the same manner as He does infused virtues. Aquinas states that grace in its broader sense refers to "something bestowed on man by God."[8] This includes that "common" grace whereby God gives humanity (and indeed all creatures) its being and thus causes human nature and all that ensues from it (habits, activities, etc.).[9] The acquired virtues are in this sense also caused by God. Yet more specifically grace refers to a "special love, according to which God draws the rational creature *beyond its natural condition* . . . and according to which love God wishes simply the eternal good of the creature, which is Himself."[10] This is true of the infused virtues but not the acquired virtues. Hence in this more precise meaning of grace we can call infused virtue "graced virtue." Labeling virtues "acquired" or "natural" does not mean God is uninvolved in them. Yet the end supplied by God in such virtues is connatural to the person, whereas with the infused virtues God inclines a person toward a good far surpassing unaided human nature.

Due to this commonality in the way God provides for the human person toward both natural and supernatural flourishing, we should expect to find significant commonalities in both acquired and infused virtues, and indeed we do. For instance, in both cases virtues serve as middle points between a person and her acts. They supply more particular principles that facilitate, even while neither necessitating nor determining, particular actions. Yet even in this clear parallel of acquired and infused virtues we begin to see important differences. For instance, the "seeds" of acquired virtue are supplied by nature. Though underdetermined, or only a beginning, nonetheless the ends of actions that constitute natural human flourishing are possessed by the person by nature. However, this cannot be the case for the infused virtues. Infused virtues orient a person toward a supernatural flourishing that exceeds the capacities of unaided human nature. So if infused virtues are truly habits that qualify a person's powers, powers that are extensions of a person's nature, what supplies that supernature?

Before offering Aquinas's answer to this question, which has important ramifications for growth in virtue, it would help to know what Aquinas cannot say. On the one hand, he cannot say that grace exists solely at the level of habit, such that what is qualified by habit is exactly the same as the infused and acquired virtues. Recall that habits qualify human powers whose ends are already—albeit inchoately—supplied by nature: "The virtue of a thing has reference to some pre-existing nature."[11] Thus there must be a change in whatever supplies those underdetermined ends to the human powers qualified by habits. On the other hand, the supernatural life toward which grace directs a person cannot simply come from the human person's rational soul. That would render God's grace no longer a gift, but simply part of nature. This participation in the Divine life would no longer be supernatural, but rather natural. Or, if a person's soul did become essentially supernatural through the bestowal of grace, there would be no continuity between the former person and the new person. How to describe the new ends supplied by grace in a manner that does not render them natural, yet depicts them as "deeper" than habits?

Aquinas's answer to this is that grace is indeed deeper than one's powers, even as qualified by infused virtues:

> Even as the natural light of reason is something besides the acquired virtues, which are ordained to this natural light, so also the light of grace which is a participation of the Divine Nature is something besides the infused virtues which are derived from and are ordained to this light.... For as the acquired virtues enable a man to walk, in accordance with the natural light of reason, so do the infused virtues enable a man to walk as befits the light of grace.[12]

Grace is "deeper," if you will, than a human power, and it abides at the soul's essence. "Hence it remains that grace, as it is prior to virtue, has a subject prior to the powers of the soul, so that it is in the essence of the soul."[13] Nevertheless, though God's grace must exist prior to the powers qualified by habits in order to supply the inchoate ends of activity, God's grace cannot simply be the essence of the soul, its nature, since grace is supernatural. "Because grace is above human nature, it cannot be a substance or a substantial form, but is an accidental form of the soul. Now what is substantially in God, becomes accidental in the soul participating in the Divine goodness."[14] Aquinas calls grace a quality, not of the soul's powers, like habits are, but of the essence of the soul itself. It is not the soul's essence, but it qualifies the essence of the person. In response to the obvious objection that as a quality, grace must then be a virtue, Aquinas replies: "Grace is reduced to the first species of quality; and yet it is not the same as virtue, but is a certain *habitudo* [habitual condition] which is presupposed to the infused virtues, as their principle and root."[15] Aquinas's position, that grace supplies the supernatural seeds prior to the person's powers that can be qualified by infused virtues, enables him to guard the continuity between acquired and infused virtues while nevertheless recognizing the sense in which grace is supernatural. This solution on the supernatural ends as qualifications rather than as natural seeds has significant implications for the possession and exercise of infused virtues.

THE DIFFERENCE GRACE MAKES "WITHIN" VIRTUE

Aquinas goes to great lengths to emphasize the continuity that exists between acquired and infused virtues. Yet he equally emphasizes the significant discontinuities between these types of virtue. In what follows we examine those continuities and discontinuities within the infused virtues. First we examine how and why Aquinas claims that the theological virtues can serve as seeds of infused virtue, even as they themselves are virtues. We then examine the impact of the supernatural end on a person's activities. It should comes as no surprise, since grace changes both the first level of "nature" and the second level of qualities, that the third level, activity, is also transformed in the case of graced virtue. Finally we examine in further detail to the relationship between habits (level two) and activity (level three), since it turns out that God's grace is needed for graced activity, even granting grace abiding in the essence of the soul and qualifying its powers through the infused virtues. We offer an account of Aquinas's thought on the gifts of the Holy Spirit to address why grace is needed to act on the infused virtues, how the habits called gifts of the Holy Spirit render one amenable to that grace, and how those habits related to the infused virtues.

Theological Virtues as Seeds and Qualities

The infused virtues, as habits in the proper sense, are rightly understood as middle points that supply particular ends (level two) between the general ends of the person and her powers supplied by nature (level one) and the particular contextualized actualization of those ends in a person's activity (level three). Yet Aquinas speaks of this dynamic for the infused virtues in two distinct ways. One way is where "grace is a certain habitual condition which is presupposed by the infused virtues, and is their source and root."[16] Grace thus qualifies a person's soul so as to provide the seeds toward supernatural acts, and the infused virtues are more specific ends than those seeds. Yet at other times Aquinas ascribes the role of supplying seeds to the theological virtues. In addressing whether or not there are infused moral virtues, Aquinas counters the position that the theological virtues alone suffice. He claims that just as nature provides principles or seeds to direct us to our natural end, from which the acquired virtues proceed, so too does God provide the theological virtues to direct us to our supernatural end, from which infused moral virtues proceed.[17]

This initially appears to be an odd claim, for two reasons. First, in other texts Aquinas distinguishes all infused virtues (including the theological virtues) from the principles supplied by the graced soul. But in this one he parallels theological virtues to the seeds of nature. Second, on the natural level it makes sense that the seeds or principles are part of nature and that habits are the qualifications of that nature. In referring to the theological virtues as seeds or principles, Aquinas says habits (which must qualify something) serve as seeds or principles.

However, there are reasons for both apparent inconsistencies. Regarding the first seeming internal contradiction: as with natural ends, supernatural ends exist on a variety of levels. Recall the connectivity of the virtues: ends supplied by moral virtues prompt means supplied by prudence, which themselves then serve as ends for ensuing acts. Similarly, God's grace recreates a person toward partaking in the Divine Nature, and one of the ways this is lived out is through the infused theological virtues whereby one believes in, has hope for, and loves God. Yet these "means" toward supernatural happiness also serve as ends that engender other means, such as the infused moral virtues. Whereas the theological virtues incline a person toward activities whose object is God directly (*in finem*), the infused moral and intellectual virtues incline a person toward activities whose objects are not God (and are accessible to unaided reason) but are done for the sake of God (*ad finem*).[18] Indeed, further on "down the line" these infused moral virtues also supply ends to the activities of the human person, ends that are executed in the deliberation and choice of (graced) practical reasoning. This dynamic explains why the theological virtues can be described both as seeds generating more specific ends and as more specific ends in relation to the graced essence of the soul.

Second, as to the "seeds" being supplied by habits (i.e., qualities) rather than nature, it is fitting in the case of supernatural life, where even the most deep-seated seed of such life is grace, itself a qualification of the soul (albeit to the essence of the soul, not simply its powers).[19] Therefore, in addition to the multiple layers of ends enabling Aquinas to speak of theological virtues as both seeds and habits, the gratuity of grace as accidental quality for the human person also makes it equally appropriate for him to refer to the qualities that are infused theological virtues not only as habits but also as seeds.

Different Ends, Different Virtues, Different Acts

Having examined further the difference that grace makes at the level of nature and of qualities, we must examine the change in activities caused by a person's orientation by grace toward the supernatural end. It is difficult to overemphasize the importance of this different end for the infused virtues. In line with Scripture and the Christian tradition, Aquinas describes a person's new life in grace as being born again, a "re-creation" or "re-generation."[20] This new life is akin to a new household or new city, namely, a heavenly one.[21] If the goal of any human life is happiness or flourishing, the graced life is a different sort of happiness.[22] Since human happiness entails a person's activities, the happiness toward which one is directed provides a distinct rule or measure for those activities.[23] If such a rule or measure provides the light by which we understand a person's actions, the graced life is a walking in a whole new light.[24] The implications of this supernatural end for human life are enormous, especially three particularly relevant ones.

First, a new life in Christ aiming toward a supernatural end demands a new set of virtues by which a person is related to that last end. Recognition of a person's last end, and its impact on all a person's activities, is a staple of classical moral thought on virtue. At the natural level there is no distinct virtue whereby one acts directly in relation to the last end.[25] Yet this is not the case in the graced life. On the supernatural level, the last end is not simply one's life "as a whole," including one's activity. The supernatural last end is God's very Self, a personal last end (indeed, a triune, "supra-personal" last end) with agency, Who bestows on humanity not only new life in grace (level one) but also infused habits (level two), whereby the person acts (level three) in direct relation to God in faith and hope and love.[26]

These are, of course, the theological virtues, and since they qualify human activity that has the living God as its "object," they are only possible with God's grace.[27] As habits (level two) they still qualify natural human powers of intellect (faith) and will (hope and love).[28] In them we see that same conjunction of intellect and will that Aquinas claims is essential for a habit in the most proper sense of making a person good: faith is a virtue of the intellect whose acts of belief are quickened by the (charity-qualified) will; charity inclines the person's will to rest in God's very Self, with whom one is united in friendship;[29] and hope inclines the person's will to move toward God as the attainable (content and cause) of one's own perfect happiness.[30] Charity and hope both qualify the will, and in both cases the will is guided by apprehension supplied by the intellect.[31] Though the theological virtues qualify the same intellect and will of a person qualified by, say, prudence and justice, the "object" of the theological virtues is God's very Self and thus there are no acquired versions of these virtues.[32]

Second, recognition of the supernatural end as a new life with a distinct rule or measure of acts toward and constitutive of that end raises the question of the relationship between the natural end of a person's humanity and the supernatural end. This area of theological inquiry is one of the most hotly debated in the twentieth century. Needless to say, it cannot be engaged in any depth here.[33] Yet one point is important as it relates to the acquired and infused virtues. Aquinas is quite clear that virtues directing one toward supernatural happiness must be infused and cannot be acquired.[34] He also claims quite clearly that the infused virtues are not oriented toward humanity's natural good as last end, but rather toward the supernatural end as last end.[35] Yet the claim that the infused virtues do not attain the natural end as last end should not be taken to indicate that humanity's natural end is obliterated, or remains unfulfilled, in the attainment of the supernatural end. Neither are true, due to the oft-cited Scholastic axiom that "grace perfects nature."[36] In short, the natural end of humanity is fulfilled, even as it is surpassed, in the attainment of the supernatural end as last end.

Third, and finally, the previous claim leads to perhaps the most important claim Aquinas makes with regard to the relationship between infused and acquired virtues, a claim he makes from the start until the end of his corpus. Through God's grace are infused not only the theological virtues directing one to actions concerning God immediately but also the infused moral and intellectual (here infused cardinal) virtues directing one toward activities accessible to unaided human reason but done in further relation to God.[37] This leads Aquinas to ask whether the infused virtues and acquired virtues are of the same species, and he consistently claims they are not.[38] Each type of virtue is ordered toward a different last end.[39] Corresponding to that last end is a different rule or measure, and thus an act of infused virtue or acquired virtue, even if it concerns the same sort of activity (e.g., sensual pleasure qualified by temperance), differs in how that activity is specified based upon that different rule or measure.[40] Since virtues are distinguished by the acts toward which they order a person, this means that the infused virtues and acquired virtues differ in species or, as we might say here, their (stable) specification. The actions of the infused cardinal virtues differ from those of the acquired cardinal virtues, even if at times they may be observably the same.[41]

In one sense the infused virtues are true habits and thus operate in roughly the same manner as acquired virtues. In another sense, since they are qualifications of human powers whose stable specification is supplied by the *causa immobilis* of one's rationality as (healed and) elevated by God's grace and thus governed by a different rule or measure, everything changes. This change entails a distinct set of virtues that do not exist at the natural level, namely, the theological virtues. Even in the case of infused cardinal virtues that have acquired counterparts, the different last end and resulting different rule or measure of action results in the different specification of the ends of the infused virtues and their actions. In addition to this change in the specification of activity in infused virtue, there are other differences in how a person acts in the new life of the infused virtues, which leads us to the gifts of the Holy Spirit.

God's Grace Needed to Act on Infused Habits: The Gifts of the Holy Spirit

We have addressed the seeds of the infused virtues (level one) and the important difference in specification of activity of the infused virtues (level three) as distinct from the acquired virtues. An examination of the gifts of the Holy Spirit continues that focuses on activity or, more precisely, the relationship between habit (level two) and activity (level three) proceeding from habits. The gifts of the Holy Spirit present one of the more subtle and contested topics in Thomistic scholarship. Some noted Thomists have even claimed that they are superfluous to Aquinas's thought on virtue, a mere add-on included out of respect for preceding authorities and a consistent interpretation of Isaiah 11:2–3.[42] This is not the position offered here. A discussion of the gifts provides occasion to address one of the most mysterious topics in moral theology, namely, the nexus between divine and human agency. Due to the mysterious nature of this topic, Aquinas's thought on the gifts, while unsurpassed in the Christian intellectual tradition, is somewhat unsettled. There is a clear evolution through his corpus regarding his thinking on the gifts, and despite some scholarly claims to the contrary, it is not clear to me that his mature thought represents a settled position.[43] His mature position lacks some of the precision that so often characterizes his distinctions and categorizations regarding the virtues. Finally, Aquinas's account leaves largely unaddressed certain questions concerning the gifts that are staples in his treatments of other habits such as virtues.

Nevertheless, I argue that the gifts of the Holy Spirit are indeed crucial to Aquinas's account of the life of grace and thus are essential to living out that life. Since they concern that inscrutable nexus of divine and human agency, they defy a more "tidy" account. Yet some of the claims here, such as the paradigm of the three levels, do aid in a deeper understanding of what the gifts are and why they are so important.

Given the focus on growing in virtue, the primary topic now is delineating the relationship between the gifts and the virtues, especially the infused virtues. What are the gifts? How are they related to level two habits and level three activity? Granting the presence of infused virtues, what is the distinctive contribution of the gifts to the graced life? I claim Aquinas presents an account of the gifts as habits (level two) that render a person amenable to the assistance of God's grace in performing the activity (level three) of the infused virtues. They are not merely occasionally operative in graced activity, nor are they only needed to perform some graced activities toward supernatural happiness but not others. The gifts of the Holy Spirit are always needed to act in a manner proceeding from infused virtue and they are always needed in order to act in a manner constitutive of that happiness in the graced journey toward supernatural happiness.

Thus the relationship between the virtues and the gifts is an appropriate subject of focus. Why are the gifts habits and not virtues? How are they enumerated? What are their paradigmatic acts? How are they amenable to growth, and in what manner are they impeded? Aquinas addresses all of these questions to greater and lesser degrees. The mystery of divine and human agency is ultimately impenetrable, and so this review will end in a somewhat unsettled manner. But much more can be said before submitting in apophatic wonder. Ten specific questions about the gifts of the Holy Spirit will guide this review.

First, why are the gifts of the Holy Spirit needed or, more specifically, why is further grace needed to act on infused virtue? The seeds of supernatural activity are not natural to a person; they are supernatural and given by God's grace. This change they cause in a person is deep, qualifying the essence of the soul itself "below" the natural powers. That said, the ends supplied by grace are still accidental, and not of the essence of the soul itself. Hence they are possessed less perfectly. Therefore, even once a person is "born again" in grace and possesses the infused virtues, a person cannot act (level three) on these habits (level two) without God's further grace.[44] One reason for this is the ongoing effects of sin on the person in this life. Yet there also is another reason that applies to the human person even in the state of original innocence as well as in the perfect happiness of the next life.[45]

Though the infused virtues are in a sense more noble than the acquired virtues in terms of their supernatural end, nevertheless the soul participates in supernatural Divine goodness less perfectly since "grace has its being in the soul in a less perfect way than the soul subsists in itself."[46] Though it may seem odd that the infused virtues, as supplied by God's grace, are not enough to enable a person to act virtuously toward supernatural happiness, our previous account of how habits supply particular principles to advance such activity (level three) without necessitating it or determining it is relevant here. There is more to be done, so to speak, than simply possessing habits, whether it be on the natural or (especially) supernatural level. Even after a person possesses the infused virtues, God's grace is needed to help the person live according to those virtues or, in other words, to perform activities proceeding from the particular ends supplied by infused virtues *qua* habits.

This is exactly the role performed by the gifts of the Holy Spirit. The gifts of the Holy Spirit are habits "whereby one becomes amenable to the promptings of the Holy Ghost."[47] Such prompting of the Holy Spirit toward particular actions is necessary even with the possession of the infused virtues. Aquinas makes this case in his treatment of the gifts: "In matters subject to human reason, and directed to man's connatural end, man can work through the judgment of his reason. . . . But in matters directed to the supernatural end, to which man's reason moves him, according as it is, in a manner, and imperfectly, informed by the theological virtues, the motion of reason does not suffice, unless it receive in addition the prompting [*instinctus*] or motion of the Holy Ghost."[48] The gifts of the Holy Spirit are not this motion itself, which Aquinas later refers to as *instinctus*.[49] Like the infused virtues, they are graced habits, not grace itself. They are habits in the human person rendering her amenable to movement by the Spirit, movement that helps the person perform activity (level three) out of the infused virtues (level two) and gifts.

Second, what do the gifts of the Holy Spirit supply that is distinct from infused virtue? Aquinas explains what exactly the gifts supply that is not supplied by the virtues, including even the infused virtues. This is especially evident in the article where he establishes the necessity of the gifts for salvation and carefully distinguishes the gifts both from the acquired (natural) virtues and from the infused (supernatural) virtues.[50] He distinguishes the gifts (and infused virtues) from human virtues by the end toward which they order a person, namely, the supernatural as distinct from the natural.[51] Yet Aquinas is particularly concerned, given the supernatural context of the gifts, to differentiate the gifts from the infused virtues. Here is where the imperfect possession of graced habits comes into play: "By the theological and moral virtues, man is not so perfected in respect of his last end, as not to stand in continual need of being moved by the yet higher promptings of the Holy Ghost."[52] These gifts are those habits that enable a person to act, proceeding from infused virtue. The gifts are called such "not only because they are infused by God [true also of the infused virtues], but also because by them man is disposed to become amenable to the Divine inspiration."[53] When a person acts according to the infused virtues, the causal influence supplied by infused virtues does not suffice without additional movement from God. The gifts are habits that render a person amenable to such movement from the Holy Spirit.

Third, what moves a person in the graced life? It is worth pausing to examine more closely Aquinas's claim about the gifts disposing one to be moved by the Divine *instinctus*. He claims that through the gifts one is habitually moved by Divine *instinctus* and that this is different from how the virtues operate. How, then, is a person who is qualified by infused virtues moved? Given that these virtues are provided by Gods' grace, is it accurate to say the infused virtues move a person by Divine *instinctus*? While it is true that the infused virtues are gifts of God's grace and orient one toward more particular activities constitutive of supernatural happiness, Aquinas claims that the infused virtues qualify a person so as to be moved by reason, even if that reason is (healed and) elevated toward the supernatural end by the theological virtues.[54] This claim is easily confused, since Aquinas uses reason in two senses.

At times when Aquinas references the measure or rule (*regulam*) of reason, he is referencing the natural end as distinct from the supernatural last end.[55] He clearly refers to this sense of reason when he claims, "In matters subject to human reason, and directed to man's connatural end, man can work through the judgment of his reason."[56] Yet at other times he refers to reason in the sense of the mover, or motive force, for a person's action.[57] In this sense reason is distinguished not from the supernatural end but from the Divine *instinctus* as mover.

At times these two distinctions can be grafted onto one another. For instance, when a person acts toward the connatural last end, human reason is the mover of the person's actions. Or when a person acts through the gifts toward the supernatural end, the person is moved by Divine *instinctus*. However, the infused virtues defy this grafting. The infused virtues orient one toward the supernatural end. Yet, as distinguished from the gifts, the infused virtues enable a person to act toward the supernatural end in a manner moved by human reason. Human reason elevated toward the supernatural end by the theological virtues, for sure, but nonetheless still with (grace-enabled) human reason as the motive force. The distinction between the three types of habit is perhaps most clearly stated when Aquinas says, "If we wish to restrict [Augustine's definition of virtue] to virtue as distinguished from the gifts, we must explain the words, "whereby we lead a good life" as referring to the rectitude of life which is measured by the rule of reason. Likewise the gifts, as distinct from infused virtue, may be defined as something given by God in relation to His motion; something, to wit, that makes man to follow well the promptings of God."[58] Here he speaks of the human virtues toward one's connatural end, as indicated by the phrase "measured by the rule of reason." Then he distinguishes infused virtues from gifts because only the latter are habits that make a person follow well the promptings of God, even though both are clearly directed toward the supernatural end.

In acts proceeding from the gifts, a person is moved from "without" by God. "From without" is distinguished from being moved "from within," as by reason.[59] However, Aquinas's claim about being moved from without should not be taken to mean that human reason is not involved in acts proceeding from the gifts of the Holy Spirit.[60] Indeed, four of the gifts of the Holy Spirit qualify human reason.[61] Furthermore, it is only those powers that are principles of properly human acts that are qualified by gifts, and these are of course the rational powers of the human person, or nonrational powers able to participate in reason.[62]

How to reconcile the claims that a person is moved "from without" through the gifts (by Divine *instinctus*) and yet it is the person's rational powers that are moved? The answer is that rational human powers can be moved movers, the interior principles of their actions, even as they are moved from the outside, assuming that exterior mover is God.[63] In treating the Rom. 8:14 text on being led by the Spirit, Aquinas claims:

> For those are led who are moved by a higher instinct. Hence we say that animals do not act but are led, because they are moved to perform their actions by nature and not from their own impulse. Similarly, the spiritual man is inclined to do something not as though by a movement of his own will chiefly, but by the prompting of the Holy Spirit.... However, this does not mean that spiritual men do not act through will and free choice because the Holy Spirit causes the very movement of the will and of free choice in them.[64]

In the movement of a person's rational powers by Divine *instinctus*, a person's rational powers are not merely moved but also moved movers. In his treatments of the gifts, Servais Pinckaers describes the noncompetitive relationship between divine and human agency as the "receptive" and the "active" (respectively) aspects of grace-enabled human action.[65] He claims: "This is the peculiar effect of inspiration or of the gifts: to achieve the unity of action between the superior principle, which is God's Spirit, and the interior principles which are the virtues, at the level of our free and reasonable will, as the source of our actions."[66] Despite the fact that the infused virtues are gifts of God's grace, and the gifts are (graced) habits possessed by a person, Pinckaers finds it helpful to align the Divine *instinctus* as source of movement with the gifts, and human reason as source of movement with the virtues. Yet he also affirms how they work in conjunction with one another, saying that "the action of the Holy Spirit is exercised [in us] *at the same time* by the virtues and by the gifts."[67] As will be noted later, an examination of the gifts of the Holy Spirit is a reflection on that inscrutable nexus of Divine and human agency.[68]

Fourth, how ought we understand Aquinas's consistent analogy on how the gifts work? In three successive articles on the gifts of the Holy Spirit,

Aquinas claims that the gifts are habits that qualify a person to be moved from the outside, in a manner akin to the way the moral virtues qualify a person to be moved by the command of reason. To use the terminology from earlier, the Divine *instinctus* moves a person in the way that one's rationality operates not "within" a habit but "across" habits. Recall how a person's appetites are impressed (with stable specification) by reason "from the outside." In the case of moral virtue, that specification is constitutive of the movement of the appetite such that it is "within" the habit. The intricate intertwining of appetite and apprehension is both within and across habits.

What is the comparison to the person qualified by the gifts? It is *not* an alignment of gifts as appetite versus Divine *instinctus* as apprehension impressing on appetite, since the gifts qualify both sorts of human powers, and Divine *instinctus* moves both.[69] Rather, it is the even more mysterious interplay of divine and human agency. The human person cannot act on her own toward the supernatural end, even having been given the infused virtues. Further help from God's grace is needed to perform activity (level three) from those virtues (level two). This is comparable to the way habits of the appetite are specified "from the outside" through practical reasoning. Yet in the case of the latter, the specification by reason, even if originating "outside" appetite, becomes constitutive of it ("within" the habit). This is where the analogy to the gifts breaks down.

Though a person moved by Divine *instinctus* is a moved mover, that Divine *instinctus* is not constitutive of the person in the manner that reasoning, as *causa immobilis,* is constitutive of appetite habits. Divine *instinctus* as grace cannot be constitutive of human activity lest it cease to be grace, supernatural.[70] In the same way that grace qualifies the soul's essence but cannot be the essence of the soul, at this other end of the causality of grace—one end being akin to level one nature, the other end level three activity—Divine *instinctus* can move human action (including human rational powers) even in a cooperative manner, yet not be constitutive of human action, lest the action cease to be gratuitous as grace always is.

Fifth, are the acts of the gifts the same as acts of the infused virtues? In other words, can you live according to the infused virtues without possessing the gifts? An examination of the contribution to graced human action made by the gifts (as distinct from the infused virtues) invites observations about two common misconceptions concerning the gifts. Aquinas is so clear regarding the distinction in motive force (even if not last end) between gifts and infused virtues that it raises the question whether or not each set of habits engenders different acts. Said differently, could one live according to the infused virtues alone, and not the gifts?[71] Some Thomistic moralists have assumed that this is indeed possible, and the claim takes one of two forms.

A first approach is to claim the gifts enable a person to act in "difficult" or "extraordinary cases." In his book on the workings of the Holy Spirit, *The Sanctifier*, Archbishop Luis Martinez refers to Aquinas's analogy of the gifts as supplying assistance for action in a manner akin to an expert doctor aiding an intern.[72] Martinez claims that the intern "has many remedies and knows much about medicine for ordinary cases" but requires the help of the expert to "handle an extraordinary case."[73] He claims that in the life of discipleship, people of faith "can attend to our own salvation in ordinary cases, but it would be impossible for us to accomplish completely the work of our sanctification without the guidance of the Holy Spirit."[74] This approach assumes that it is possible in ordinary matters to live the graced life of discipleship through the infused virtues alone, whereas the gifts are necessary for "extraordinary" cases.

A second approach is to claim that acts prompted by the Holy Spirit through the gifts follow a different rule or measure than those of the infused virtues. Speaking in the context of faith and thus the infused virtues, Martinez claims: "The norms of the gifts are different from the norms of the virtues," that of the gifts being a "supernatural norm."[75] Romanus Cessario claims that "once an action comes under the influence of the gifts, the action acquires an entirely new moral character or species."[76] He says that for some justified persons in a state of grace, "human reason remains the dominant directive rule or measure for the virtues, even for the infused moral and theological virtues. However, in other persons the Holy Spirit, like a prompter on a theatrical set, inspires a virtuous action in accord with a measure that surpasses that of human reason."[77] These claims suggest the activity of the infused virtues is measured by the rule of human reason, whereas activity of the gifts is according to a "supernatural norm," a "measure that surpasses that of human reason." These statements confuse human reason as rule or measure for human action (which is true only of the acquired virtues) and reason as motive force for action (which is true of acquired and infused virtues).

Both of these approaches assume it is possible to act from the infused virtues without the aid of the gifts, and that the acts of the infused virtues differ from acts of the gifts. Yet this position conflates Aquinas's careful delineation of the distinct contributions of the infused virtues and the gifts, with the assumption that one could act out of infused virtue but not the gifts. Aquinas explicitly denies this, claiming (as noted earlier) that a person requires additional grace to act out of habitual grace.[78] Thus even in "ordinary" matters of salvation, the Divine *instinctus* is necessary to help move a person to action.

Furthermore, Aquinas explicitly denies that the gifts and infused virtues concern different sorts of action. In discussing the infused virtues, he is quite clear that they are measured by the Divine rule, just as the gifts are.[79] In his treatment of the necessity of the gifts for salvation, Aquinas explicitly denies one way to describe how the gifts surpass the perfection of the virtues: "The gifts surpass the ordinary perfection of the virtues, not as regards the kinds of works (as counsel surpass commandments), but as regards the manner of working, in respect of man being moved by a higher principle."[80] Jean-Pierre Torrell helpfully interprets this passage with the following: "When one speaks of the necessity of the gifts and their connection to the virtues, one should not imagine that it means going *beyond* the virtues. On the contrary, according to the formula that Thomas often repeats, the gifts are granted "to help the virtues (*in adiutorium virtutum*)" to attain their final goal, despite our timidities, lukewarmness, pettiness. Certainly nothing goes beyond faith or charity."[81] Torrell notes the same "final goal" (and thus measure) of the gifts and virtues and rejects the position that the gifts lead to different sorts of activities. As Pinckaers notes, the action of the Holy Spirit is exercised at the same time by the virtues and the gifts, according to two complementary modalities—active and receptive—with the gifts necessary for the development of the virtues and the virtues forming the basis of the gifts.[82]

In sum, one cannot live according to the infused virtues alone, without the gifts. Though this should be obvious, given Aquinas's claims about the necessity of God's grace beyond habitual grace so as to act on the infused virtues, certain Thomistic moralists have articulated an inadequate account of the gifts that requires this reminder. The necessity of the gifts to be able to act out of the infused virtues should be clear given Aquinas's claim that the gifts are infused with charity and the other infused virtues.[83] This also explains Aquinas's claim that assistance from the Holy Spirit happens *always* in the activities of the infused virtues.[84]

Sixth, why are the gifts of the Holy Spirit *habits*? Notice that what has been established is the necessity of God's grace, as Divine *instinctus,* to help a person act (level three) toward the supernatural end even after the possession of infused virtues (level two). But the gifts are not this Divine *instinctus*; rather, they are habits, by God's grace infused with charity and the other infused virtues. Why are the gifts themselves *habits*? Ever tightening that nexus of divine and human causality without sacrificing the gratuity of grace, Aquinas claims that the gifts of the Holy Spirit are indeed (super)human habits. Certainly God's grace can move a person in a manner that does not require habits, such as the graces of conversion or repentance or the gratuitous graces not given to all (e.g., prophecy). So why are the gifts habits?

Aquinas's first answer to this is that the Holy Spirit abides in people, which indicates a stable presence.[85] Yet, since there are graces that do not abide (e.g., actual grace, gratuitous grace), and since the infused virtues are graced habits that do abide, this answer is not enough on its own. Second, Aquinas claims that something moved must be made proportionate to its mover, and the something moved is moved most perfectly when it has a disposition to be so moved.[86] Since a human person is not simply a (moved) instrument but rather one moved by the Holy Spirit and also a mover with free will, the person is more fittingly moved through the possession of a habit to be so moved.[87] Though such moved movement is possible without a habit, the abiding habit makes activity proceeding from such more the person's own, even as she is moved from without.

We have reached here the inscrutable nexus of divine and human agency. A person may not need a habit to be a moved mover, but activity is most fully the person's own when it proceeds from the person's own (gifted) habit. And even then it requires movement from without, the Divine *instinctus*, which is precisely that to which the habits that are gifts of the Holy Spirit render one amenable.

Seventh, if the gifts are habits, why are they not also virtues? The challenge of depicting the nexus between divine and human agency also suggests why Aquinas claims that the gifts are graced habits that nonetheless are not virtues. This is a very strange claim since in Aquinas's thought virtue can usually be equated with habits that are good, and certainly the gifts are good habits. But a virtue is also the highest reach of a power, and since the power of acting out of a gift comes from the outside but in a manner that does not then become constitutive of the person's activity (unlike with the moral virtues), Aquinas adopts the strange position that the gifts are good habits yet not virtues.[88]

Eighth, how are the gifts enumerated? Having established that the gifts are good habits that render the person amenable to the Divine *instinctus* and enable her to act out of infused virtue, certain other questions common to Aquinas's treatments of habits come into play, questions to which he provides varying degrees of attention. One such question concerns the enumeration of the gifts. The traditional seven gifts of the Holy Spirit—wisdom, understanding, counsel, fortitude, knowledge, piety, fear of the Lord—are found in Isaiah 11:2–3, so for Aquinas there is no question that they are suitably enumerated.[89] Yet enumeration also raises the question of *why* this enumeration, why *these* seven?

It is noteworthy that throughout his corpus Aquinas offers various accounts of the enumeration of the seven gifts of the Holy Spirit, accounts that are always attuned to human anthropology (as is his account of the cardinal virtues) though in significantly different ways.[90] Aquinas increasingly aligns the seven gifts with the three theological and four cardinal virtues, which makes sense given the account of the gifts offered here as aiding the acts of the infused virtues in what Pinckaers calls a "complementary" way. Yet Aquinas's alignment of gifts with infused virtues changes even within the *Summa Theologiae* and never reaches one-to-one correspondence between virtues and gifts. Most notably, in his treatment of particular infused virtues in the *Secunda secundae,* Aquinas aligns both understanding and knowledge with faith, and assigns no gift to temperance. However, though his enumeration in the *Prima secundae* is in some ways less developed, he clearly associates fear of the Lord with temperance, which leads Pinckaers to align fear of the Lord not only with hope but also temperance.[91] It is for this reason that Aquinas's position on enumerating the gifts in relation to the virtues is labeled "unsettled." Of course, that should not be any indictment of the centrality of his main point about the virtues and gifts, namely, the nexus of divine and human agency. Hence Torrell claims it is "enough for us to see that this is nothing more or less than a demonstration of the extent to which the spiritual life is under the total and constant motion of the Spirit."[92]

For this reason it is more difficult to specify acts of the gifts in a manner whereby they together comprehensively "cover" all types of morally significant activities of the person, as Aquinas does with the virtues. This does not of course mean we cannot identify characteristic acts of each gift. Perhaps it is not unfair to expect a lack of complete precision in describing the always ultimately mysterious movement of Divine *instinctus,* since the Spirit, like the wind, "blows where it wills" (Jn 3:8). This leads to the next topic, regarding the object, or paradigmatic act, of each gift.

Ninth, what are the objects of the habits called gifts of the Holy Spirit? Another topic where the use of habits to describe the causal influence of divine agency on human activity seems to reach its breaking point is this naming of the objects, or paradigmatic acts, of the habits called gifts of the Holy Spirit. In one sense the naming of the acts of these habits is not in question; the names of the gifts are found in the highest authority to Aquinas, namely, Sacred Scripture. Those names represent describable activities. In fact, Aquinas's *Secunda secundae* treatment of the gifts offers a rich examination of such acts. For instance, what is the relationship between gifts such as wisdom and knowledge and understanding, on the one hand, and their acquired intellectual virtue counterparts, on the other?[93] What is the relationship between an infused virtue and a gift that shares the same name, as in fortitude?[94] What are the different types of fear, and which of those fall under the gift of the Holy Spirit called fear of the Lord?[95]

That said, while the gifts *qua* habits are revealed through identifiable acts, those acts are not other than the acts of the infused virtues.[96] Aquinas claims that what the gifts have as distinct from the virtues are not a separate realm of delineated activities, but rather a different manner of movement.[97] Given that Aquinas so commonly claims that habits are distinguished by their objects, this is once again an unusual claim regarding the gifts.[98] At this point it may seem more understandable why Thomists such as Dom Lottin did not regard the gifts as distinct from the infused virtues. Nevertheless, given not only scriptural authority but also the value in describing the gifts as habits in order to address the nexus of divine and human causality, Aquinas's position seems propitious despite the difficulty of delineating their objects in relation to the infused virtues, akin to what occurs on the question of enumeration. The Spirit blows where it wills.[99]

Finally, do the gifts grow? There are a series of further questions that arise, given the gifts' status as habits. These questions Aquinas commonly treats with regard to habits that are virtues but with less detail (though to varying degrees) concerning the gifts. For instance, Aquinas unsurprisingly claims the gifts are connected to one another, as they are to the infused virtues, given that they are bestowed with charity.[100] He also explains in what ways the gifts endure in heaven (and in what ways they do not) in an article quite similar to his treatment of the endurance of the virtues in heaven.[101]

Considering our topic, what can be said about growth in the gifts? Though Aquinas devotes extensive attention to growth (and corruption) of habits with regard to virtue, he does not offer comparable attention to growth in the habits that are the gifts. Nonetheless, Thomistic moralists speculate that there must be some sort of growth in the gifts. Martinez rightly notes that Aquinas claims fear of the Lord increases with growth in charity.[102] Pinckaers likewise claims that the gifts, while existing in all persons with the infused virtues, exist in different people to varying degrees of realization.[103] Andrew Pinsent even claims that the gifts are compatible with contrary dispositions in a manner akin to charity, which seems both correct and also another arena for growth in the life of grace.[104] Presumably the contributions of this study to the dynamics that impede the exercise of the infused virtues could apply to the gifts as well.[105] These topics suggest there is more to be done in articulating the central role of the gifts of the Holy Spirit in the life of graced discipleship. Pinckaers's comment on Aquinas's development of the scriptural witness provides warrant for ongoing work on the gifts today: "This is a good example of development of a spiritual teaching based on the gospel, uniting catechesis, spirituality, and theological reflection."[106]

THE DIFFERENCE GRACE MAKES "ACROSS" VIRTUES

The previous section explored how the three-level dynamic of seed, habit, and act exists with virtues that are infused by God and yet also changes significantly. Similarly to the acquired virtues, infused virtues are properly human habits and thus stably (supra-)rationally specified. This occurs not only "within" a habit (supplying the *causa immobilis*) but also "across" habits, such that the virtues are connected.

There are some rather arresting differences in the connectivity of the infused virtues as distinct from the acquired virtues. But these (and other) important differences can cloak certain important commonalities in the connectivity of the infused virtues, and so we begin with these similarities.

As an infused virtue, charity is bestowed gratuitously by God. Thus charity, along with all the other virtues infused with it and connected by it, is bestowed at once, without necessarily any preceding actions. While the lack of necessary connection to prior actions is indeed important, the fact that charity, and thus the other virtues given the connectivity it engenders, arrives at once, is actually importantly similar to the acquired virtues.

The claim that charity is bestowed at once does not necessarily mean that God's grace is not active before its possession. It only means that God's grace is simply not possessed habitually.[107] Nor does it necessarily mean that none of a person's activity is oriented toward the person's supernatural end before the attainment of charity, though of course that would only be possible with God's (nonhabitual) grace. (Dynamics such as these will be addressed in the following chapter's examination of St. Augustine's conversion.) It simply means that at some point a person crosses the line so as to possess charity. Once again granting the significance of the possibility (though not necessity) of a lack of any graced action toward the supernatural prior to the possession of charity, the fact that charity is suddenly possessed and with it connectivity to other virtues is in certain ways very much like the possession of the acquired virtues.

One comes to possess a properly human habit when the source of stable specification of the particular end at level two is a *causa immobilis*, the person's rationality. Of course, it is notoriously difficult to identify when a person crosses the line to possess properly human virtue, but that does not disprove the fact that at some point it happens.[108] What this means with acquired virtue is that at some point a power becomes qualified "enough" so as to be stably inclined to activity in a manner characteristic of a properly human act, that is, with a grasp of its end, in relation to other ends for the sake of further ends and with attention to life as a whole. Though beforehand there may be progress (and increasing connectivity) toward that attainment, and of course progress can continue afterward, the very features that "qualify" possession of a properly human habit are those that necessitate connectivity of the acquired virtues. Reason and will are involved in the specification of the level two end "within" the habit, and this can occur only in relation to, connectivity with, the stable specification of other habits.

This is precisely what happens with the infused virtues, though of course the *causa immobilis* supplying stable specification is rationality as qualified by grace, so Aquinas calls grace the cause of such virtues. Aquinas insists that with charity are bestowed all of the other infused virtues and the gifts of the Holy Spirit. Infused virtues "are connected because of charity, because no such virtue can be had without charity and, if charity is had, all of them are had."[109] When we say one is given charity and all other virtues as well, we can easily lapse into the error of regarding virtues as substantial forms akin to artifacts. We might imagine infusion of the virtues as the reception of a set of tools, but this is not correct. Receiving charity is more precisely worded as having rationality, especially the will by charity but never without the intellect by faith, qualified by God's grace so as to be stably inclined to act in specific manners where the person's last end is the uncreated God. After all, infused virtues are also habits, "good qualities of mind."[110] The person gifted with charity is qualified to stably act toward God and do all other activities for the sake of God.

Whatever the preceding (or succeeding) acts in relation to that bestowal of charity, reaching a point where the person is stably ordered toward God works not only within the virtue (i.e., in her relationship to God in friendship) but also across virtues. Most obviously, once a person's rational powers (i.e., the will) are qualified by charity, they are also qualified by faith (intellect) and hope (will, also toward God but under a distinct formality). And it is those same rational powers that are qualified by the cardinal virtues. Hence the infused moral virtues are obtained with the bestowal of charity. Though it may seem that with one artifact/substantial form (charity) a person is (extrinsically) bestowed additional substantial forms/artifacts (that is, the other theological virtues, the infused moral virtues, and also the gifts), in reality the qualification that occurs in one's rational powers with the bestowal of charity necessarily requalifies all human powers where stable specification is able to be provided by those rational powers. Gérard Gilleman describes this dynamic in a way that avoids regarding infused virtues as distinct things (substantial forms) that are added to a person's powers: "Neither are the supernatural virtues things added to the faculties, but supernatural qualities of those faculties; they are those faculties inasmuch as they are elevated and supernaturalized. When we say that an act proceeds from an infused virtue, we mean that it proceeds from the faculty elevated by that virtue: it springs entirely from the faculty and entirely from the virtue."[111] When the other infused virtues and gifts of the Holy Spirit are bestowed at once with charity, it is not as if a person receives a scattered assortment of entities (akin to artifacts) that are only accidentally related. Rather, rationality is requalified so as to be ordered toward the end of friendship with God in charity, a friendship that reorients everything in the person's life.

Once again we find the connectivity of the infused virtues closely mimicking the acquired virtues, even as the specification of acts of these virtues differs. As noted earlier, there is an inherent connection between the rationality within virtues and across virtues. And, in a similar way, the supernatural happiness toward which charity directs the person entails a new divine measure of action specifying activities directed toward (and constitutive of) that happiness.[112] With acquired virtues the objects of the virtues are specified in line with the measure of human reason, attentive to "various modes, in respect of the various matters . . . and according to various circumstances."[113] That feature necessarily renders the person's virtues connected.[114] Jean Porter uses language of balancing a "general standard of reasonableness" with "domain-specific" rationality.[115] This same dynamic occurs with the bestowal of charity, whereby a person is oriented toward God as ultimate end and the "general standard" is now the divine rule as the rational powers are (healed and) elevated by God's grace. That new general standard informs specification of all properly human habits and activity, and thus the "domain-specific" rationalities are changed accordingly.[116]

Granting the important commonalities between the connectivity of the acquired and infused virtues, there are also significant discontinuities. One of the most commonly discussed in the context of treatments of growth in virtue is the different ways that contrary dispositions can persist alongside the infused virtues, a topic that is addressed later. Another is Aquinas's claim that when charity is gained or lost, so too are all of the other infused virtues. However, though it is a significant point of difference from the acquired virtues that this may occur for the infused virtues without any preceding action on the part of the person, the fact that all the virtues are gained or lost together once the "line" is crossed is actually true of the acquired virtues as well.[117] The one difference that remains to be examined is that the infused virtues are not connected by prudence or another intellectual virtue like faith, but rather by charity, a virtue of the will. To that topic we now turn.

Why does charity, a virtue of the will, connect the theological virtues, whereas prudence, a virtue of the (practical) intellect, connects all the cardinal virtues?[118] A person's rationality is the *causa immobilis* that provides the stable specification of the level two ends of virtues, and since specification is supplied by powers of apprehension, virtues always entail human reasoning. Furthermore, virtues also make their possessor good, and so properly human virtues always involve the will not only in exercise (as with other intellectual virtues) but even in specification of activity (as seen in prudence and faith). Thus, to note again an important continuity between acquired and infused virtue, it is wrong to regard acquired virtues as connected by prudence without the involvement of will, or to regard the infused virtues as connected by charity without the involvement of the intellect. Prudence relies on an appetite well qualified by the moral virtues, and charity is never infused without faith and infused prudence.[119] However, the way the intellectual virtues supply specification to the infused virtues of the appetite does indeed differ. Therefore, what is the difference in connectivity for the acquired as distinct from the theological virtues, and what is the significance of that difference?

The infused virtues are connected by charity, and Aquinas's reason for this flows directly from the reasons he names for the necessity of the infused virtues. Virtues that direct us toward supernatural happiness *must* be infused because they are directed toward an end that far surpasses the capacity of unaided human reason. Aquinas offers this same reason as to why this renders a virtue of the appetite more appropriately the basis of connectivity rather than an intellectual virtue:

> Because the theological virtues have an object surpassing the human soul: whereas prudence and the moral virtues are about things beneath man. Now in things that are above man, to love them is more excellent than to know them. Because knowledge is perfected by the known being in the knower: whereas love is perfected by the lover being drawn to the beloved. Now that which is above man is more excellent in itself than in man: since a thing is contained according to the mode of the container. But it is the other way about in things beneath man.[120]

Aquinas distinguishes prudence's role in "forming" the moral virtues from charity's role in "forming" the theological virtues: "In moral matters, which concern things below man, the cognitive virtue informs the appetitive virtues, just as prudence informs the other moral virtues. But in the theological virtues which concern God, the virtue of the will, viz., charity, informs the virtue of the intellect, viz., faith."[121] This claim does not deny the sense in which charity as a virtue of the will depends upon faith to "show the object" of charity, namely, God.[122] Charity is never bestowed by God without faith. Nevertheless, since the infused virtues are directed beyond man toward God both immediately (as theological virtues) and ultimately (as infused cardinal virtues), they are connected by charity.

This is not to say that in the practical matters "below" the person has complete comprehension. Practical matters concern contingents, and thus there is always room for and need for ongoing growth. This room for growth is even more obviously the case with the theological virtues, whose object is "above" the person, "surpassing the human soul." Clearly there is room for and need for ongoing growth in the theological and infused cardinal virtues. We see another commonality in acquired and infused virtue as to their room for growth.

Furthermore, again in a way similar to the acquired virtues, Aquinas recognizes a sense in which the infused virtues can exist as not connected; but then, of course, they are not virtues. When the moral virtues exist without the *causa immobilis* of rationality, and thus in an unconnected manner, they are not properly called virtues but rather dispositions.[123] These dispositions are likely less stable, but even if relatively stable they are not specified with a person's rationality or with ends attentive to "various modes, in respect of the various matters . . . and according to various circumstances."[124] Something similar happens with faith and hope without charity. They are not virtues.[125] Given that the object of these dispositions is God, their specification is not merely sensory. They are likely less stable, but might be relatively stable, and they dispose a person to acts that are observably acts of faith and hope. What lacks? Given that their object is God, any rational engagement with an object that lacks the (grace-enabled) love of God in the friendship of charity is as lacking as a disposition toward moral virtue that is inattentive to various modes and circumstances. The person is not acting in a manner that makes her good, with attention to the whole.

A further interesting question is how charity forms the cardinal virtues, given that they concern matters "below" humanity yet are in relation to God, Who is "above" humanity. Since the cardinal virtues pertain to types of activities that are accessible to unaided reason, they can exist without charity as true virtues, acquired and directed toward the person's natural end as last end. Nevertheless, in the life of grace, charity "forms" these virtues too, ordering them toward the supernatural end of friendship with God. We must address later what remains of such infused cardinal virtues after the loss of charity, but first an account is needed of how charity orders those virtues and their activities toward their last end, to which we now turn.[126]

THE INFUSED VIRTUES AND ONE'S LIFE AS A WHOLE: CHARITY AS FORM OF THE VIRTUES

The difference made by grace "within" a virtue necessarily entails differences "across" the virtues due to connectivity. Connectivity applies to both acquired virtue and infused virtue. The connectivity of the acquired virtues also necessarily includes their orientation toward the last end. A comparable dynamic exists with the infused virtues, and once again there are continuities and differences in how the infused virtues (as distinct from the acquired virtues) are ordered toward a person's last end.

The last end is both something out there and something one does. Human action is more or less coherently ordered to the last end—that is, more or less constitutive of happiness—and such happiness consists in something. In the current context of infused virtue, the last end is granted to be that supernatural happiness made possible only by God's grace, a destiny in which we participate through the graced actions of the virtues. The uncreated God is our last end (out there), and the grace-enabled virtues and gifts make possible our activity constitutive of the attainment of that end, initially in this life and fully in the next. The various features of a last end described earlier apply here as well, namely: its singularity; its inherent relation to properly human action; its relation to all activities in a person's life; and the possibility of growing coherence of a person's activities toward the last end (see chapter 4). Given that all these features apply to the supernatural last end, and that the identification of the last end in the context of infused virtue is a given, in some sense this treatment of the last end in the context of infused virtue is more straightforward.

Yet that supernatural context also raises additional questions. Just as with the acquired virtues there is a question of how the myriad activities and goods of human life are related to the natural last end (e.g., inclusivity, exclusivity, etc.), there is comparable debate among Christian moralists on how to describe the relationship between the personal uncreated God as last end and the myriad non-ultimate ends in human life.[127] This debate is primarily an analysis of the last end as something "out there" sought as happiness. More specifically, it is a debate about how the last end can be one, and yet related to the various goods sought in any person's life. These debates are not expansively addressed here, though note that how a person regards the unification of various goods in a human life is closely related to an accounting of the coherence of a person's practical reasoning in seeking those goods.[128] The task here is to understand how charity as the virtue orienting us toward our last end relates to the other virtues, an important topic for growing in virtue.

The last end in the life of grace is personal, and the recipient of grace receives a set of (theological) virtues whereby she relates to God directly. The central theological virtue is charity, whereby one loves God in friendship.[129] Charity is arguably the defining feature of the Christian life. Charity in one sense is God's very Self (1 Jn. 4:16). Charity is also the means by which human persons can partake of the Divine Nature (2 Pet. 1:4).[130] Jesus names charity as the greatest commandment (Mt. 22:37–39). There is a sense in which all acts of a person living toward supernatural happiness are acts of charity (Col. 3:14, 1 Cor. 10:31).

Therefore a distinct challenge of Christian reflection on the last end is to supply an account of how the theological virtue of charity relates to the cardinal virtues and their activities, which have as their objects not God but rather activities accessible to unaided reason, even if done for the further sake of God. Though Aquinas is far from the only or even the first Christian thinker to offer an account of how charity can govern a person's entire life, he offers a particularly developed account of this dynamic in deploying the notion of virtue.[131] As noted earlier, charity connects all the infused virtues (and gifts). Pinckaers calls charity the "sap" or the "lifeblood" of the Christian life.[132] It "assembles" the virtues and directs them toward God as one's last end.[133] And this is precisely what Aquinas means when he claims that charity is the "form of the virtues."

Though Aquinas recognizes that charity can be called "root," "motor," or "mother" of the virtues, he most commonly describes charity as the "form of the virtues."[134] In a mature treatment of charity as form of the virtues, he describes this role with reference to a person's last end: "It is charity which directs the acts of all other virtues to the last end, and which, consequently, also gives the form to all other acts of virtue: and it is precisely in this sense that charity is called the form of the virtues, for these are called virtues in relation to 'informed' acts."[135] Charity has as its object the last end, God. It also moves, or commands, the acts of other virtues toward that last end.[136] As Aquinas says, charity "draws" the other virtues toward the last end.[137] At times he describes this using language of means/ends: "Charity, inasmuch as it has the last end for object, moves the other virtues to act. For the habit to which the end pertains always commands the habits to which the means pertain."[138] Thus charity is *form* of the virtues, "informing" acts of the other virtues, since it directs them toward the further end of God as supernatural happiness.[139]

What Aquinas achieves in this claim is a description of the unity of a person's life, oriented toward the last end of supernatural happiness, with all activity directed there by one virtue, namely, charity. In other words, we have simply a reaffirmation of Aquinas's claims about the last end in general—that each person has only one last end and that all actions are directed toward it—but now achieved through a distinct virtue, charity. In a real sense, then, all acts of the graced life toward God as last end are acts of charity. However, even in achieving this unity through charity, Aquinas is equally clear that charity does not replace the other virtues. In other words, even though the life of grace is unified through charity, it is not reduced to charity alone. There are two ways Aquinas describes this distinct role for charity and other virtues in the coherent human life.

Before turning to those two ways, a reminder is in order regarding the original claim that virtues are not substantial forms. The task of depicting charity's relationship to other virtues at times can seem mechanical. But we are always talking about one unified person with her properly human powers qualified by virtues. As Gilleman reminds us, the infused virtues are not "things added to the faculties, but [rather are] supernatural qualities of those faculties; they are those faculties inasmuch as they are elevated and supernaturalized."[140] So when charity "forms" other virtues, it is not some entity attached to the person that then relates to other entities similarly attached. Possessing charity means that one clings with one's will to God as last end, and charity forming the other virtues means the person's properly human powers are "elevated and supernaturalized" and, unsurprisingly, they are qualified such that all of their activities are done in a manner shaped by clinging to God as last end.[141] This is the sense that all acts of a person with charity are (or should be) acts of charity.[142]

Yet the myriad activities in a person's life and the virtues that incline one toward those activities retain a finality that is not reduced to charity, even as those activities are further referred to God as last end. At times Aquinas uses the distinction between elicited acts and commanded acts. While charity commands the acts of other virtues, ordering them toward God, those acts are elicited by the (theological or cardinal) virtues informed by charity.[143] A virtue's elicited act is toward the arena of activity proper to that virtue, with its own immediate finality and specified with regard to the rule or measure for such action. A commanded act is ordered by the will toward some further end, specified by that same rule or measure.[144] To say that charity informs a virtue is simply to say that the act of that virtue is performed from the perspective of the acting person with its own immediate finality, in a manner further ordered toward God as last end.[145]

Aquinas also describes this dynamic using the language of "special form" and "general form" of virtues. When a virtue is commanded by charity,

charity gives it its general form even as it retains its special form: "God makes in us virtues that are formed with a special form and virtues that are formed with a general form. The special form is derived from the object and the end, but the general form is derived from charity."[146] Different virtues are specified according to their object and immediate end. So an act of temperance or fortitude remains an act of temperance or fortitude even as it is ordered by charity toward the further end of God. The immediate end is the special form of the virtue, while the further end of God is the general form.[147] "Each virtue has a special form from its proper end and its proper object, by which it becomes this virtue. But it has from charity a certain common form, by which it can merit eternal life."[148] Of course charity as a special virtue has its own proper acts as well, one of which is commanding the other virtues toward the last end of God.[149] But in that role of commanding the other virtues it serves as a general form of those virtues, not their specific form. This is once again why all virtues are not reduced to or replaced by charity, even as in a real sense all acts of the person possessing charity are acts of charity.

Before concluding, a mention of the special form of virtues commanded by charity to God provides occasion to revisit Aquinas's argument for the necessity of infused cardinal virtues.[150] After all, given this role of charity in commanding the cardinal virtues, it seems that there is no need for infused cardinal virtues; why can't the acquired virtues be ordered to God as last end by charity?[151] This topic brings us full circle to the start of the examination of infused virtue, since Aquinas's argument for the necessity of infused virtue begins with reference to the seeds of virtue (level one). Whereas the acquired virtues "arise from certain natural principles preexisting in us," we require a different set of principles to order us toward the supernatural end, namely, the theological virtues. The acquired cardinal virtues "are not proportionate to the theological virtues" or the supernatural end, so in addition to theological virtues, God infuses in us cardinal virtues proportionate to that end.[152] Since the life of grace involves not only activities toward God directly (through the theological virtues) but also activities in relation to God, the infused cardinal virtues are necessary and gifted along with charity and the gifts.[153] Just as the acquired virtues are oriented toward the natural end as last end, all virtues that are oriented toward supernatural happiness as last end, even when they are cardinal virtues, are infused. Thus it is clear that when charity commands the acts of other virtues, those virtues, formed by charity, are infused and not acquired.

Whenever Aquinas offers this argument in support of the necessity of the infused cardinal virtues, he immediately examines whether the acts of those virtues are the same as those of the acquired virtues.[154] His answer is always that the acquired virtues are not of the same species as the infused virtues. In other words, their particular objects (level two) differ from one another. They concern the same sort of activity, for certain. At times Aquinas refers to this as having the same "matter," as when both acquired temperance and infused temperance concern pleasures of touch.[155] One recent Thomist calls this the same "field of operation."[156] Yet Aquinas claims that the different rules or measures of actions of these two sorts of virtues result in different "forms" or "species" or "objects" of the acts of these distinct virtues, based on the different sorts of happiness to which they incline a person.[157] This argument further solidifies Aquinas's position that only the infused virtues are formed by charity, since only the acts generated by infused virtues have a divine rule or measure, and as such they differ from acts of acquired virtue, which have the rule or measure of human reason. Indeed, when "higher" virtues (such as charity) order virtues with more immediate "fields of operation," both sets of virtue must share the same measure, as supplied by the last end or happiness to which they are directed.[158]

In sum, the objects of the infused and acquired virtues (level two), and thus the acts proceeding from those virtues (level three), differ in species due to their differing last ends and the resulting different rule or measure for their respective acts.[159] Consequently, the acquired virtues are unable to be ordered to supernatural happiness. Aquinas's account of charity as a form of the virtues, ordering them toward God as last end, is an account of the infused virtues. This point is actually obvious, granted the recollection that the person clinging to God as last end has her powers "elevated and supernaturalized," such that all acts of those powers are also oriented toward her last end. Of course this does not also mean there is no room for growth in the life of infused virtue, or occasions when activity fails to be actually ordered toward God as last end. This dichotomy leads to the following discussion on growth in infused virtue, to which we now turn.

NOTES

1. For a succinct account of this dynamic, see Knobel, *Aquinas on the Infused Moral Virtues*, 17–21. For another insightful recent example of attention to this issue, see Decosimo, who argues that the more Aquinas is Aristotelian the more he is Augustinian, and vice versa (*Ethics as a Work of Charity*, 253–72). See also Casey, *Pagan Virtue*, 211.
2. ST I–II 51,4.
3. ST I–II 62,1. See ST I–II 51,4, ST I–II 63,3; *De virt* a. 10; and *Sent.* l. 3 d. 33 q.1 a. 2 qa. 3. See also *De virt.* a. 9: "But man is not only a citizen of the earthly city, but is also a participant in the heavenly city of Jerusalem whose ruler is the Lord and whose citizens are the angels and all the saints, whether they reign in glory and are at rest in the heaven or

are still pilgrims on earth. . . . A man's nature does not suffice for him to be a participant of this city; he must be elevated by the grace of God. For it is manifest that the virtues that are man's as a participant in this city cannot be acquired by him through his natural powers; hence they are not caused by our acts but are infused in us as a divine gift."

4. For a helpful treatment of how God's grace elevates human nature, see Sherwin, *By Knowledge and By Love*, 121–31.
5. It should be clear that the last end distinction regarding virtues (natural or supernatural) is perfectly correlated to the efficient cause of virtues (acquired or infused). All supernatural virtues are infused and all natural virtues are acquired. For more on this, see Mattison, "Thomas's Categorizations of Virtue," 213–29. Though the infused virtues perfect (rather than obliterate or leave untouched) nature, they are not oriented toward the natural end as last end. See *De virt. card.* a. 4 ad 3.
6. In addition to the following quotations, see *De virt.* a 10; ST I–II 62,1; and ST I–II 110,3.
7. ST I–II 110,2. See also *De virt.* a. 10, which is where Aquinas even parallels the gift from God of the rational soul far exceeding the capacity of matter/the body to the gift of grace and the infused virtues far exceeding the capacity of the rational human soul. This reaffirms a point in next paragraph about there being a "grace" to nature as well. See *De virt.* a. 10 for language of humanity's "first perfection" as acquired from God: so, too, does the human person have her ultimate perfection, that is, complete happiness, from God immediately.
8. ST I–II 110,1.
9. For a penetrating inquiry into various types of grace, see Meinert, *The Love of God Poured Out*, 102.
10. ST I–II 110,1 (emphasis added). Huetter puts it thus: "In its most proper sense . . . *gratia* denotes a strictly supernatural gift of God to the rational creature for the purpose of salvation, divinization, and eventual union of the rational creature with God. This is *gratia gratum faciens*, sanctifying grace. This supernatural gift is either actual or habitual." See Huetter, "Grace and Charity," 179–80.
11. ST I–II 110,3. See also ST I–II 54,3.
12. ST I–II 110,3. See also *De virt.* a. 10: "In order that a man might perform actions ordered to the end of eternal life, there is divinely infused in him first grace, by which the soul has a kind of spiritual existence, and then faith, hope, and charity."
13. ST I–II 110,4. See also *De ver.* XXVII.6.
14. ST I–II 110,2 ad 2.
15. ST I–II 110,3 ad 3: "*Gratia reducitur ad primam speciem qualitatis. Nec tamen est idem quod virtus, sed habitudo quaedam quae praesupponitur virtutibus infusis, sicut earum principium et radix.*" Note Aquinas's use of *habitudo* here, which he does quite infrequently in his work on virtue (only a handful of times in his ST I–II 55–70 and *Disputed Questions on Virtue*). The term is used when the entity at hand has some feature making it dissimilar from a habit (level two) in the most proper sense, which is also the case here (e.g., ST I–II 56,5). Hence the English Dominican translators use "disposition," which is better than "habit" but still a level two entity. Freddoso offers the best term, "habitual condition."
16. ST I–II 110,3 ad 3. See also *De car.* a. 3 ad 19.
17. ST I–II 63,3.
18. ST I–II 63,3 ad 2. For more on Aquinas's consistent use of the Scholastic terminology *in finem* to describe human activity ordered toward God immediately (e.g., I–II 62,1) and

ad finem to refer to human activities toward objects in further relation to God (e.g., I–II 63,3 ad 2), see Mattison, "Thomas's Categorizations of Virtue," 215. For the description of the activities of the moral and intellectual virtues as accessible to (unaided) human reason ("*Objectum autem virtutem intellectualium et moralium est aliquid quod humana ratione comprehendi*"), see ST I–II 62,2.

19. For a more detailed treatment of Aquinas's conception of the "seeds" of virtue, with attention to both acquired and infused virtue, see Knobel, *Aquinas on the Infused Moral Virtues*, 26–33, 77n16. Concerning the acquired virtues, Knobel says: "I will be concerned to argue that Aquinas does not equate the 'seeds' of virtue with our various natural inclinations, but rather with the very principles that make virtue possible: with our natural habitual knowledge of the first principles of practical reason" (26). Given that Aquinas understands *synderesis* as a habit, there is even greater commonality between the seeds of acquired and infused virtues as habits.
20. ST I–II 110, 3 and 4.
21. *De virt.* a. 9.
22. ST I–II 51,4, 62,1.
23. See ST I–II 3,2 on happiness entailing human activity. For the connection between different sorts of happiness and the resulting different rules or measures, see ST I–II 63,2. For an excellent treatment of this, see Knobel, *Aquinas on the Infused Moral Virtues*, 17–18.
24. ST I–II 110,3. The enormous topic of the relation between the twofold human end is obviously beyond the scope of this project But it must be said here that the supernatural end of humanity fulfills the natural end even as it surpasses it. Aquinas notes the continuity between those ends in the context of treating the infusion of virtue: "That God works in all things according to their mode does not hinder God from doing what nature cannot do; but it follows from this that God does nothing contrary to that which is suitable to nature" (ST I–II 51,4 ad 2). See also *De virt.* a 10 ad 13. For a helpful treatment of how grace perfects nature even as the natural is not obliterated, see Porter, *Nature as Reason*, 378–400.
25. Perhaps it could be argued that in a unity-of-the-virtues approach akin to the Stoics, where all virtue is reduced to *phronesis*, *phronesis* is directed toward a person's last end. Yet the Stoic account of *phronesis* is not an account of a virtue directed toward the last end as distinct from other virtues not so directed, which is the case with the theological virtues. And the Stoic last end, while intelligible, is not personal, as with theological virtues. For more on this see Annas, *Morality of Happiness*, 388–411, and Irwin, "Stoic and Aristotelian Conceptions of Happiness."
26. For a powerful comparable claim about this interpersonal union in the context of virtue, see Pinsent, *The Second Person Perspective in Aquinas's Ethics*, 98–99.
27. See ST I–II 62,1–2 for the claim that the theological virtues all have God as their "object" and are possible only through God's grace since they are beyond the capacity of unaided human rational powers. The scare quotes recognize the problems in referring to God as an "object," but here object means something like "immediate target of activity" rather than any objectification or indication of something circumscribable.
28. Thus there are comparable natural-level human activities. For instance, the central act of faith is belief but acts of belief that do not have God as object are possible. See ST II–II 2,1. (For a reflection on this continuity between religious faith and ordinary everyday acts of belief, see John Paul II, *Fides et ratio*, 31–32, and Pope Francis, *Lumen Fidei*, 18.) Acts of love that are not facets of the theological virtue of charity are possible, even if that

theological virtue of charity represents the height of human (grace-enabled) love. See ST I–II 26,3. Though the object of the theological virtue hope is God, Aquinas describes more broadly applicable dynamics of hope as well as the way in which it may be reasonable to hope in things other than God. See ST II–II 17,1 and 17,4.

29. See ST II–II 23,1 and *De car.* a. 2.
30. See ST I–II 62,3; and ST II–II 17,8. On God as the object of hope in a twofold sense see ST II–II 17,1 17,4.
31. ST I–II 62,4. For an in-depth study of the interpenetration of reason and will in the theological virtues, see Sherwin, *By Knowledge and By Love,* 147–203.
32. ST I–II 62,1 ad 3.
33. For perhaps the most important recent contribution to this debate, see Feingold, *The Natural Desire to See God.* For placement of this debate in relationship to questions pertaining directly to virtue, see Knobel, *Aquinas on the Infused Moral Virtues,* 23–24.
34. In addition to the myriad texts regarding the need for infused virtues, see *De virt card.* a. 4: "The acquired virtues, of which the philosophers spoke, are ordered only toward perfecting man in civil life."
35. See *De virt. card.* a. 4 ad 3: "The civil good is not the ultimate end of the infused cardinal virtues of which we speak, but of the acquired virtues of which the philosophers spoke." It is for the reasons given in this note and the previous one that Aquinas claims the acquired cardinal virtues do not persist in the next life, whereas the infused cardinal virtues do.
36. ST I 1,8 ad 2.
37. See ST I–II 63,3 (esp. ad 2). For the description of the activities of the moral and intellectual virtues as accessible to (unaided) human reason see ST I–II 62,2; and Mattison, "Thomas's Categorizations of Virtue," 215. The existence of the infused moral virtues granted by God existing along with the theological virtues is a staple of the Thomistic moral tradition, even if recent scholarship has had to reemphasize their importance. There is a significant strain in the Christian tradition that denies the need for these virtues, especially inspired by the thought of Scotus. For a helpful account of these various accounts of virtue in historical context, see Kent, *Virtues of the Will.*
38. ST I–II 63,4. See also *De virt.* a. 10 ad 7–10, and *Sent* l. 3, d. 33, q. 1, a. 2, qa. 4.
39. ST I–II 63,4 ad 1; *Sent* l. 3, d. 33, q. 1, a. 2, qa. 4; and *De virt.* a. 10 ad 9.
40. *De virt.* a. 10 ad 8; ST I–II 63,4 ad 2; and *Sent* l. 3, d. 33, q. 1, a. 2, qa. 4 ad 3.
41. For a more extended treatment of this claim directed toward a broader audience, see Mattison, "Moral Virtue, the Grace of God, and Discipleship."
42. Torrell notes this position, with which he disagrees, and attributes it to Dom Lottin. See *Thomas Aquinas, Vol. 2,* 414–24. Pinckaers notes this same claim from Lottin in "Morality and the Movement of the Holy Spirit," 388.
43. Cessario describes Aquinas's alignment of gifts and virtues in the *Summa Theolgiae* as "definitive." See Cessario, *Christian Faith and the Theological Life,* 162. However, there are even different such depictions within the *Summa Theologiae,* so it may be better to refer to Aquinas's "later" treatments rather than suggest a clear settled position. For a helpful overview of the different alignments of the gifts throughout Aquinas's corpus, see O'Connor, "The Evolution of St. Thomas's Thought on the Gifts," 110–30 and especially the helpful chart at 130.
44. ST I–II 109,9: "In order to live righteously, a man needs twofold help from God. First, a habitual gift whereby corrupted human nature is healed and after being healed, lifted

up so as to work deeds meritorious of eternal life, which exceed the capacity of nature. Second, man needs the help of grace in order to be moved by God to act."

45. See, e.g., ST I 95,1 and 95,3 and ST I–II 68,6.
46. ST I–II 110,2 ad 2. See also I–II 68,2: "Now man's reason is perfected by God in two ways: first, with its natural perfection, to wit, the natural light of reason; secondly, with a supernatural perfection, to wit, the theological virtues. . . . And, though this latter perfection is greater than the former, yet the former is possessed by man in a more perfect manner than the latter: because man has the former in his full possession, whereas he possesses the latter imperfectly, since we love and know God imperfectly." Note that the theological virtues are depicted as serving the role of seeds akin to the natural light of reason. See also I–II 68,3 ad 3.
47. ST I–II 68, 3. For insightful treatments of the gifts of the Holy Spirit in Aquinas, see: O'Connor *Summa Theologiae*, 80–147; Pinckaers, "Morality and the Movement of the Holy Spirit," 385–95; Torrell, *Saint Thomas Aquinas, Vol. 2*, 206–15; Meinert, *The Love of God Poured Out*; Cessario, *Christian Faith and the Theological Life*, 159–80, and *Introduction to Moral Theology*, 205–12; Stroud, "Thomas Aquinas' Exposition of the Gifts of the Holy Spirit"; and McKay, "The Infused and Acquired Virtues in Aquinas's Moral Philosophy." Anyone familiar with this scholarship will see this as an endorsement of, and additional support for, the argument on the constant (rather than sporadic) need for the gifts. For another recent affirmation of the position see Spezzano, *The Glory of God's Grace*, 243n102.
48. ST I–II 68,2. See also I–II 109,9–10. For an excellent treatment of how Aquinas's question on the gifts (I–II 68) and the so-called treatise on grace can be read in mutually illuminating ways, see Meinert, *The Love of God Poured Out*. Meinert argues in detail how the gifts of the Holy Spirit render one amenable to the divine *instinctus*, which is best understood as postjustification *auxilium* (103–13). See chap. 7 for other distinctions regarding grace, including actual grace as distinct from habitual grace, and operative as distinct from cooperative grace.
49. For more on Aquinas's use of *instinctus* to describe the movement supplied by God's agency through the gifts of the Holy Spirit, see O'Connor, "*Instinctus* and *Inspiratio*," 131–41. See also Pinckaers, "Morality and the Movement of the Holy Spirit," 385–88; and Stroud, "Thomas Aquinas' Exposition of the Gifts of the Holy Spirit," 173–86. See also Stroud, "*Instinctus* and the Gifts of the Holy Spirit," where Stroud gives further attention to the growing use of *instinctus* as part of Aquinas's countering of semi-Pelagianism.
50. ST I–II 68,2. For extended treatments of the distinct roles of acquired virtues, infused virtues, and gifts, see Stroud, "Thomas Aquinas' Exposition of the Gifts of the Holy Spirit," 197–212; and Meinert, *The Love of God Poured Out*, 252–63.
51. See ST I–II 68,2, as well as 68,1: "Human virtues perfect man according as it is natural for him to be moved by his reason in his interior and exterior actions. Consequently man needs yet higher perfections, whereby to be disposed to be moved by God." See also I–II 68,1 ad 3, where the natural end is described as "measured by the rule of reason."
52. ST I–II 68, 2 ad 2. The English Dominicans' translation of *semper* deploys "continual," which is best translated as "always."
53. ST I–II 68,1.
54. ST I–II 68,2.
55. See for instance 68,1 ad 3. See also the term *regulam* in I–II 63,4.
56. ST I–II 68,2.

57. See, for instance, ST I–II 68,1: "Human virtues perfect man according as it is natural for him to be moved by his reason in his interior and exterior actions." See also I–II 68,2: "In matters directed to the supernatural end, to which man's reason moves him, according as it is, in a manner, and imperfectly, informed by the theological virtues, the motion of reason does not suffice."
58. ST I–II 68,1 ad 3.
59. ST I–II 68,1.
60. Certain texts can be taken to suggest this. Consider ST I–II 68,1: "Even the Philosopher says in the chapter *On Good Fortune* [*Ethic. Eudem.*, vii, 8] that for those who are moved by Divine instinct, there is no need to take counsel according to human reason, but only to follow their inner promptings, since they are moved by a principle higher than human reason."
61. ST I–II 68,4.
62. Aquinas states such powers are qualified by *both* virtues and gifts: "*In omnibus viribus hominis quae possunt esse principia humanorum actuum, sicut sunt virtutes, ita etiam sunt dona.*" In these powers, "just as there are virtues, thus there are also gifts" (I–II 68,4). The English Dominicans' translation is confusing on this point: "Whatever powers in man can be principles of human actions can also be the subjects of gifts, even as they are virtues." The Freddoso translation is spot on: "And so just as there are virtues for all the human powers that can be principles of human actions, viz., reason and the appetitive powers, so too there are gifts for all those powers."
63. See ST I–II 10,4. Torrell offers a helpful treatment of this in the context of the gifts (*Thomas Aquinas, Vol. 2*, 209–11), as does Pinsent, *The Second Person Perspective in Aquinas's Ethics*, 35.
64. See Aquinas, *Commentary on Romans*, c. 8 l. 3 (635).
65. Pinckaers, *La vie selon L'esprit*, 207.
66. Pinckaers, "Morality and the Movement of the Holy Spirit," 389.
67. Pinckaers, *La vie selon L'esprit*, 207 (emphasis added).
68. For an excellent review of how the gifts serve as the nexus of divine and human causality, see Herdt, *Putting on Virtue*, 90–91.
69. See ST I–II 68,4 on the enumeration of the gifts and how they qualify human powers of both apprehension and appetite.
70. For the case that the Divine *instinctus* that moves a person through the gifts of the Holy Spirit is best understood as the actual grace called *auxilium*, see Meinert, *The Love of God Poured Out*, 98–113. For Aquinas's own reference to grace (and law) as "extrinsic principles" of human action, see ST I–II 90, Prologue.
71. Texts such as this support this claim: "The gifts perfect man for acts which are higher than acts of virtue." However, Aquinas is here contrasting acts of the gifts from acts of human acquired virtues, which are addressed in the immediately preceding lines. See ST I–II 68,1.
72. For this analogy, see ST I–II 68,2.
73. Martinez, *The Sanctifier*, 143. It is unclear if Cessario holds this position. Cessario claims that the infused moral and theological virtues "enable a believer to act properly in the commonplace experiences of the Christian life" (*Christian Faith and the Theological Life*, 163) and that the gifts "represent seven distinct ways in which the individual believer receives divine impulses or movements that assist him or her to perform *specific kinds of action*" (*Introduction to Moral Theology*, 206 [emphasis added]). If by "specific kinds

of action" he means each gift corresponds with actions of distinct types, he is, of course, correct. If he means the gifts concern specific types of action distinct from the types of actions of the infused virtues, his position would be akin to Martinez's.

74. Martinez, *The Sanctifier*, 144.
75. Martinez, 142.
76. Cessario, *Introduction to Moral Theology*, 207. In *Christian Faith and the Theological Life* he calls action of the gifts "an entirely new sort of action" as compared to actions of the infused virtues, citing John of St. Thomas (164). The context makes clear that Cessario does not mean once activity of the acquired virtues comes under the influence of the gifts it gains a new species (which is true), but rather action of the infused virtues comes under that influence.
77. Cessario, *Introduction to Moral Theology*, 209. He offers as an example believers who pray to fulfill what is required versus those who pray with intensity and for longer periods. There is a suggestion of commandment and counsel here that Aquinas explicitly denies in relation to infused virtue and gift. See also Cessario, *Christian Faith and the Theological Life*, for the claim that "human reason ordinarily remains the rule or measure for the infused moral and theological virtues" (166).
78. ST I–II 109,9.
79. ST I–II 63,4.
80. ST I–II 68,2 ad 1. Cessario's distinction between requisite prayer and prayer beyond what is requisite, and comparison of these to the virtues and gifts, respectively, falls prey to Aquinas's argument against understanding the virtues and gifts as akin to the commandments and counsels (*Introduction to Moral Theology*, 209). Lest one think Aquinas is contrasting the human virtues and gifts, this cannot be the case since the acts of the former are distinct from graced acts according to the divine rule (I–II 63,4), and in the next objection he makes it clear he is distinguishing between the infused (theological) virtues and gifts. The principle of movement is also clearly the basis of his distinction between gifts and infused virtues, not between gifts and acquired virtues (I–II 68,1 ad 3).
81. Torrell, *Thomas Aquinas, Vol. 2*, 214.
82. Pinckaers, *La vie selon l'Esprit*, 207. See also Pinsent, *The Second Person Perspective in Aquinas's Ethics*, on this point: "Aquinas holds that the gifts extend to all the things to which the virtues extend" (32).
83. See ST I–II 68,5 ad 3, where Aquinas makes this observation regarding Gregory's consideration of the gifts as distinct from one another. Aquinas explicitly says that doing such does not actually mean one gift can be possessed without the others. Though he is referencing the gifts as distinct from one another rather than the gifts as distinct from infused virtues, he makes a similar claim and conceptual distinction between the latter not implying the possibility of them being actually possessed in such a manner.
84. Note that the English Dominicans misleadingly translate *semper* in ST I–II 68,2 ad 2 as a person standing in "continual" need of movement by the Holy Spirit, rather than "always" needing such prompting, as rightly translated by Freddoso. After all, something can be continually needed though not always needed. See also I–II 68,3 ad 1, where *semper* appears three times and yet not once in the English Dominicans' translation (which uses "ever"). Freddoso appropriately uses "at all times." For other recent treatments of how the gifts are "always" needed, see Pinckaers, "Morality and the Movement of the Holy

Spirit," 391; Stroud, *Thomas Aquinas' Exposition of the Gifts of the Holy Spirit*, 208–11; Meinert, *The Love of God Poured Out*, 267–69; Pinsent, *The Second Person Perspective in Aquinas's Ethics*, 32; Spezzano, *The Glory of God's Grace*, 244; and McKay, "The Infused and Acquired Virtues in Aquinas's Moral Philosophy," 95. This position on the gifts being always necessary for acts of the infused virtues is in part a correction of John of St. Thomas's classic metaphor of the gifts of the Holy Spirit being akin to sails on a boat otherwise propelled by oars (virtues). Though there are aspects to commend in this metaphor (e.g., the noncompetitive account of divine and human causality), its affirmation of only a sporadic role for the gifts in the graced life is problematic. For a contemporary account that relies on this metaphor but betrays its problems, see Cessario, *Introduction to Moral Theology*, 207–9. For a fair but critical treatment of this metaphor see Pinsent, *The Second Person Perspective in Aquinas's Ethics*, 32, 36–38.

85. ST I–II 68,3 s.c.
86. ST I–II 68,1: "Whatever is moved must be proportionate to its mover; and the perfection of the mobile as such, consists in a *disposition* whereby it is disposed to be moved well by its mover" (emphasis added).
87. ST I–II 68,3 ad 2.
88. See I–II 68,1, and 68,3.
89. For a helpful translation of the words used for the gifts, see O'Connor, "The Scriptural Basis for the Doctrine of the Gifts."
90. For a review on the enumeration of the gifts in Aquinas's thought, see O'Connor, "The Evolution of St. Thomas's Thought on the Gifts," 130. For recognition of change in Aquinas's thoughts on enumeration, see Torrell, *Saint Thomas Aquinas, Vol. 2*, 212. See also Cessario, *Christian Faith and the Theological Life*, 163n11. Cessario argues that the basis of enumeration in ST I–II (alignment with the theological and cardinal virtues, with two gifts—knowledge and understanding—aligned with faith and none with temperance) is "definitive" (*Christian Faith and the Theological Life*, 164) though we can only say with confidence that it is Aquinas's last enumeration.
91. See ST I–II 68,5 for *Prima secundae* indications of the link between temperance and fear of the Lord. See Pinckaers, *La vie selon l'Esprit*, 207, for this made explicit. Compare to Torrell, who does not align fear of the Lord with temperance (*Spiritual Master*, 212n35).
92. Torrell, *Spiritual Master*, 212.
93. See ST II–II 8,1, 9,1, and 45,1.
94. See ST II–II 139,1.
95. See ST II–II 19,2 and 19,9.
96. Perhaps the most promising way to address the acts of the infused virtues and gifts is through the beatitudes, as Aquinas indicates in ST I–II 69,1.
97. ST I–II 68,1 ad 1. Recall Aquinas's claim that the acts of the gifts are not distinct from those of the virtues, as counsels are to commandments (I–II 68,2 ad 1). The difference is in movement, not specification of activity.
98. See ST I–II 49,3 and 54,2. In the latter Aquinas notes that habits differ specifically by their object and nature but also "in respect of the active principles of such dispositions."
99. See Aquinas's interpretation of the Jn 3:8 passage about the wind as referring to the Holy Spirit (*Commentary on the Gospel of John*, C. 3, L. 2, 452–55).
100. ST I–II 68,5. Pinsent rightly notes the "gifts can never be present without infused virtues and vice versa" (*The Second Person Perspective in Aquinas's Ethics*, 34).

101. ST I–II 68,6. Compare to I–II 67, esp. a. 1.
102. ST II–II 19,10. See also Martinez, *The Sanctifier*, 145.
103. Pinckaers, *La vie selon l'Esprit*, 207, 391. Though Pinckaers's treatment of Aquinas's three stages of growth in charity describe the third stage as "dominated" by the gifts (199), it is clear from his overall treatment that he does not think activity aided by the gifts characterizes only that third level of growth.
104. Pinsent, *The Second Person Perspective in Aquinas's Ethics*, 34.
105. In addition to the presence of contrary disposition, as noted by Pinsent, see also the next chapter for an account of habitual ordering in the case of venial sin. The fact that one could possess the gifts yet not act in a manner moved by the Holy Spirit—something true of the infused virtues as well—provides "room for growth" in the gifts and also explains the tendency of certain moralists to postulate the possibility of living out of the infused virtues alone and not the gifts.
106. Pinckaers, *La vie selon l'Esprit*, 207.
107. See chap. 7 for different Thomistic terms for describing the effects of God's grace with and without the infusion of a habit.
108. In fact, identifying the occasion of that line may at times be easier with the infused virtues given certain ways God bestows them, such as through baptism.
109. *De virt card.* a. 2. See also ST I–II 65,1, as well as 68,5 on the gifts.
110. *De virt.* a. 10 ad 11.
111. Gilleman, *The Primacy of Charity in Moral Theology*, 16. Gilleman manages both to distinguish what are labeled here level one and level two and emphasize their tight connection. Gilleman's book is in certain ways a remarkably prescient account of charity as a virtue that appeared well before the turn to virtue in moral theology decades later. Though at times it evidences certain inadequacies that characterize moral theology of its day, in many ways it is ahead of its time.
112. See ST II–II 24,1 ad 2 on this new measure. See also I–II 63,4.
113. ST I–II 63,1.
114. Recall Decosimo's comments in *Ethics as a Work of Charity* about the connectivity of the moral virtues, which applies also to the infused virtues: "Connection inheres in virtue's *being* virtue" (157 [emphasis in original]); and "Stability and unity [i.e., connectivity] mutually implicate one another and are inextricably related, inhering in virtue's *ratio*. . . . [Connectivity is not] an independent addition that turns imperfect virtue perfect. Unity, *difficile mobile*, *recte ratione*, true virtue—these rise and fall together" (156).
115. Pinckaers, *La vie selon l'Esprit*, 207.
116. ST I–II 63,4.
117. For the claim that charity and all the infused virtues can be lost in one act, see ST II–II 24,12 and *De car.* a. 13.
118. I use "cardinal" virtues to "cover" all moral and intellectual virtues that are virtues in the full sense of making their possessor good, a move Aquinas makes in ST I–II 61 and even in *De virt. card.* aa. 1–4.
119. For a helpful account of the interpenetration of intellect and will in practical reasoning as well as in the infused virtues, see Sherwin, *By Knowledge and by Love*, 152–84.
120. ST I–II 66,6 ad 1.
121. *De car.* a. 3 ad 13. Here Aquinas makes a similar claim to the previous quotation about matters "above" humanity: "When the things are above the one who understands, then the will rises higher than the intellect is able to attain."

122. ST I–II 66,6 ad 1.
123. ST I–II 65,1.
124. ST I–II 63,1.
125. See ST I–II 65,4 regarding both hope and faith without charity. For more on "unformed faith" or "dead faith," see ST II–II 4,4 and 6,2, and *De ver.* XIV.6. See also *Comm. Sent.* l. 3 d. 23 q. 3 a. 1 qa. 2 on how unformed faith is not a virtue, and ad 1 ad 3, where Aquinas refers to it as a disposition. See esp. qa. 3 on this point, where Aquinas claims formed and unformed faith differ "as perfect and imperfect in the same species in the way that a disposition to virtue and a habit to virtue differ." For a treatment of dead faith in the context of debates over virtue, see Mattison, "Revisiting the Relationship between Infused and Acquired Cardinal Virtues." On a living hope as distinct from a hope without charity, see ST II–II 17,8 ad 2. See *De spe.* a. 3 on "unformed" hope.
126. For Aquinas's claim that charity orders both infused cardinal virtues (level two) and their activities toward the last end (level three), see Gilleman, *The Primacy of Charity in Moral Theology*, 29–45, esp. 29–30, citing ST II–II 23,8.
127. A recent and lively example of such debate is the scholarship prompted by controversial claims by Grisez and Ryan about the Kingdom of God, rather than God alone in the beatific vision, as constituting humanity's last end. For a helpful summation of that argument (and a bibliography of the previous decade's worth of contributions to that discussion), see Grisez, "The True Ultimate End of Human Beings." Jensen offers a critique of Grisez's view in *Sin*, 41–65. See also Sullivan, "Seek First the Kingdom."
128. See Jensen, *Sin*, 43–49. Jensen describes various approaches to practical reasoning that correspond with different accounts of God as a person's last end.
129. For Aquinas's claim that charity is friendship, see ST II–II 23,1. On charity as greatest of the virtues, see ST II–II 23,6.
130. For Aquinas's distinction between charity as Uncreated God and charity as created, grace-enabled virtue, see ST I–II 23,2 and *De car.* a. 1.
131. For his classic account of love of God in relation to other loves, with a thoroughly teleological view of practical reasoning, see Augustine, *Teaching Christianity*, book 1.
132. The former term is from Pinckaers, *Sources of Christian Ethics*, 370; the latter is from Pinckaers, *La vie selon 'L'esprit*, 208.
133. Pinckaers, *La vie selon 'Esprit*, 208.
134. For all four terms see *De car.* a. 3 (though McInerny translates *motor* as moving power). For Aquinas's other treatments of charity as a form of the virtues, see *Sent.* l. 3 d. 27 q. 2 a. 4 qa. 3 and ST II–III 23,8.
135. ST I–II 23,8. See also *De car.* a. 3. As evident in this quote, Aquinas calls charity a form of the virtues and a form of the acts of virtue. The language of levels in this project helps clarify these distinct claims, given that habits are specified by their objects (paradigmatic acts), Aquinas's use of charity as form of both is unsurprising. For extended treatment of this idea, including relevant texts, see Falanga, *Charity*, 1–15. For a treatment of this issue that is more concerned with distinguishing the ways that charity informs other virtues and informs acts of those virtues, see Porter, "Moral Virtues, Charity, and Grace," 57.
136. That is, charity as form of the virtues, not as essential form or exemplar form but rather as mover and efficient cause. See ST II–II 23,8; and *De car.* a. 3 ad 16 and ad 18. For more on this idea, including attention to developments in Aquinas's thought, see Falanga, *Charity*, 29–45; and Sherwin, *By Knowledge and by Love*, 192–202.

137. See *De car.* a. 3 ad 18: "*Quod trahit alias virtutes ad suum finem*" (author's translation).
138. ST I–II 114,4 ad 1. In that same article Aquinas claims: "Everlasting life consists in the enjoyment of God. Now the human mind's movement to the fruition of the Divine good is the proper act of charity, whereby all the acts of the other virtues are ordained to this end, since all the other virtues are commanded by charity. Hence the merit of life everlasting pertains first to charity, and secondly, to the other virtues, inasmuch as their acts are commanded by charity."
139. For explanation of why charity is rightly said to be the form of even the theological virtues, which have God as their object, see *De car.* a. 3.
140. Gilleman, *The Primacy of Charity in Moral Theology*, 16. On how the act of a faculty (power) is not other than the act of a virtue, Gilleman claims: "In our virtuous activity, the virtue does not elicit an act different from that of the faculty; that which elicits the act is the faculty bettered by the virtuous quality. And in turn, the faculty is but an instrument of the will, and finally, of the soul" (15). This idea sets up the next claim on how elicited acts, proper to a virtue (or better: virtuous faculty), are commanded by the will, which is always ultimately toward one's last end.
141. See *De car.* a. 5 ad 11.
142. Aquinas is aware of the obvious ways that one's actions may not seem to be acts of charity even when a person is ordered toward God as one's last end. One way he addresses this topic is through his notion of "habitual ordering" (discussed later). Another is through "virtual ordering," whereby a person acts for the sake of a further end even without thinking of that further end while acting. For example, a person not thinking of the destination during each step of his trek, even though that destination is ordering his walk (ST I–II 1,6 ad 3); or a doctor searching for herbs for a potion, who may not be thinking of her patient's cure, even though that further end drives her action (*De car.* a. 11, ad 2). See also *Sent* l. 2 d. 40 q. 1 a. 5 ad 7 and *De Perf. Spirit.* 5. For more on both habitual and virtual ordering, see Mattison, "Habitual Ordering in Aquinas." Virtual ordering is part of an explanation of how the "automaticity" of habitual action can seem less reflective of, while in reality is actually driven by, a person's rationality. Snow calls this dynamic the "effacing" of reason. See Snow, *Virtue as Social Intelligence*, 29–30.
143. See *De car.* a. 5 ad 3: "Charity does not produce the acts of the other virtues by eliciting them, but only by commanding them." For more on elicited vs. commanded acts, see ST I–II 8–17. On these in the context of charity, see Sherwin, *By Knowledge and By Love*, 180–81.
144. For the necessity of elicited and commanded acts sharing the same rule or measure, see Knobel, *Aquinas on the Infused Moral Virtues*, 112; and Porter, "Moral Virtues, Charity, and Grace," 48.
145. This dynamic also occurs in acts of acquired virtue, though in the absence of a distinct virtue, such as charity ordering a person toward the last end as its object, there is no need for an account of how one virtue serves as the form of the virtues with regard to acquired virtue.
146. *De car.* a. 3 ad 10.
147. For a helpful treatment of this, see Gilleman, *The Primacy of Charity in Moral Theology*, 43–44.
148. *De car.* a. 3 ad 9.
149. For charity as a special virtue, see *De car.* a. 3 ad 17 (on the beatific vision as act proper to charity), esp. *De car.* a. 5; and ST II–II 23,4.

150. The term "infused cardinal virtues" (rather than Aquinas's "infused moral and intellectual virtues") indicates that virtues like art and those of the speculative intellect (other than faith) are not virtues in the fullest sense. Thus their objects are not transformed through charity and orientation toward God as last end in the same manner that virtues in the fullest sense are so transformed. For the (more limited) sense in which art and virtues of the speculative intellect are formed by charity in their exercise rather than through specification, see Falanga, *Charity*, 125–35. The term "cardinal virtues" excludes these, yet is meant to include virtues in the fullest sense that "fall under" the cardinal virtues understood in their general sense (e.g., patience, truthfulness, chastity, etc.).
151. This position is indeed held in the tradition. See, for instance, Duns Scotus, *Duns Scotus on the Will and Morality*, Ordinatio III, Distinction 36.
152. ST I–II 63,3. See also *De virt.* a. 10 ad 9.
153. See ST I–II 63,3 ad 2 on the need for virtues not only concerning God directly (*in Deum*) but also "in regard to other things in relation to God" (*ad Deum*). Elsewhere Aquinas describes these activities, which may (or may not) be done in relation to God, as activities "comprehensible to human reason" (I–II 62,2). He of course means in principle, since when they are infused, these types of activities remain accessible to unaided reason, but the specification of their objects requires God's grace, as does acting out of those virtues.
154. See *Comm. Sent.* l. 3 d. 33 q. 1 a. 2 qa. 4; ST I–II 63,4; and, *De virt.* a. 10 ad 8–10.
155. See *De virt.* a 10 ad 8.
156. Porter, "Moral Virtues, Charity, and Grace," 43–44.
157. See, respectively, *De virt.* a. 10 ad 8; ST I–II 63,4; and ST I–II 63,4 ad 1. Porter refers to this happiness as having a different "normative standard" ("Moral Virtues, Charity, and Grace," 51).
158. Though the emphasis here is on charity and the cardinal virtues it forms possessing a common divine rule or measure, this dynamic can be present on the natural level too, as when Aquinas claims that there can be various ends of prudence ordered to one another (ST II–II 47,11). However, he is also clear there that the various levels of prudence share a common last end (ad 3), in this case a natural one. For a contrasting read of these passages in Aquinas, one in which the infused cardinal virtues command the acquired cardinal virtues, see Decosimo, "More to Love," 48–55. For a critique of Decosimo on this point, see Porter, "Moral Virtues, Charity, and Grace," 48, 51–52. This topic is addressed in great detail in the appendix.
159. Charity and its accompanying infused virtues are not measured by the rule of human reason: "Charity is regulated, not by the reason, as human virtues are, but by God's wisdom, and transcends the rule of human reason" (ST II–II 24,1 ad 2). However, charity transcends but does not defy the (natural) end of human reason. That natural end is attained even as it is surpassed. This is what Porter references in saying, "Right reason does not set the normative standard for the infused virtues, but rational considerations are incorporated into its operations whenever they are relevant and appropriate to the standards set by the New Law" ("Moral Virtues, Charity, and Grace," 51n13).

CHAPTER 7

GROWING IN INFUSED VIRTUE

Crossing the Line and Various Ways of Growing

One of the main underlying themes of this project is addressing the continuities and discontinuities between acquired (natural) and infused (supernatural) virtues. One danger in identifying the discontinuities is allowing them to occlude the continuities. This is nowhere more true than with growth in, or loss of, infused virtue. There are some striking differences in the case of infused virtues, such as the possibility of receiving them not only all at once but with no preceding actions on the part of the person, especially obvious in traditions that practice infant baptism. Another striking difference is the possibility of losing all infused virtue with one act of mortal sin. To be clear, these are indeed significant differences. It is also the case, as has already been emphasized, that in a sense the infused virtues are a part of a whole new life with concomitant radically different actions. Nevertheless, differences such as these can mask commonalities.

In order to adequately identify both commonalities and differences, the sections of this chapter track those of chapter five on acquired/natural virtue. Section one offers accounts of growth in graced virtue. It starts with an account that closely mimics the attainment of acquired virtue, before noting a more obviously different path to infused virtue. Section two examines the possibility of persistent contrary dispositions in the person with infused virtue, another commonly mentioned difference from the acquired virtues. Section three directly addresses various ways a person grows in infused virtue. Finally, section four examines the loss of infused virtue, with special attention to explaining any persistent "good" action in the person who has lost the infused virtues.

BEGINNINGS OF A THOMISTIC ACCOUNT OF FORMATION IN THE GRACED LIFE OF DISCIPLESHIP

Earlier the work of Katharine Breen was deployed in a basic account of how children grow to the attainment of virtue. Breen describes how children's natural dispositions (*mores*) are cultivated (at times redirected) into good *consuetudines*. Communal practices, what Aquinas calls customs in the first sense, lead children into activities (level three) that develop in them customs in Aquinas's second sense of the term, as more or less stable dispositions (level two) to activities of a certain sort. As noted, custom dispositions can be quite complex, particularly in humans as linguistic animals. What, then, is added in order for there to be a "full blown" habit, especially when both the complexity and the second nature stability indicative of habit are already present? Breen claims the "internal" state changes. Aquinas would say there is no longer simply *causa transmutabilis* but also *causa immobilis*. Specification of level two habits is supplied by one's rationality such that one can holistically or "systematically relate [their rational powers] to their actions."[1] Though sensory dispositions can continue to exert causal influence on a person's activity, at some point one crosses the line such that the ends of the person's habits are more fully her own due to the involvement of reason and will. The ongoing attunement effect that a person's level three activity has on level two engenders a human habit at level two, when activity that is properly human, attentive to life as a whole with a person's ends as her own, results in an object of the level two habit that is so attuned. With the acquired virtues, granting the important influence of natural dispositions and especially social accustomization, a person's habits are indeed caused by her own properly human actions.

Does something of this sort happen with the infused virtues? The most obvious answer is no, for the reasons described earlier. The infused virtues are toward a supernatural end that cannot be ascertained (let alone attained) without God's grace. To act toward and participate in that end, grace is required at the level of the soul (level one), in habits of the powers (level two), and in activity (level three). There are even further differences in the attainment of infused virtues. Yet before proceeding so quickly to those differences, it is worth pausing to identify certain commonalities, especially on the process of accustomization toward the full actualization of infused virtues.

Something similar to the social formation of acquired virtue commonly occurs with the infused virtues. Such formation occurs with individuals possessing their own natural dispositions. One reason it is delightful to read (auto)biographies of the saints is the display of the ongoing causal influence of such natural dispositions in the life of graced discipleship. There are also myriad ways that children are accustomed to Christian faith in active Christian communities. Children grow up saying prayers, singing hymns, making the sign of the cross, and reverencing devotionals before being able to engage in these activities in a properly human way, with their rationality fully engaged. They "get used to," in a sensory manner, not only these most obviously religious activities but also faith-animated care of sick family members, service to the vulnerable, moderation of consumption, and honest, charitable communication, among other activities. These familial and social influences on a person's formation mimic in many ways the sort of formation toward virtue that occurs with the acquired virtues. We might even say that before the child is able to possess properly human habits caused by their own acts, the community "supplies" formation with an intelligibility that surpasses the child's own abilities and serves to form the child in the activities of the infused virtues.[2]

Granting a similarity in communal formation in virtue, two important differences should be noted. First, the entire process, whatever the level of involvement of the child, is permeated by God's grace. An earlier point clarified that "graced" in the context of infused virtue means not simply God's agency (which is, of course, present through creation and through "common" grace in the acquired virtues) but also orientation toward supernatural flourishing in a manner not possible without God's grace. That definition continues. But some additional Thomistic distinctions with regard to grace will also help. Relying on Augustine, Aquinas distinguishes between operative and cooperative grace. Both are God's agency, but operative grace is where "God is the sole mover," whereas with cooperative grace "our mind both moves and is moved; the activity is not only attributed to God but also to the soul."[3] Depicted in the brief account of formation in virtue is God's operative grace—operating as it commonly does through the secondary causality of family, priests, community members, and others—with increasing activity of the child in cooperative grace.

Aquinas also distinguishes between what has come to be termed "actual" grace on the one hand and "habitual" grace on the other.[4] These correspond to what here are termed level three activity and level two disposition/habit. "A person is aided by God's gratuitous will in two ways: first, inasmuch as one's soul is moved by God to know or will or do something, and in this way the gratuitous effect in man is not a quality, but a movement of the soul; for 'motion is the act of the mover in the moved.' Secondly, one is helped by

God's gratuitous will, inasmuch as a habitual gift is infused by God into the soul."[5] This first type of grace Aquinas later calls "actual"; the second he calls "habitual." Actual grace is God's help to activity at level three.[6] Habitual grace is God's help to possession of a level two habit.[7] Note that all four permutations with these two distinctions are possible. So habitual grace can be operative (as when infused virtues are given to us "without us") and cooperative (as when we act on the infused virtues), and actual grace can be operative (as when God works on us "without us") and cooperative (as in our activity when we are both moved and mover).[8]

Why mention here these scholastic categorizations of grace? My first point is to note the important difference between formation in acquired virtue and in infused virtue: the latter is only possible with God's grace. For this claim to be more than stipulative, and to adequately depict the various causal forces at work in such formation, these distinctions can help "sort out" the various ways God's grace is present in the journey of formation in infused virtue. So, for instance, the gift of infused virtues (habitual grace) does not imply that ongoing (actual) grace is not needed to act on and grow in infused virtue. And the various (often communal) forces of formation, along with varying degrees of active involvement by the child, are helpfully examined with the operative/cooperative grace distinction. In short, the claim that formation in infused virtue is only possible with God's grace is not a claim inattentive to distinct (though noncompetitive) roles for divine and human agency or the various levels (activity and habit) on which grace operates.

There is a second difference between the basic account of formation in infused virtue and formation in acquired virtue, an even more obvious difference. It is not that one suddenly crosses the line to possess all the infused virtues, since this is true of the acquired virtues as well. Yet with the infused virtues, there need be no (cooperatively graced) activity on the part of the person leading up to that line crossing. This is particularly obvious in the practice of infant baptism, but presumably also evident in more stark stories of conversion, such as that of Saul on the road to Damascus. Sticking with the former: in the sacrament of baptism a person is justified and sanctified through God's grace. A person is not only healed, but elevated so as to be equipped (qualified) to live a life directed toward supernatural happiness, a life made possible by the possession of charity and all the infused virtues. Aquinas teaches quite clearly, in line with the Christian tradition, that faith and love—and indeed all the infused virtues—are granted at baptism.[9] How is it possible that infants can rightly be said to possess virtues as habits in the properly human sense, if they are incapable of properly human action?

Aquinas addresses this question directly and, interestingly, does so in the context of the three levels referenced throughout this project. In response to the question of whether or not children (presumably those before the age of reason) should be baptized, he observes some have taught that children do not receive "grace and virtues" at baptism but simply the "imprint of the character of Christ," to which would be added grace and virtues when they grow old enough. Though this position speaks of graced virtue arriving only with appropriate age, its affirmation of an imprint of Christ's character on the baptized infant suggests something akin to baptism changing a person at level one but not level two. Aquinas claims this position is false, appealing to a distinction between what is called here level two and level three: "The source of their error was that they did not recognize the distinction between habit and act."[10] It is obviously true that there is some lack in the ability of baptized infants to live out the infused virtues. But Aquinas ascribes that lack to the level of activity, not habit. He claims: "This inability of children to act is not due to the absence of habits, but an impediment on the part of the body: thus also when a man is asleep, though he may have the habits of virtue, yet is he hindered from virtuous acts through being asleep."[11] Of course, there is an important difference in the analogy with the sleeping person, whose prior acts could have engendered a habit even as sleep at the present moment prevents her from acting on the habit. With the virtues infused at baptism there is no such prior activity. But the cases are analogous since in both the sleeping habituated person and the baptized infant there is a lack of activity (level three) which need not indicate the lack of a habit (level two).

This raises a host of issues pertinent to sacramental theology that cannot be addressed in the scope of this project. For our purposes it is important to note that Aquinas affirms that the infused virtues can indeed exist without activity, indeed without any prior activity on the person's part. However, besides the fact that an example of lack of activity (e.g., sleeping) yet with the presence of a habit does not *prove* that a habit is present where there is no activity (rather, only that it might be present), does this solution not create more problems than it solves? After all, if a habit is the stable specification of a person's habituation-amenable power by a *causa immobilis*, what *causa immobilis* is present in this case and what sort of stable specification is present? Two things can be said in response to these questions.

First, Aquinas evidences a beautifully communal understanding of the human person. This is unsurprising for someone who affirms Aristotle's claim that the person is a social animal.[12] It is also unsurprising for someone who affirms the corporate identity of the believer in the Body of Christ that is the Church. Yet it is here that Aquinas uses some of his more beautiful and poetic language to describe the way that baptized infants have their agency "supplied" by the Church: "The spiritual regeneration effected by Baptism is somewhat like carnal birth, in this respect, that as the child while in the mother's womb receives nourishment not independently, but through the nourishment of its mother, so also children before the use of reason, being as it were in the womb of their mother the Church, receive salvation not by their own act, but by the act of the Church."[13] Aquinas relies on Augustine for several equally powerful statements regarding the Church supplying agency to baptized children.[14] Aquinas indicates how the childhood process of grace-enabled accustomization is aided by the possession of infused virtues when he claims, "It was fitting that children should receive Baptism, in order that being reared from childhood in things pertaining to the Christian mode of life, they may the more easily persevere therein."[15] Aquinas thus guards the relationship between habits at level two and activities at level three by beautiful affirmations of the corporate situated-ness of human agency.

Beautiful though it may be, this solution for activity-free habits raises further questions about the relationship between individual agency and the community or, as more commonly depicted today, between individual agency and social structure. After all, if pre-rational children can possess infused virtues due to their membership in the Church community, why cannot something similar be said about acquired virtues, or even vices, in the pre-rational child?[16] Indeed, there are treatments of social theory today that seem to do exactly this, conflating individual agency and social structure such that the latter governs the former.[17] Alternatively, recent work in critical realism is attentive to the causal influence of social structure yet careful to distinguish such influence from properly personal agency.[18] Is Aquinas somehow able to simultaneously distinguish the impactful role of social formation that can happen with acquired virtue and vice—in which case the child is not properly said to possess habits—from the child with infused virtues—whose ecclesial situated-ness does indeed supply habits in the properly human sense?

The answer is yes, because with the infused virtues the *causa immobilis* stably specifying the child's powers is not ultimately the community *qua* community but rather God's grace operative through the Church as Body of Christ. In this very context of infant baptism Aquinas indicates this divine agency operative through the Church: "But the faith of one [Christ, contrasting Him to Adam], indeed of the whole Church, profits the child through the operation of the Holy Ghost, Who unites the Church together, and communicates the goods of one member to another."[19] Personal agency is indeed requisite for the possession of properly human (or, of course, superhuman) habits, and this is supplied by the *causa immobilis* of God's grace.

The initial task here is to establish commonalties between childhood growth in both the acquired virtues and the infused virtues. Many of the dynamics of both are similar as to natural temperament and communal accustomization. In many ways an upbringing in the infused virtues is indeed observably similar to habit formation more generally. But in another way everything changes. One obvious is in the "content," if you will, of the graced life of discipleship. A life oriented toward supernatural union with God and others in God looks different in obvious ways from one ordered to pleasure or money or fame or even natural human flourishing. Even where there is no observable difference, the formal objects of actions in the graced life will differ to the extent they are indeed commanded by charity and actually ordered toward supernatural happiness. Furthermore, the entire attainment of and growth in the infused virtues is initiated and moved by God's grace. This is particularly evident in the case of infant baptism, with its infusion of all the graced virtues that are initially possessed solely in habit and not in act. But it is also true in all accustomization and personal formation that results in the increasing possession of the infused virtues, not only in habit but also in act. Before turning to additional issues regarding growth in (or loss of) the infused virtues, a word on the adult convert is in order.

The case of infant baptism presents specific challenges to an account of graced virtue since there is no prior activity on the part of the infant to cause the infused virtues. Yet in the case of the adult convert there are indeed prior actions and presumably also habits and dispositions preceding the reception of infused virtue. This presents one obvious distinct challenge, namely, explaining what transpires with those previously attained habits and dispositions. What can be said about the path toward infused virtue when it is not bestowed in early childhood and "grown into," as with the case of infant baptism? Let's call this situation the adult convert, and appeal to St. Augustine's story in Book VIII of *Confessions* as an example.

The first thing to be said about the adult convert is that though her prior activities engender dispositions and habits, her actions are in no way the cause of the infused virtues. In line with the Christian tradition's anti-Pelagian (and anti-semi-Pelagian) stream, the infused virtues are a total gift from God that can be caused only by God.[20] This does not preclude the possibility of receiving actual grace before the reception of the infused virtues as habitual grace. And the actual grace that prepares one for infused virtue, while always operative, may indeed also be cooperative. Yet, to the extent that any preparation for habitual grace does occur, "every preparation in a person must be by the help of God moving the soul to God."[21] In no case can a person cause the infused virtues by her own acts.

We see this in the widely known autobiographical account of Augustine's conversion. If anything is clear from that description, it is that Augustine regards his conversion as possible only through the grace of Christ. The "brute force of habit" was dragging him down, and he exclaims that only "grace through Jesus Christ" was able to save him.[22] He narrates the buildup to his conversion and describes the ways that God drew him to God's Self. At times God's grace is more obviously operative, seemingly without Augustine's involvement, such as when Augustine hears Ponticianus's story of the conversion of two court officials, and relates, "You were wrenching me back toward myself, and pulling me round from that standpoint behind my back. You set me down before my face, forcing me to mark how despicable I was, how misshapen and begrimed, filthy and festering."[23] At other times God's grace was working more cooperatively, as when Augustine relays, "You inspired in me the idea that I should go to Simplicianus, and even I could see the sense of this. I regarded him as your good servant, a man from whom grace radiated."[24] Indeed, while still vacillating before conversion, Augustine reports that "a new will had begun to emerge in me, the will to worship you distinterestedly and enjoy you, O God, our only sure felicity."[25] The Divine passive here leaves little doubt as to the origin of this will, yet nevertheless it is Augustine's own will as well. When the climactic moment of conversion comes there is no doubt who the agent is. Augustine praises God, saying, "You had converted me to yourself," and reports that through his mother, Monica, God has "the power to do more than we ask or understand."[26]

The claim that the infused virtues are caused by God's grace and not by a person's acts need not mean that there is no prior activity of the person before reception of habitual grace, and certainly need not mean God's actual grace is not present. Yet, even so, the infused virtues are pure gift. Granting this, what about the person's prior dispositions and habits? It is granted that before the reception of habitual grace a person does not possess the infused virtues. What might qualify such a person's habituate-able powers toward specific activity? There are various options. A person might have possessed vices, as indeed Augustine reports of his own unchastity. Or a person might be virtuous but in a manner ordered toward natural human flourishing. Finally, a person may be characterized by mere dispositions (indeed bundles of them), whether they be from natural temperament, custom, properly human activity (though without stability), or any combination thereof. The adult convert, especially given Aquinas's claim that any action disposes a person one way or another, is not a "blank slate." What, then, of the existing habits and/or dispositions?

This brings us back to a persistent question in this study: can dispositions become habits? The consistent answer offered here is no. Once a person is granted the infused virtues through God's grace, her habituate-able powers are stably specified by her rationality as (healed and) elevated by God's grace. It is through faith (in speculative reason) and infused prudence (in practical reason) that such specification is supplied, and through charity (operating along with hope and the infused moral virtues) that her virtues are connected and stably oriented toward the supernatural happiness of union with God and others in God. Thus, properly speaking, if the adult convert's habituation-amenable powers are merely qualified by dispositions prior to conversion, those dispositions do not "become" infused virtues. Rather, the habituate-able powers that were qualified by dispositions become qualified by infused virtues. These infused virtues stably specify those powers with paradigmatic acts (more particular ends) informed by the measure of the Divine rule, with specification supplied by the *causa immobilis* of one's reason and will elevated by God's grace.

In a moment we examine the question of whether contrary sensory dispositions are more possible with the infused virtues, and if so, how they can be eliminated. Unlike in the case of a child attaining a properly human habit, the adult convert raises the question as to what happens not to prior dispositions, but to prior habits, be they virtues or vices. Neither previously acquired vices nor virtues are able to remain in the person who possesses the infused virtues. Although contrary sensory dispositions are compatible with habits when the former dispose a person without dislodging the stable rational specification of the person's habits, properly human habits all require stable rational specification of habituation-amenable powers. Whether the habit be a vice, an acquired virtue, or an infused virtue, it is a qualification, a stable specification, of rational human powers. Aquinas takes it as axiomatic that the same powers that propel a person toward the same type of activity (e.g., eating) cannot be stably rationally specified by both a virtue and a vice.[27] With the understanding of habit depicted here as the stable specification of habituate-able powers by the *causa immobilis* of the rational soul, it should be clear why the same person cannot be stably specified toward the same sort of activity by the same rational soul according to both the measure or mode of natural human flourishing *and* the measure or mode of supernatural human flourishing. Actions directed toward the supernatural end differ in formal object from actions directed toward natural human flourishing, even if at times the latter may be observably the same. Furthermore, if properly human action is always directed toward the last end, and if each person has only one last end, it cannot be the case that a person acts toward both, toward natural human flourishing as an overall view of things (i.e., last end) *and* toward supernatural flourishing as an overall view of things.

This is, of course, an argument against what has recently been called "coexistence," or the position that a person can possess both acquired and infused cardinal virtues at the same time (see the appendix for an extensive discussion on the debate).[28] But what happens to the previously possessed habits of a person who receives the infused virtues? In earlier writings on this topic I claimed that the acquired virtues "are literally trans-formed" so that they become infused virtues.[29] The use of "literally" and the inserted hyphen in "trans-formed" emphasize that the infused virtues are directed toward actions with a different formal object than the acquired virtues. This I continue to affirm. Yet I was mistaken in saying the "acquired virtues" are *literally* transformed. This term implies that they remain in some sense, even though changed, while in reality the natural powers persist and the stable specification that is acquired virtue ceases. To recall an earlier image from Aquinas, to say so is to claim that a boy becomes a man, whereas most properly a person who is a boy becomes a person who is a man. So, to put it more precisely: with the reception of the infused virtues a person whose powers were qualified by the acquired virtues becomes a person whose powers are (re) qualified by the infused virtues. She now possesses virtues that are indeed formally different (even if at times observably the same). Acquired virtues do not become infused virtues (nor are they "literally trans-formed" into them) any more than dispositions become habits.

Yet there can remain *relictae,* or residual dispositions, from the previously possessed acquired virtues. As part of the attainment of the acquired virtue, a person's senses are connaturalized to certain types of action. Just as from natural temperament or custom there can remain sensory dispositions that continue to exert causal influence on a person with acquired virtue, so, too, from previously acquired virtues there can remain *relictae* that continue to exert causal influence on the habituated person with infused virtue. If such residual dispositions either reflect a lack of stability in rationality or are vehement enough to dislodge the stable rational specificity, then the person does not possess infused virtues. Yet, if they do neither of these, residual dispositions from previously acquired virtues can be contrary dispositions for the person with infused virtue.[30]

Though it may seem odd to label *relictae* from acquired virtues as contrary dispositions, since they dispose a person to good acts in the acquired virtue sense, this position is a necessary consequence of the formal difference between acquired and infused virtues. Much as "good" dispositions from nature or nurture can dispose a person toward acts that are observably good but in actuality unformed by practical reasoning (and thus at times reckless like a blind horse), for the person with infused virtue, *relictae* from previous acquired virtues can dispose her to observably good action.[31] To the extent these dispositions are unformed by charity, they are at times only accidentally supportive (if at all) of infused virtue and may misleadingly suggest the ongoing presence of acquired virtues.

In presenting a basic account of the attainment of infused virtue, the comparison has been made between the baptized infant and the adult convert. Both present distinct challenges to accounts of attainment of virtue, where acquired virtue serves as the paradigm for virtue. The former requires explanation as to what it means to possess a virtue without prior or even immediately ensuing activity. The latter raises questions about what happens to previously possessed habits after the reception of infused virtue, which is formally distinct from any previously possessed dispositions or habits, even if they were acquired virtues. Presumably there are a variety of other ways that infused virtues are received, or even re-received. Whatever the particulars of these accounts, which are likely as various as there are graced lives, there are important commonalities.

The infused virtues are completely gratuitous and not caused by the person's acts. Furthermore, a careful understanding of the various ways God's grace works helps us better understand how infused virtues are given and actualized, both without us and with our involvement and with and without habits possessed by the person. A nuanced understanding of the ways grace operates enables us to see how many of the dynamics involved in acquired virtues—such as natural temperament, accustomization, and properly human acts—are also involved in the attainment and actualization of infused virtues. Finally, in whatever way the infused virtues are received, there remains room for growth in them. Certain topics regarding the growth of, or loss of, infused virtue require further treatment. To these we now turn.

INFUSED VIRTUE AND CONTRARY DISPOSITIONS

A consistent topic in studies of Thomistic virtue is the possibility of contrary dispositions persisting even following the reception of the infused virtues. Perhaps due to common experiences of people living (presumably) graced lives yet struggling with persistent contrary inclinations or due to a text in Aquinas noting this very possibility, studies of the infused virtue in Aquinas's work always recognize and grant the compatibility of the infused virtues with contrary inclinations.[32] The oft-cited text in Aquinas is this: "Sometimes the habits of moral virtue undergo difficulty in activity, by reason of certain [contrary] dispositions remaining [*relictas*] from previous acts. This difficulty does not occur in respect of acquired moral virtue: because the repeated acts by which they are acquired, remove also the contrary dispositions."[33] The reason for this is obvious, given the previous examination of why repeated acts can cause a virtue. Repeated acts enable reason to be "impressed" upon the appetite since the appetite is by nature directed "to many things."[34] This is especially true with the sensitive appetite, which naturally obeys reason but also has "something of its own" such that it does not obey reason slavishly.[35] Therefore it is more possible for the infused virtues to be possessed along with contrary dispositions, given that infused virtue need not entail prior acts.

This is indeed true, and Aquinas affirms it elsewhere as well.[36] It is a necessary consequence of the giftedness of the infused virtues in a manner that is not dependent upon prior acts of the person.[37] Furthermore, there is something deeply attractive to modern sensibilities about this feature of infused virtue: it is utterly egalitarian.[38] Recognition of the importance of formation in order to attain virtue, a recognition as old as Aristotle, raises questions of elitism.[39] After all, if people are bereft of such formation through no fault of their own, the life of virtue may be unavailable to or at the very least far more difficult for them.[40] The fact that infused virtue is not dependent on such prior activity can alleviate the concern that virtue is elitist, even if that same feature can render contrary dispositions more likely. In short, the claim that infused virtue is more compatible with contrary dispositions is here granted.

This recognition ought to be understood carefully, however, at least in comparison with a comparable claim about the acquired virtues. It is too often bluntly assumed that acquired virtues are not accompanied by contrary dispositions, but that infused virtues are. While granting the aforementioned difference, acquired virtues *are* compatible with contrary dispositions and it is *not* the case that infused virtues are always accompanied by contrary dispositions. Furthermore, it is not the case that if infused virtues are unaccompanied by contrary dispositions than it is only due to something other than infused virtues, such as the additional presence of acquired virtues.[41]

Consider first the compatibility of acquired virtue with contrary dispositions. Aquinas states quite clearly that, "Passions inclining to evil are not taken away completely by either acquired or infused virtue. . . . There always remains the struggle between the flesh and the spirit, even with moral virtue. The Apostle speaks of this in Gal 5:17: 'For the flesh lusts against the spirit, and the spirit against the flesh.'"[42] As previously noted, it is striking that Aquinas explicitly states this as true of acquired virtue, given the context of the passage in an article on infused virtue. Given that context of acquired virtue (though certainly applicable there from a Christian perspective on anthropology), such contrary movements will always remain in this life due to the *fomes peccati* that persist as an effect of original sin.[43] Nevertheless, one might note that Aquinas describes the compatibility of passions and acquired virtue and that passions are *movements* of the sensitive appetite (level three) rather than dispositions. Does he ever claim contrary *dispositions* (level two) are compatible with acquired virtue?

He does indeed. Aquinas claims that the very same actions that lead to the attainment of acquired virtue also "diminish" or even "totally remove" a contrary disposition.[44] Even more decisively, Aquinas addresses the ways virtue can differ as to the degree of perfection in different people, and he claims this is due to the differences in the same four causes of virtue that have largely structured this project, namely, natural temperament, custom, properly human acts, and grace.[45] The clear implication is that dispositions obtained from nature or custom continue to exercise causal influence even once a habit is possessed, and these can of course be contrary dispositions. Therefore, granting that there is a greater possibility of having contrary dispositions when possessing the infused virtues, nevertheless the possibility of such contrary dispositions exists with both acquired and infused virtue, and part of growth in the virtuous life is a lessening or even a removal of such dispositions.

This claim could suggest that elimination of contrary dispositions is the main focus of growth in infused virtue. Angela Knobel has recently made a case that this is not so. Lessening or eliminating contrary dispositions, she claims, is not a process of increasing the virtue per se but more akin to removing impediments to the exercise of the virtue.[46] There is good textual support in Aquinas for Knobel's view. Indeed, in one of the places where Aquinas addresses the greater compatibility of infused virtue with contrary dispositions, he claims: "Although habits as such make someone act promptly and with pleasure, this can be impeded by something supervening, as one having the habit of knowledge is sometimes impeded from using it by sleepiness or drunkenness or something of the like. Therefore, one who repents receives by grace charity and all the other virtues but because of the lingering dispositions from his prior sins [*relictas*] he experiences difficulty in the performance of virtues which he has received habitually."[47] Getting some sleep or sobering up do not lead to growth in knowledge. Rather, they remove impediments to the exercise of one's habitual knowledge. Similarly, since a person who possesses infused virtue is stably specified in her acts by her (grace-enabled) rationality, it is granted that the contrary dispositions have not dislodged that stable specification and therefore in a sense can be considered "external" to the habit in the manner of being sleepy or drunk. Knobel is right to claim that the main focus of growth in infused virtue does not equal the removal of contrary dispositions. Unfortunately, Aquinas's most frequent term to describe growth in virtue is *intensio,* and its English cognate (and common translation) "intensity" can misleadingly suggest growth by more emotional desire, that is, greater support by the sensitive appetite. As noted earlier regarding acquired virtue, removal of contrary inclinations—and even sensory formation to foster greater passion in support of good action—are not the primary ways one grows in infused virtue.

However, what happens when contrary sensory dispositions are eliminated or removed or when passions are formed to support virtuous activity? Though Aquinas rightly adduces sleepiness and drunkenness as analogous to how contrary dispositions are "external to" a possessed habit, the analogy fails on the positive side, precisely due to Aquinas's position on the unicity of forms. The rational soul governs contrary sensory dispositions, so a person can possess a virtue even when these are present. But when sensory movements support virtuous activity, to the extent that they do so as participating in reason, they are not simply removed as impediments. Rather, they are formed in support of the virtue. Aquinas most commonly describes such sensory movements as "participating in reason," and when they act their intelligibility (formal cause) is informed by a person's rationality even as the movements remain sensory.[48] Such sensory movements are not external to the habit, and certainly not a parallel habit, but part of the habit possessed.

Granting with Knobel that elimination of contrary dispositions is not the main focus of growth in infused (or acquired) virtue, it is indeed an important facet of growth in any virtue that the sensory facets of habituation-amenable powers be formed in line with rationality. It is true that when contrary sensory dispositions exist, they are like external impediments, as Aquinas says (as long as they neither reflect rationality nor dislodge the stability of rational specification). In fact, I would extend this line of thought beyond Aquinas to claim that some persistent contrary sensory dispositions (e.g., from eating disorders, phobias, addictions) that are entrenched enough not to be able to be removed in a person with infused virtue (though of course not able to dislodge stable rational specification), can persist as such impediments yet be compatible with the virtue, akin to how sleepiness or drunkenness does not dislodge being knowledgeable.[49] However, the participation of sensory movements in reason such that they support virtuous activity is an important facet of, even if not the primary manner of, growth in virtue.

The assumption that growth in virtue is primarily constituted by growth in facility as supplied by movement of the sensitive appetite is particularly strong in virtue ethics scholarship today.[50] This is because there is some truth to it for the reasons already described (i.e., the greater possibility of infused virtue existing alongside contrary dispositions due to its bestowal without the necessity of prior acts). However, when sensory facility is viewed as the primary marker for possession of or growth in virtue, certain problems attend. First, there is a neglect of what *is* the primary locus of growth in virtue. And second, there is a suspicion that "the infused virtues cannot really be considered virtues at all."[51] For instance, one recent Thomistic moralist claims that the "infused virtues, without the facility or ability that comes with acquired virtues, are habits only in an analogous sense. For they lack the ease or facility of operation that characterize a habit in the strict sense."[52] The assumption that sensory facility is the primary marker for possession of virtue, where Aquinas contrasts acquired and infused virtue on facility, seems to support the view that infused virtues are not full virtues: "Acquired virtue prevails in this, that the struggle is felt less, and this is due to its cause, since it is by frequent acts that a man is accustomed to virtue, and a man becomes unaccustomed to obey such passions when he has learned to resist them and that is why he feels their troubling less. But infused virtue prevails in this, that while such passions are felt they in no way dominate."[53] If sensory facility is the marker for increased virtue, the claim that a person with infused virtue can continue to experience contrary passions but that they do not dominate offers little consolation.

Aquinas himself seems to recognize this view of virtue, where lack of contrary disposition is the characteristic feature. He indicates that sensory connaturalization is not unimportant when he describes what infused virtue offers with regard to sensory movements, even if at the outset contrary sensory dispositions exist: "Because from the outset infused virtue does not always take away the feeling of the passions like acquired virtue, they are not from the outset performed with pleasure, but this is not out of keeping with what is meant by virtue, because sometimes it suffices for virtue that we act without sadness, and it is not required that we act with pleasure or fail to feel annoyance."[54] This reply to the objection responds to concerns about contrary sensory dispositions by saying, "You are still virtuous even if annoyed at acting virtuously, or doing it without pleasure, so long as you are not sad doing so!" Small consolation indeed.

However, just because Aquinas addresses how one with infused virtues might "feel" while acting, this does not mean that sensory facility is the essence of a virtue. As should be most clear by now, a virtue offers stable rational specification of a habituation-amenable power toward good action that makes its possessor good. Of course, if all works well, a good action will entail pleasant sensory movements. This is why acting with pleasure is commonly adduced as a marker for possessing a virtue. That said, such pleasure is not essential.[55]

The virtue must incline a person to activity that is good or constitutive of full flourishing. It must be stable, and specified rationally, thus attentive to various ends and indeed life as a whole. There must be some completion or rest attained by the activity, since the end toward which the virtue directs the person has become second nature. And this is why virtuous activity is commonly pleasant in a sensory way. Yet such pleasure can be impeded without dislodging the virtue if the essential features (stable specification by the *causa immobilis* of a person's rationality) remain. There must be good reason for a lack of such pleasure. For instance, sadness in acting virtuously could signal a lack of stable rational specification toward such activity, which would indeed indicate a lack of virtue. But circumstances in life can make virtuous activities unpleasant.[56] Or features of the self (even at level two) could render virtuous activity unpleasant, such as sensory dispositions from natural temperament or prior acts. If this latter occurs, then so long as such dispositions are on the way toward corruption to the extent that such lessening or even removal is possible through participation in reason, then lack of pleasure in acting virtuously need not disqualify a person from possession of virtue.[57] We turn now to understand better what is essentially supplied by infused virtue, and therefore the primary focus of growth in infused virtue.

GROWTH IN INFUSED VIRTUE: WITHIN, ACROSS, AND IN RELATION TO THE WHOLE

One theme of this book is the important differences and commonalities between acquired and infused virtue. For instance, infused virtues are caused not by a person's own actions but rather by God's grace. Yet, despite this enormously important difference, many dynamics of attaining infused virtue or becoming active in the living of infused virtue mimic those of acquired virtue. We find something similar here with regard to growth in infused virtue.

One of Aquinas's more consistent claims regarding virtue is that virtues are increased, or grow, in the same manner that they are attained.[58] Therefore, the first thing to be said about growth in infused virtue is that it is not caused by a person's actions, but it is a gift from God's grace. "Just as acquired virtues are increased by the acts which cause them, so infused virtues are increased by the action of God by whom they are caused."[59] But, as noted previously, affirming that such virtue is given by the grace of God does not necessarily mean that there is no role for human action in attainment or, for that matter, in growth. Indeed, Aquinas claims that "our acts can merit an increase of charity, insofar as they presuppose charity which is the principle of meriting. But no one can merit charity at the outset, because without charity there can be no merit."[60] Actions can lead to an increase in charity, albeit only because they are already (cooperatively and habitually) graced acts of charity. In fact, given the "mechanics" of how habits operate at the natural level, it is not at all surprising that human activity is involved in the growth of infused virtue even if, of course, that growth is ultimately a gift from God.

In terms of the ways Aquinas describes growth in virtue, the same terminology is used for both acquired and infused virtues.[61] These terms mainly counter errors in thinking that the virtues grow in actual size, or even that they grow primarily by extension, to a greater number of objects.[62] Aquinas claims that virtue, which again is an accidental quality and not a substantial form, grows by greater participation, or greater rootedness, of the subject in the virtue.[63] Common terms Aquinas uses for this growth is that virtue becomes more "fervent" or "vehement."[64] These terms in English have an emotional connotation, which likely contributes to the assumption that growth in infused virtue happens mainly through greater sensory facility. Aquinas appears to support this when he says that charity increases when something is "loved more."[65] But this is a misread of these terms. Aquinas equates "vehemently" to a greater participation by the subject and says that the meaning of both phrases is to be more reduced to act, or acting more perfectly. Since action is made perfect by attaining its end, this is a claim not about emotional intensity (though that may be included) but about most fittingly attaining the person's end.

This leads to the most common and important term Aquinas uses for growth in virtue, namely, *intensio*. As noted earlier, despite the obvious English cognate "intensity," the Latin term *intensio* is best understood not as referencing some sort of emotional intensity. Rather, Aquinas equates it with "growth" (*augeri*) and greater participation in a virtue.[66] The term has a sense of tautness, stretching, extending, or aiming. A more helpful translation could be "extension."[67] Given the account offered here of habit as stable specification, we might think of this extension in two ways. First, a virtue can become more stable, and extend further "back into" the person (or her powers). This can occur through elimination of contrary dispositions, since greater impression of any appetitive powers by rational specification grants further stability. Second, there can be growth in specification such that the level two virtue's object better extends "outward toward" the end of the level one natural power. The particular principle or paradigmatic action supplied by the virtue can be more attuned to various modes, circumstances, and so forth, thus enabling the person's powers to better achieve her ends in level three activity. Aquinas at one point claims that a virtue provides a person a "right estimation of an end."[68] Therefore *intensio*, or extension, of a virtue occurs when the appetitive inclination supplied by the habit's particular principle is better attuned to the end of a person's habituation-amenable powers. In that sense *intensio* is quite similar to what happens in growth of acquired virtue. However, infused virtue not only increases as caused by God's grace but its better attunement is according to the measure of the Divine rule, in a way that is formally different from the attunement that occurs with acquired virtue.[69]

It may help to provide a concrete example of growth in an infused virtue. Consider a believer who grows in her prayer life. This person is in the regular practice of spending time each day reading from the lectionary, especially the day's gospel. Through this practice she learns more about God, is encouraged and sustained in her relationship with God, is challenged to repent, and is more aware of God's mercy and forgiveness. Through this virtue of prayerfulness God nourishes her relationship with Him and guides her in living her life accordingly.[70]

God also stirs in her a desire for greater intimacy and friendship with Him. Perhaps through the suggestion of a friend or prior awareness of Ignatian prayer, she begins to practice meditative prayer on the gospels (and scripture more broadly), with regular conversation with a spiritual director. As she grows into this practice she finds herself better attuned to the ends of her prior prayerfulness. Rather than attaining only basic knowledge about God and morality, her meditative prayer with the scriptures fosters greater intimacy and friendship with God. She is enabled to grasp more fully who God is and see and desire more fully how her friendship with God relates to various areas of her life. Ends attained by her earlier prayer life are extended as she develops appetitive inclinations more attuned to them. She also experiences a greater stability in her prayerfulness—not only in less hesitance (even sensory resistance) to praying (e.g., "I don't feel like it") given the greater fruitfulness of her prayer but also as an extension of stability turning back into her as she experiences facility in being more inclined to do a composition of place and enter into a scripture passage so as to encounter the Word there. Her facility may indeed contain sensory facets, but the "rest" she attains in her prayer is not simply sensory or emotional. It should be noted that not only her possession of this virtue but also its growth is clearly a gift possible only through God's grace. The gift may entail her (cooperative) activity, and indeed may mimic acquired virtue in repeated activity and even growth in fits and starts, but none of this means the growth in her prayerfulness is not a gift of God's grace.

It is worth pausing to ask whether the growth depicted here is primarily growth in skill and technique rather than virtue. This example does indeed entail technical aspects, just as growth in parenting can be aided by reading books or growth in temperance can be aided by certain diets. Yet growth in virtue is neither reduced to nor necessarily entails technical growth. What makes this woman more prayerful is a more stable specification of her ability to render God His due, and of her capacity for friendship with Him. Although she had already possessed an appetitive inclination toward activity attaining God as object (in charity) and end, that particular principle becomes more stable and more attuned in its specificity toward that end. Obviously the practice of Ignatian prayer is not the only way to become more prayerful; countless other ways are possible.[71] Furthermore, the emphasis here has been on growth "within" a virtue. Unsurprisingly, given the relationship between growth within virtue and growth across virtues, it is easy to imagine this specific growth being related to other areas of growth. For instance, considerations of career decisions could be brought as material to prayer and informed by prayer (just as anxieties about work—or excessive ambition, distrust, rancor, etc.—can impede prayer). A person's activities regarding sensual pleasures can be brought to prayer and nourished by it (or impede the ability to be moved by God in prayer, or even be deflected from prayer). In sum, growth in virtue is not merely a technical exercise. Rather, it makes its possessor even more good by better attaining the end of virtue. Such growth happens not only within virtue but also across virtues. Indeed, this points to growth in coherence of life as a whole, a topic to which we now turn.

Though there is important commonality between growth in acquired and growth in infused virtue in Aquinas's thought, there are certain topics addressed by Aquinas as necessary for treatment of growth in charity and the concomitant other infused virtues. It is already clear that he affirms the possibility of further growth after the attainment of virtue. Yet this claim with regard to charity presents additional questions in the context of the graced life of discipleship.[72] One example of this is when he delineates where there is "room for growth" in charity. The fact that we are commanded to love God with our whole hearts (Deut. 6:5), to do all for God's glory (1 Cor. 10:31), and to "be perfect" (Mt. 5:48; cf. 19:21), raises the question of whether perfect charity is possible and what sort of perfection is required.[73]

In an often overlooked but spiritually enriching mini-treatise on perfection in charity, Aquinas examines many ways charity may be called perfect.[74] Some forms of perfection are possible only for God or for people in the next life; others are possible in this life but not required for all. These forms are not addressed here. Yet there is one form of perfection for the person with charity which is not only possible in this life but also required, namely, "removing any inclination contrary to charity," by which inclination Aquinas means "turning one's self away from God by mortal sin."[75] Aquinas grants that we are unable to avoid all venial sin in this life: "We are not able to love God perfectly in this life so that we are always actually directed toward him." Yet, he continues, it is possible for one to be "never directed to what is contrary to God."[76] Granting this obligation to avoid mortal sin, Aquinas also indicates here an arena for ongoing growth in charity, namely, being "actually" directed to God rather than sinning venially. Aquinas's reference to being "actually" ordered to God points us toward what he calls "habitual" (as distinct from actual) ordering, which is both an arena for growth in charity and an occasion to probe the relationship between habits (level two) and activities (level three) in a manner that may be relevant for growth in acquired virtue as well.

A full review of Aquinas's writings on habitual ordering is beyond the scope of this book.[77] For the purposes of examining growth in virtue, what is most interesting about habitual ordering is its contribution to his account of the relationship between a habit and an activity. Normally a habit provides a particular principle that contributes to activity in that its stability and specification enable one to choose a particular act (level three) with more consistency and promptness. Of course, even when possessing such a habit, a person need not act in accord with that habit. Habitual ordering is Aquinas's explanation for how a habit causally influences activity even when activity is not in accordance with the habit.[78]

In the dozen or so times Aquinas addresses habitual ordering, nearly all address venial sin.[79] Venial sins are those chosen acts that are contrary to charity yet do not dislodge the virtue of charity. Thus venial sin provides the perfect occasion to address how a person can act with a habit but not out of it, and how the possession of a habit causally influences an act even when the act is not out of the habit.[80] After all, Aquinas does not simply say a person who sins venially does not lose charity, though that is true. He claims that venial sins are actively ordered to God by the person. In the *Commentary on Colossians* we read that the one sinning venially "refers all things to God, not actually but habitually."[81] In other passages the referral of the venial sin itself is more explicit: "He that sins venially cleaves to temporal good, not as enjoying it, because he does not fix his end in it, but as using it, *by referring it to God,* not actually but habitually."[82] How can Aquinas claim a venial sin is referred to God when what makes it sinful is its being *not* ordered to God?

Aquinas grants that the venial sin is not "actually" ordered to God, by which he means it is not "in reality" ordered to God.[83] Yet he claims that it is indeed "habitually" ordered to God, emphasizing the relationship between the finality of the particular principle one habitually possesses (level two) and one's activity, even as in reality the act does not accord with the habit's finality. What is that relationship? It cannot be simply that the person possesses the habit while doing the act, true though that may be. Such a meaning of habitual ordering would refer solely to the person performing the act and not to the ordering of the act itself.[84] Aquinas is clear that the venial sinner habitually orders the *act* toward God. What this must mean is that the person does the act for the sake of God ("referring it to God"), even though in actuality it is not referred to God. What does this mean?

One way to habitually refer something to God is indicated by Aquinas's active description of this referral. It is reminiscent of the previous treatment of the last end. A person does all she does for the sake of her last end. We see here how this can be true even when the act is not actually ordered toward the last end. It is habitually so ordered when the person actively orders it, or "narrates" it, toward her last end. Think of how commonly this occurs in sinful acts. We tell ourselves (explicitly or implicitly) that this act in pursuit of pleasure fits in with our various virtuous ends, even when it does not. We choose an act in a relationship or at work that we tell ourselves advances the goals at hand when in fact it strains them. In these cases the habit "does work," if you will, in how we narrate the act, prompting us to narrate the act as toward the end of the habit even when it doesn't. Additionally, presumably the habit does work in "parametering" chosen activity so as to avoid actions that dislodge the end we claim to pursue. This second aspect is a necessary aspect of habitual ordering, since narration of the act toward God cannot alone constitute habitual ordering. After all, people self-deceptively rationalize not just venial but even mortal sins, and Aquinas is quite clear that mortal sins are not habitually ordered to God. They dislodge the habit and thus are not habitually ordered. This stark reality is both a cautionary note about the power of human self-deception and a reminder that particular principles (level two) causally impact but do not determine chosen activity (level three).

Aquinas here offers an account of the relationship between habit and practical reasoning with attention to occasions when activity does not accord with (but does not dislodge) the habit possessed. More relevant for our purposes, it offers an account of "room for growth" in charity. If one of the acts of charity is to order all activities toward God as supernatural happiness, in accord with a person's overall view of things or last end, then Aquinas's treatment of habitual ordering offers another way that a person can grow in charity, namely, when habitually but not actively ordering her activity to God.[85] The venial sinner possesses charity but has room for growth (as we all do in this life), and one arena for such growth is changing activity only habitually ordered toward God into activity actually so ordered.

Before turning to loss of virtue, another aspect of habitual ordering should be noted. Though nearly all Aquinas's texts on habitual ordering concern venial sin, one does not, and it is found in his treatment of the various ways charity can be perfected in this life. When he claims that virtually ordering all to God falls under the precept but habitually ordering all to God does not, he is addressing a different matter (about what falls under the precept to charity "do everything for the glory of God," 1 Cor. 10:31). He claims in passing that one habitually refers something to God when doing nothing or intending nothing. There are challenging questions raised by this text, questions I take up elsewhere.[86] For our purposes it suffices to note that the reference to not intending anything suggests another arena where there is "room for growth." A person retains her habit while doing nothing, but also while acting without intending anything, presumably in the sense of non-properly human activity. In the latter case especially, the habit plays the important role of habitual ordering, namely, parametering the non-properly human action so that habit is not lost. Habitual ordering thus includes both actively yet venially sinfully ordering activity to God and acting when "not intending anything" (at least in a properly human way), perhaps instead acting out of nature or custom. Such realms of activity, proceeding from, to use M. F. Burnyeat's words, "pockets of thought in us which can remain relatively unaffected by our overall view of things," constitute room for growth for the person with charity.[87]

Aquinas's thought on habitual ordering provides (a currently untapped) resource on where there is room for growth in charity and infused virtue, and how possession of the habit charity can influence a person's activity even when she is not acting in accord with that habit. Is there something in Aquinas's thought on habitual ordering that is applicable to acquired virtue as well? I suspect there is. Any treatment of commonality between infused and acquired virtue should equally emphasize the crucial differences. So it must be noted at the outset that, unlike acquired virtue, charity is granted solely as a gift from God and can be lost by mortal sin and even possibly without any prior contrary acts. Yet despite these important differences, Aquinas's account of how a person with charity habitually orders her actions seems applicable to a person with acquired virtue. Not only can a person with acquired virtue act with but not out of that virtue, there is also clearly "room for growth" in the life of acquired virtue, as when she brings those "pockets of thought" into conformity with her overall view of things, in this case oriented toward natural human flourishing. Recall Elijah Millgram's description of growth in the life of (surely acquired) virtue in just this sort of way:

> At one extreme, someone in whom action is triggered by whatever impulse happens to come over him, without any regard to other concerns or interests he may have, is a mere collection of reflexes rather than a cohesive acting self. At the other, the thoughtful deliberator whose every decision is appropriately informed by the full range of considerations available to him is the *phronimos* . . . [an] ideal of practical intelligence, unified agency, and virtue. Between the extremes of infancy and wisdom lies the modicum of coherence that we demand of responsible adults.[88]

If at some point people cross the line to a coherence sufficient for connected virtue, there surely remains room for growth toward the *phronimos,* "whose every decision is appropriately informed by the full range of considerations available to him." Though more detailed analysis of application of habitual ordering to acquired virtue cannot be offered here, these quotes from Burnyeat and Millgram suggest that Aquinas's notion of habitual ordering may offer a resource for explaining the tight connection between a person's habits and activities, even where there is room for growth due to the presence of activity not proceeding out of habit.[89]

We began exploration of *intensio* or extension "within" a virtue and shifted to how such attunement of the stable rational specification supplied by the habit occurs not only within but also across virtues, as connected by charity. We now culminate with (related) attention to a person's life as a whole, the last end, with room for increasing coherence of activities. This attention to "the whole," to "one's overall view of things," seems like growth in the whole life of virtue rather than simply any one virtue. Possession of virtue in a properly human (and, of course, superhuman) sense is indeed intrinsically related to connectivity of virtue and the last end. In the graced context of infused virtue, increasing coherence of one's life as a whole is a facet of growth in charity, given its role as connecting the virtues and as form of the virtues. In light of the comments of Burnyeat and Millgram, presumably in the case of acquired virtue there is a role for justice and prudence comparable to the role played by charity in the case of infused virtue (never without living faith and infused prudence). Before turning to the less edifying topic of loss of virtue, we can note Steven Jensen's more inspiring depiction of the ongoing need for growth in the life of infused virtue:

> If everyone in a state of grace did indeed order all of his actions virtually toward the divine good, then there might be little room for spiritual growth. As it is, not everyone in a state of grace does order all of

> his actions virtually to the divine good. Those in a state of grace are themselves ordered habitually to the divine good, but not all of their actions have a virtual order to this good. As such, they often lead disjointed lives; they often pursue a multiplicity of goods, independent of the divine good. They are ready to curb these pursuits when the goods exclude the divine good (else they would commit a mortal sin), but as long as these independent goods do not eliminate the divine good, they are often pleased to pursue them. Eliminating these independent goods, ultimately seeking to subordinate everything virtually to the divine good, is the work of the spiritual life.[90]

Amen.

LOSING INFUSED VIRTUE

Completing this chapter's paralleling discussion with chapter 5, we conclude this discussion on growth in infused virtue with an examination of the loss of infused virtue. According to Aquinas there are some striking differences between the loss of acquired and the loss of infused virtue, differences that prompt him to ask questions that make little sense in the context of acquired virtue. For instance, he asks whether charity can be lost, and answers by noting several reasons why it cannot be lost, which seems unintelligible in the case of acquired virtue. He also asks whether or not charity can be lost through one act, the answer to which would clearly be no concerning acquired virtue. Questions such as these reveal how intent Aquinas is to describe the important differences between acquired and infused virtue. This analysis will identify these differences but not neglect the important commonalities and conclude with a look at what dispositions or habits remain after the loss of infused virtue, a topic where we see even more commonality with the acquired virtues.

In his two most important treatments of this topic, Aquinas asks whether charity can be lost.[91] This is a rather stunning question, since it seems obvious that a habit, as second nature (or, in this case, supernature), is not possessed necessarily. The reader's puzzlement is only supported when in these two treatments Aquinas begins his response by explaining the varying ways in which we *cannot* say that charity can be lost. What becomes quickly evident is that Aquinas's main concern is the efficacy of God's agency. After all, if, as repeatedly emphasized, the infused virtues are caused not by human action but by God's grace, then it seems the loss of the infused virtues is also caused by God or, if it were caused by us, it would signify an inefficacy in God's agency. Thus Aquinas emphasizes that "the movement of the Holy Spirit is always efficacious according to its own intention."[92] Nonetheless, he goes on to say, "if a gift can be taken away by violence, then it seems that the giver . . . is defeated. But if he to whom the gift is given voluntarily rejects it, it does not seem that this causes the donor, who ought not to force men to virtue, to be defeated."[93] Such comments indicate that a person's refusal of the initial gift of charity does not defeat God's will. What about the loss of charity once possessed?

Aquinas claims that charity cannot be lost by charity itself, or even by a person's will as informed by charity. These claims emphasize not only that the refusal of charity is not a failure on God's part, but also that once charity is received, the habit itself and even a person's will as qualified by it are not defective. However, "Charity is not always to be in operation, otherwise when one sleeps, he would not have charity."[94] As already mentioned, even though a person may possess charity, she need not always act out of charity.[95] Furthermore, though in the next life no one in the presence of God will be able *not* to love Him, in this life the end of perfect happiness to which charity directs us is not evident to us in His full essence. Therefore, "although the cause of charity is incorruptible, the influence of this cause is impeded by sin which separates us from God."[96] Since the cause of infused virtue is God's grace, Aquinas must devote more attention to how it can be lost. In the end it can be lost due to the person's action, not God's, and for reasons in accord with Divine Providence.

Granting the important difference as to the cause of infused virtue, and the impossibility of acting contrary to charity in the next life, there are important similarities between failing to act out of charity and failing to act out of an acquired virtue in this life that should not be missed. Aquinas offers an observation in the context of loss of charity that is as true of the acquired virtues as it is of charity. "The habit of virtue inclines one to act rightly according as through it one has the right estimation of the end."[97] Therefore, properly speaking, one never acts contrary to any virtue when acting "out of" that virtue.[98] However, he continues, with a claim as true of acquired virtue as of charity, "one who has the habit of virtue sometimes acts contrary to the inclination of his proper habit; for a thing seems to him to be otherwise, according to some other mode, such as through passion or anything that entices him from the correct estimation."[99] Something may "seem otherwise," or as not contrary to one's (natural or supernatural) good, due to passion or due to some other "internal" cause of sin such as ignorance or malice.[100] But it is precisely due to the distinction between habit/disposition (level two) and activity (level three) that it is indeed possible to act contrary to either the acquired or infused virtues in this life. Yet this leads to another significant difference between infused and acquired virtue.

In all of his mature treatments of loss of charity, Aquinas asks whether or not it is possible to lose charity through one act of mortal sin. He affirms it is indeed possible.[101] In one sense this is not at all shocking, granting an accurate understanding of mortal sin. Recall that charity directs a person not to one end among many but to the last end of God as perfect happiness. Mortal sin is not simply the inordinate pursuit of a lower good but rather the pursuit of some temporal good in a manner more than God, thus displacing God as last end.[102] Understood as such it is clear why mortal sin by definition results in the loss of charity. It also makes clear why mortal sin results in the loss of all infused virtues. All infused virtues, as informed by charity, concern particular activities done for the further sake of love of God as last end. In displacing love of God above all things, mortal sin precludes the possibility of any infused virtue. This does not mean that the loss of charity immediately results in the possession of contrary vices. Rather, as Aquinas claims, "it is not necessary to say that a man loses the habit of one virtue only when the habit of the contrary vice is generated in him."[103] What a person does possess after the loss of charity is addressed later, but a proper understanding of mortal sin makes it obvious that it necessitates the loss of charity.

Yet what is rather striking in the difference between loss of charity and loss of acquired virtue is that charity is lost through one act of mortal sin. Once again we see a ramification of the fact that God, rather than a person's acts, causes infused virtue.[104] After all, the graced life toward supernatural happiness requires not only the initial gift of habitual grace but ongoing grace to support that habit and its activity. As Aquinas says, "God does not cause charity in our soul so that He is the cause only of its becoming and not of its preservation; as the builder is the cause of a house only in its becoming, and when he is taken away, the house still remains. God, however, is the cause of charity and of grace in the soul both as regards their becoming and their preservation."[105] Reminiscent of his discussion of the gifts of the Holy Spirit, Aquinas also describes this dynamic using the analogy of the removal of the source of light, resulting in darkness for that which had been illuminated: "If any intervening obstacle prevents the direct rays of the sun, the light in the air fails. Likewise, when mortal sin enters, which obstructs the soul's direct sight of God—and through this something else is preferred to God—the flow of charity is stopped, and charity is then lacking in man, as is said (Is. 59:2), 'Your iniquities have divided between you and your God.'"[106] The person is no longer able to act out of, nor even continue to possess, her infused virtue, both of which were dependent on God's habitual and actual grace. This is not some arbitrary change in the person, but rather the cessation of the person's stable specification toward God as last end because "something else is preferred to God."[107] Presumably that loss could vary in terms of duration or degree, but nevertheless at some point one crosses the line to lose infused virtue.

Before turning to examine the *relictae* after the loss of infused virtue, it is worth noting that although infused virtue is lost through one mortal sin, it is possible that the mortal sin was preceded by acts leading toward that loss. A person can (even repeatedly) sin venially, thus disposing herself to mortal sin.[108] As with the loss of acquired virtue, loss of infused virtue always entails a moment when the person crosses the line. When that loss is preceded by acts of venial sin disposing toward it, there is even more similarity between the loss of acquired virtue and the loss of infused virtue.

The possibility of losing infused virtue raises the question of what qualifies the person's powers after the loss of infused virtue. We will find that what occurs is strikingly similar to what happens in the loss of acquired virtue, though with infused virtue there are added considerations. Recall that when acquired virtue is lost, the two obvious possibilities for level two dispositions or habits in the person are the acquisition of vices contrary to the lost virtues, or a lack of stable rational specification such that the person possesses only dispositions. In line with Aquinas's claim that "it is not necessary to say that a man loses the habit of one virtue only when the habit of the contrary vice is generated in him," such an immediate formation of contrary vice at the loss of acquired virtue is unlikely.[109] It would require not only loss of the acquired virtue but thoroughgoing repudiation of right practical reasoning and stable specification by contrary practical reasoning. Even if there were immediate contrary practical reasoning, at the very least there would be "lag time" in which the appetitive powers would need to be impressed by contrary practical reasoning. Thus it is more likely that the person who loses acquired virtue would be disposed, not habituated. Any persistent activity that is observably similar to activity of the lost habit would be caused by residual sensory dispositions, or "customs," reflective of what the person had "gotten used to" while possessing the acquired virtues.

The same thing happens when one loses infused virtue. The immediate formation of contrary vice is unlikely since, even after a mortal sin, such a formation would require sudden stable rational specification in a manner opposed to charity and to natural human flourishing. Thus the person would be merely disposed, and any persistent level three activity after the loss of virtue would be caused by level two *relictae,* residual sensory dispositions or customs, reflective of what the person had gotten used to while possessing the infused virtues.[110] Yet there are two additional considerations related to infused virtue.

First, since presumably the residual dispositions after the loss of infused virtue are toward observably good action, one could claim that the person now possesses acquired rather than infused virtue (a possibility obviously not available in the loss of acquired virtue). In fact, this position is offered in support of the coexistence of acquired and infused virtues (see appendix).[111] After all, assuming a persistent good action is due to acquired virtue, it seems unbecoming that a person who sins mortally would gain even acquired virtue by that act, and thus it seems likely the acquired virtues were there all along, "underneath" or "coexisting" with the infused virtues. However, whether the acquired virtues already coexisted with infused virtues or simply originated at the loss of infused virtue, the positing of acquired virtue as a solution to the problem of persistent (observably) good action in the one who loses infused virtue is untenable.

Once again the reason for this position is seen through a proper understanding of habit. Virtues are stable specifications of a person's powers toward activity constitutive of happiness, where the stable specification is supplied by the *causa immobilis* of the person's rationality. The intelligibility (or formal object) of such activities is according to a rule or measure, which in the case of infused virtues is the divine measure, dependent upon grace as oriented toward supernatural happiness. Therefore the activities performed out of infused virtue acquire their intelligibility in relation to that supernatural end. Even when sensory accustomization occurs as part of infused virtue, which indeed it can and should despite the possibility of contrary dispositions, even that sensory accustomization is intelligible in light of supernatural happiness. It is sensory, yet it is also annexed to a person's rational specification, and thus its intelligibility, or meaning, is defined through the perspective of the acting person, who does all she does for the sake of supernatural happiness. In more obviously supernatural instances she may get used to rising earlier to pray and meditate or come to savor the smells and sounds of liturgy. Or, in not necessarily supernatural instances, she may be accustomed to seeing the needs of the vulnerable and responding or desiring ordinate amounts of food or drink. Though in these examples there exists sensory accustoming, and even although in the latter case they are possible as part of acquired virtue, in all these cases they had developed along with infused virtue and participated in reason measured by the divine rule. What developed was not just a savoring of the smell of candles or the dim light of morning liturgy but these as constituting occasions of worship. Though moderate consumption and serving the vulnerable are possible for a person possessing acquired virtue, in *this person* they developed as part of offering herself in service to God and serving others as encounters with Christ, seeing the other as *imago Dei*. Therefore, if she were to lose infused virtue, and thus "prefer something else" to God, residual sensory dispositions would lose their prior intelligibility as having participated in reason (in this case reason measured by the divine rule from the perspective of this acting person). These dispositions may not immediately (or possibly ever) be stably inclined to an alternate intelligibility or rule, but they also no longer retain their former intelligibility because, with the loss of infused virtue, it is no longer present, at least in its stable specification.

All this is to say that any dispositions to persistent (observably good) action after the loss of infused virtue are best understood as sensory *relictae* from prior accustomization as part of infused virtue whose rational intelligibility is now lost. To claim that such observably good action evinces possession of acquired virtue is to neglect its origin as annexed to infused virtue with that corresponding intelligibility. The fact that a desire to arise early to pray or to savor the smells of a church are no longer intelligible when not oriented toward God as last end is more obvious. But even a desire for moderate consumption or service to the vulnerable does not mean the same thing absent orientation to God as last end.

This is why Knobel makes the striking argument that the acquired virtues can form in a person sensory dispositions that function in a manner akin to "contrary dispositions" in the context of infused virtue.[112] She is exactly right. Switching the direction to the reception of (rather than the loss of) infused virtue, the moderate or service-oriented convert may retain sensory dispositions toward these activities, but in the context of friendship with God and oriented toward supernatural happiness, these dispositions, to the extent that they participate in reason, need to be reimpressed by reason and changed in their intelligibility. "Contrary" dispositions is not the best term to describe these *relictae*, since in many cases the sensory dispositions will incline one toward acts that are more observably continuous with and closer in their intelligibility or meaning to the intelligibility of the acts of newly bestowed infused virtues. The convert's new graced virtues not only share the same "matter" as her previous acquired virtues but they do share a formality that is closer to her new virtues than, say, that of a person who had been vicious. That said, even for this convert, since the acts of infused virtue differ in formal object from those of acquired virtue, the immediate paradigmatic acts (not just the further ends) to which the infused virtues incline a person differ.[113] Any prior sensory dispositions, to the extent that they participated in reason as governed by the measure of human reason, now are impressed with human reason as healed and elevated by God's grace in accordance with the divine measure.

In the loss of infused virtue, the *relictae* would need to be reimpressed (or requalified) by a person's rationality as measured by the rule of human reason toward natural flourishing if they were to become acquired virtues. Perhaps in time they will be. But the point here is that residual formation from a person's life of infused virtue, once that infused virtue is lost, is not accurately described as acquired virtue.

Yet before moving on to a second added consideration of the loss of infused virtue, it should be noted that there is understandably a reason people assume that what persists after the loss of infused virtue is acquired virtue. This is due to the continuity between natural and supernatural flourishing. Indeed, supernatural happiness is not unnatural, but supernatural. Supernatural happiness fulfills natural flourishing, and exceeds it. How could fasting, sexual abstinence, or sacrifice (even of one's life) ever be constitutive of natural flourishing? Besides the fact that there are natural analogues to each of these (e.g., preparing for medical procedures; an "I can wait; I'm worth it" account of sexual abstinence; military service), supernatural flourishing can further illuminate and surpass natural flourishing but never defy it.[114] While it is completely true, as Aquinas claims, that the activities of the infused virtues differ from the acquired virtues in intelligibility in formal object, it is also completely true, as Knobel as has recently argued and people have too long failed to acknowledge, that there is a sense in which formation in acquired virtue actually supplies "contrary dispositions" to an ensuing life of infused virtue.[115] That said, due to the continuity between nature and grace, requalification of sensory dispositions that occurs in a convert is clearly more drastic for a convert from a life of vice than a convert from a life of acquired virtue. Indeed, such continuity is also the reason why it is unlikely that the person who loses infused virtue would be immediately stably rationally specified (even if lagging in the impressing of the appetite) by right practical reasoning toward natural human flourishing. Mortal sins, whereby one loses infused virtue (e.g., corruption, adultery, etc.), generally oppose natural flourishing. If mortal sin did not oppose natural flourishing, it is conceivable that there would be a sort of "un-version" (as opposed to *con*version) whereby a person rationally renounces the divine good in favor of natural flourishing. Note that even were this to occur, it would still require requalification of the appetitive powers accordingly and thus repeated acts. It seems more likely, certainly initially, that the person who relinquishes God as highest good, perhaps due to experience of inexplicable suffering, is more lost, rather than coherently ordered toward natural flourishing.[116] In conclusion, persistent observably good acts following the loss of infused virtue are not accurately explained by the possession of acquired virtue.

Though we have noted commonalities between the loss of acquired virtue and the loss of infused virtue, one consideration in the loss of infused virtue is the possibility of explaining ensuing good action by possession of acquired virtue, a possibility rejected here. A second issue is how to describe, after the loss of infused virtue, an activity characteristic of theological virtue in that it is observably similar to that of infused theological virtue but is not able to be such due to the loss of charity. Thus far the answer posited here is dispositions by accustomization. In the case of lost infused cardinal virtues, this is readily imaginable, since even if any observably good actions are not from acquired virtues, there can be dispositions to such activity akin to those supplied by nature and custom to chastity, meekness, and so on. But what about faith and hope, theological virtues with no analogues supplied by nature and toward (merely) natural human flourishing? Can these exist without charity and, if they can, what are they?

Aquinas claims that faith and hope can indeed exist without charity, though since he devotes most attention to faith, it will be the focus here as well.[117] This more extended attention to faith, due in part to Scriptural references (e.g., 1 Cor. 13:2; James 2:19–26), labels faith without charity as "unformed," lifeless," or "dead." The latter term is used here due to its prominence, even though "unformed" is most technically accurate, given charity's role as form of the virtues. Faith is a virtue of the speculative intellect. Yet faith is unlike other speculative intellect virtues. Others can be possessed without making their possessor good, since their activities can be specified without the involvement of the will. Faith is a virtue of assenting to true things about God and God's relationship to creation. Its act, belief, is essentially an act of the intellect.[118] But since the intellect is not moved to assent simply by what is known (since things known by faith are not able to be seen), the intellect is prompted by the will to its act of assent. In the case of living faith, it is the will qualified by charity that prompts the intellect, thus informing its act of assent toward God. Therefore, since living faith requires a good (charity-informed) will, faith is a virtue in the fullest sense since it makes its possessor good.

Though faith can exist without charity, is this dead faith a virtue? Consistently throughout his corpus Aquinas claims it is not.[119] Dead faith is still rightly called faith because it entails persistent (observably accurate) accurate assent of the intellect to truths about God. However, that assent does not come about in the way it should. Aquinas consistently likens dead faith to moral virtue without prudence. A person possessing the moral virtues without prudence (say, from nature or custom) can perform acts observably similar to acts of the moral virtues. But those acts are lacking the specification supplied by practical reasoning. Though the moral virtues qualify appetites, they do so as participating in reason. Lacking that source of stable specification, they are not virtues in the proper sense. Something similar happens in dead faith, though in the opposite direction. With dead faith the speculative intellect is specified accurately. Yet that assent is not prompted by the will as informed by charity. All virtues "in the fullest sense" rely on both appetite and apprehension in the rational specification of their object.[120] Just as so-called moral virtues gained through nature or custom are not virtues in the proper sense, neither is dead faith, despite the accuracy of assent.

My argument is that dead faith is akin to a disposition rather than a habit.[121] At times Aquinas describes dead faith as a disposition, distinguishing from living faith as a habit.[122] This is corroborated by his consistent comparison of dead faith to moral virtues without prudence, the latter of which he understands as dispositions. In fact, he makes claims about dead faith that harken back to his foundational treatment of the disposition/habit distinction.[123] He claims that dead faith may be compared to living faith as imperfect is to perfect.[124] He also analogizes the change of dead faith to living faith as a boy becoming a man.[125] All of these textual references suggest that dead faith is best understood as a disposition not a habit.

Though this position is affirmed here, admittedly it is not always clear in Aquinas's work, in part due to complexity of a disposition to activity of a theological virtue and in part due to some lack of clarity in Aquinas's earlier work on infused virtue. What problems are there for the interpretation offered here that dead faith is best understood as a disposition? The first is that throughout his works Aquinas repeatedly describes dead faith as a habit.[126] This is not a significant issue, since, as was the case with moral virtues obtained through nature or custom, at times Aquinas deploys the term virtue in a broader, less precise sense to indicate the commonality in arena of activity to which one is inclined by these dispositions and full-blown moral virtues. This occurs when describing dead faith as a habit. Indeed, when Aquinas uses habit and disposition more precisely in relation to one another, he calls dead faith a disposition rather than a habit.[127]

Yet in the case of dispositions to moral virtue gained from nature or custom, what is lacking is stable specification by the *causa immobilis* of rationality. Yet that does not seem to be lacking in dead faith. After all, what is known in faith cannot be known by the senses alone. In this sense dead faith may seem like intellectual virtue, such as skill or wisdom, which involves the person's rationality but are not virtues in the proper sense since they do not make the possessor good. Aquinas is able to call them virtues (even if not in the fullest sense) because they do not require the involvement of the will in the specification of their acts. Yet this does not apply to dead faith, since the act that is central to faith—belief—requires the involvement of the appetitive powers not just in its exercise but in its specification. At one point Aquinas describes the knowledge of dead faith as akin to opinion.[128] For dead faith still to be aptly described as faith, there must be some appetitive involvement in specification of the act of belief. By calling the knowledge of dead faith opinion, Aquinas seems to be suggesting that a person's appetite is not directed toward God in the proper way, which would be not only as true (with the intellect) but as a person's greatest good (with a charity-informed will). Thus, even though Aquinas consistently claims that in dead faith the essence of the act of faith is present (assenting to true things about God), the absence of charity is not extrinsic to the act of faith in the same way that the absence of charity is for the moral virtues, which can exist as true virtues without charity. Faith cannot exist as a proper virtue without charity.

Thus we are back to the comparison to moral virtue absent prudence. The claim here is that dead faith is best understood as a disposition, obviously attained through accustomization and not from nature. The specification of the object of dead faith is a failure in rationality; it is not a failure of apprehension (reason) but rather a failure of appetite (will). Akin to the way pre-rational children can (voluntarily) act in a manner that is observably the same as those operating rationally (since what these children lack is supplied by custom), those with dead faith can perform observably the same acts as those with living faith, yet without charity (since what they lack is supplied by *relictae*, as from their previously possessed faith).

A concrete example of dead faith may help. Consider a person whose living faith becomes dead. Aquinas describes this case by saying, "When someone sins mortally, grace and formed faith are taken away. Still, we see that faith remains."[129] We might imagine someone who after sinning mortally continues to affirm truths about God and may continue to attend liturgy and say the creed. These persistent observably accurate acts of assent to truths about God are bereft of charity. The intellect is prompted to such acts of assent not by a charity-qualified will but by seemingly having "gotten used to," or accustomed to, such acts. The activities (level three) may involve rationality. But the acts lack the involvement of the (charity-qualified) will as rational appetite in specifying the assent to God not only as first truth but also as greatest good. This is not perfect faith. To reference Aquinas's analogy, it is akin to a person possessing moral virtue from nature performing observably good acts that are not rationally specified.

This also helps explain Aquinas's consistent, initially perplexing claim that dead faith is a gift.[130] If dead faith is lacking, such that it is not a virtue, how could it be a gift from God? Aquinas notes that dead faith is not the only gift from God where charity lacks. Citing 1 Cor. 13 he mentions prophecy as also possible without charity.[131] In fact, given that what is known in faith is beyond the capacity of unaided reason, it must be the case that dead faith is a gift. It is a gift not in the sense that God gives this lesser good to some as an end in itself. It is a gift in that the specified content of its act (e.g., saying "God is Father, Son, and Holy Spirit") is beyond unaided human reason and so must have come from God somewhere along the way. Nevertheless, despite the fact that it is clearly God's agency that has made such knowledge possible, it is not by God's agency that the person with dead faith has rejected or surrendered the charity that makes faith living. It is not the deadness that comes from God, but the faith.[132]

This examination of the loss of theological virtue bears striking similarities to the loss of the infused cardinal virtues.[133] In both cases, when charity and all infused virtues are lost, observably good actions may remain. There may be even some grasp of the end of such actions that makes them voluntary and rational. Yet they seem to be "pockets of thought in us which can remain relatively unaffected by our overall view of things," lacking attunement to "various modes, in respect of the various matters, . . . according to various circumstances" and lacking the animation of friendship with God that charity supplies.

An examination of growth in and loss of infused virtue represents the culmination of this project. The account offered here depends on an accurate grasp of habit and command of disposition/habit, drawing on the various causes of habit. It addresses how contrary dispositions can be compatible with a habit and how they are lessened or even removed, while presenting an account of growth (*intensio*) that is not limited to the removal of contrary dispositions. It also addresses the ways that grace heals and elevates human rationality, not only as *causa immobilis* "within" virtue but extending across virtues to the believer's last end, the living God—putting on full display the commonalities between acquired and infused virtue even as the two are (quite literally) radically different. Having brought the constructive project on habit, virtue, and growing in virtue to completion, we turn to the recent debate over the possibility of the acquired and infused virtues "coexisting" in the same person.

NOTES

1. Breen, *Imagining an English Reading Public*, 48.
2. At the end of the last century MacIntyre's enormously important *Dependent Rational Animals* both granted the difference between human and nonhuman animals with regard to rationality and explored how that seemingly clear binary evidences aspects of a continuum, especially in higher-order mammals. The treatment of children here can seem

too blunt and suggestive of a clear binary rather than continuum. While there are reasons to continue to maintain that an agent is either rational or not, it is obviously the case that rationality in children is developmental. Such an inquiry is beyond the scope of this project, though on the topic of when one crosses the line to be rational, recall Russell's work on *satis* concepts (see chap. 5), including the difference between vague *satis* concepts and boundary *satis* concepts (*Practical Intelligence and the Virtues*, 113–23).

3. ST I–II 111,2.
4. For a helpful overview of the various types of grace in the context of the virtues (and gifts), see Meinert, *Love of God Poured Out*, 14–46.
5. ST I–II 110,2. This quotation appears immediately before mention of how God provides no less at the supernatural level than at the natural level.
6. ST I–II 111,2.
7. Though God paradigmatically gives habitual grace as the infused virtues and gifts, there is a sense in which a disposition can be called a gift from God, as seen with regard to dead faith.
8. The language of "without us" hearkens back to the definition of virtue Aquinas reports from Augustine. See ST I–II 55,4.
9. ST III 69,6.
10. ST III 69,6.
11. ST III 69,6.
12. ST I–II 61,5.
13. ST III 68,9 ad 1. See also ST III 71,1 ad 1, where Aquinas claims catechizing must always precede baptism. In response to an objector who claims infants cannot be catechized, Aquinas replies: "Just as Mother Church, as stated above [III 69,6 ad 3], lends children another's feet that they may come, and another's heart that they may believe, so, too, she lends them another's ears, that they may hear, and another's mind, that through others they may be taught. And therefore, as they are to be baptized, on the same grounds they are to be instructed."
14. See, especially, ST II 68,9 ad 1, for this beautiful statement from Augustine: "The Church, our mother, offers her maternal mouth for her children, that they may imbibe the sacred mysteries: for they cannot as yet with their own hearts believe unto justice, nor with their own mouths confess unto salvation . . . And if they are rightly said to believe, because in a certain fashion they make profession of faith by the words of their sponsors, why should they not also be said to repent, since by the words of those same sponsors they evidence their renunciation of the devil and this world?" (*On Merit and the Remission of Sins*, i).
15. ST III 68,9.
16. For consistent recognition and analysis of how every "moral philosophy . . . presupposes a sociology," see MacIntyre, *After Virtue*, 23, and MacIntyre's more recent *Ethics in the Conflicts of Modernity*.
17. On *habitus* see Bourdieu, *Outline of a Theory of Practice*, 72–95. For the charge of "conflationism" against Bourdieu, in contrast to critical realists like Margaret Archer, see Elder-Vass, *The Causal Power of Social Structures*, 89, 104–6.
18. See Finn, *Moral Agency within Social Structures*; Smith, *What Is a Person?*. Daly, *The Structures of Virtue and Vice*, brings critical realism and virtue into dialogue.
19. ST III 68,9 ad 2.
20. ST I–II 112,1: "The gift of grace surpasses every capability of created nature, since it is nothing short of a partaking of the Divine Nature, which exceeds every other nature. And

thus it is impossible that any creature should cause grace." See also ST I–II 63,2 and *De virt.* a. 10.

21. ST I–II 112,2. See also ST I–II 109,6.
22. See Augustine, *Confessions,* at VIII.5.12. Augustine never uses the term *habitus* in Book VIII, only *consuetudo,* though he clearly means by this term what Aquinas would mean by a properly human habit, as he describes "willingly" becoming habituated (VIII.5.11). What Augustine's account lacks as to the precise distinctions found in Aquinas is more than compensated by the power of his account.
23. Augustine, *Confessions* VIII.7.16.
24. Augustine, VIII.1.1.
25. Augustine, VIII.5.10.
26. Augustine, VIII.12.30.
27. *De virt.* a. 10 ad 16. For more on this point, see Knobel, *Aquinas on the Infused Moral Virtues,* 226–27.
28. For an article that takes on this question directly and surveys prior scholarship addressing it, see Mattison, "Can Christians Possess the Acquired Virtues?." See also Mattison, "Aquinas, Custom, and the Coexistence of Infused and Acquired Cardinal Virtues." For works from the past decade that address this question directly, see: Knobel, "Can Aquinas's Infused and Acquired Virtues Coexist in the Christian Life?"; Knobel, "Two Theories of Christian Virtue"; Knobel, "Relating Aquinas's Acquired and Infused Virtues"; Knobel, "Elevating Virtue?"; Porter, "Moral Virtues, Charity, and Grace"; Decosimo, "More to Love"; Decosimo, *Ethics as a Work of Charity,* 190–97; Pinsent, "Who's Afraid of the Infused Virtues?"; and Austin, *Aquinas on Virtue,* 180–85.
29. Mattison, "Can Christians Possess the Acquired Virtues?," 567. For a helpful corrective to my claim, for which I am grateful, see Knobel, *Aquinas and the Infused Moral Virtues,* 183–84. I make the same error of wording in the following: "When charity arrives the acquired cardinal virtues become infused cardinal virtues. There is continuity but change. They are perfected, given a new form ('transformed') by charity" ("Revisiting the Relationship between Infused and Acquired Cardinal Virtues," 27). I should have said that habituation-amenable powers that are qualified by acquired cardinal virtues become *qualified by* infused cardinal virtues.
30. In recent work on this topic Knobel has explicitly made the case that residual dispositions from acquired virtues can act as contrary disposition to the infused virtues. See Knobel, *Aquinas on the Infused Moral Virtues,* 180–82, 212–29. She claims: "It is conceivable that the achievement of the former [acquired virtue] might in some circumstances even detract from one's ability to pursue the latter [infused virtue]" (212–13; see also 222). She is exactly correct in this claim, a claim not seen elsewhere in the literature. In fact, as she rightly notes, what can be found on this topic is the claim that Aquinas's argument on the possibility of contrary dispositions persisting even with the reception of infused virtue is true only of previously attained vices, not acquired virtues (65, 167, citing Sherwin, "Infused Virtue," 40).
31. In rightly noting the difference in formal object between acquired and infused virtues, Knobel assumes that any residual disposition from acquired virtue has "nothing at all" to do with the attainment of or degree of possession of infused virtue (*Aquinas on the Infused Moral Virtues,* 212, 221). While rightly indicating the formal difference in infused virtue, this wording is too strong. The sensory connaturalization that occurs as part of the attainment of acquired virtue can continue to exert causal influence in the manner that a

natural disposition can cause different degrees of possession of a virtue. See ST I–II 66,1. This is a claim about the continuity between natural and supernatural happiness (as with the sensory and rational) rather than a denial of the formal difference between acquired and infused virtue.

32. For examples of such recent treatments, see Sherwin, "Infused Virtue," 49–51; Mattison, "Can Christians Possess the Acquired Cardinal Virtues?," 576–80; and Knobel, *Aquinas on the Infused Moral Virtues*, 118–20. For expanded thoughts addressing this point, see the appendix, obj. 13.
33. ST I–II 65,3 ad 2. The English Dominicans' translation is modified here, since its use of "experience" and "their works" suggests the virtues themselves are agents: "Sometimes the habits of moral virtue experience difficulty in their works" (*Habitus moralium virtutum infusarum patiuntur interdum difficultatem in operando*).
34. See ST I–II 51,3 for reference to reason "impressing" its likeness on the appetites; and *Sent* l. 3 d. 33 q. 1 a. 2 qa. 1 ad 3 for "*ad multa*."
35. See ST I 81,3 for reference to the passions having "something of their own"; as well as Aquinas's analogy to the passions being ruled politically, rather than despotically, by reason.
36. See *De virt. card.* a. 2 ad 2: "Although habits as such make someone act promptly and with pleasure, this can be impeded by something supervening, as one having the habit of science is sometimes impeded from using it by sleepiness or drunkenness or something of the like. Therefore, one who repents receives by grace charity and all the other virtues but because of the lingering dispositions from his prior sins he experiences difficulty in the performance of virtues which he has received habitually. This does not happen with virtues acquired through the practice of acts, which at the same time remove contrary dispositions and generate the habits of the virtues."
37. Note that while one could assume it is the attainment of infused virtues all at once that leads to this greater possibility of contrary dispositions, the "all-at-once arrival" is actually true of acquired virtues as well. The differentiating factor is the lack of preceding acts on the part of the person. In his two key texts on this dynamic, Aquinas references the lack of preceding actions, not the suddenness of the attainment of the virtues (ST I–II 65,3 ad 2; *De virt. card.* a. 2 ad 2).
38. For this claim with regard to Augustine and graced virtue, see Herdt, *Putting on Virtue*, 66. Of course, while this account does not privilege one over another as to ability to receive the infused virtues, it raises other theological questions as to whom God's grace is given and why. For (a rare) treatment of predestination in the context of virtue, with particular attention to whether one could know or not that one lives in grace, see Herdt, *Putting on Virtue*, 198–202.
39. Aristotle describes the importance of good upbringing for the attainment of virtue in *Nicomachaen Ethics*, i.4.
40. For various concerns in contemporary philosophical virtue ethics about elitism as marring the possibility of formation in virtue in relation to our contingent identities and especially intellectual ability, see Korsgaard, *Self-Constitution*, 24–25, 43; Annas, *Intelligent Virtue*, 30–31; and, Russell, *Practical Intelligence and the Virtues*, 28. See also an account of how income inequality can be an impediment to formation in virtue in Ward, *Wealth, Virtue, and Moral Luck*. For a more critical account of virtue ethics with this concern in mind, see Tessman, *Burdened Virtues*.
41. For some who posit the possibility of the coexistence of infused and acquired cardinal virtues, the possession of acquired cardinal virtues is requisite for facility of action while

possessing the infused cardinal virtues. See for instance Inglis, "Aquinas's Replication of the Acquired Moral Virtues," 22; Dell'Olio, *Foundations of Moral Selfhood*, 137–38, 141; Sherwin, "Infused Virtue," 49–51; Mirkes, "Aquinas's Doctrine of Moral Virtue," 217–18; and Miner, "Non-Aristotelian Prudence in the *Prima Secundae*," 421. See appendix, obj. 13.

42. *De virt.* 10 ad 14.
43. For Aquinas's treatment of the *fomes* peccati, see ST I–II 91,6; and *Commentary on Romans*, 586–90. For a helpful treatment of this topic, see Johnson, "St. Thomas and the 'Law of Sin.'" See also Aquinas's treatment of the "four wounds" as effects of sin, at ST I–II 85,3.
44. *De virt.* a. 9 ad 21. See also ST I–II 53,2, and *De virt.* a. 11 ad 13.
45. ST I–II 66,1, and *De virt. card.* a. 3.
46. See Knobel, *Aquinas on the Infused Moral Virtues*, 87, 225.
47. *De virt. card.* a. 2 ad 2, with *scientiae* changed from "science" to "knowledge." See also *De virt. card.* a. 3 ad 13.
48. For certain important examples of Aquinas's oft-repeated claim that the passions can participate in reason, see *Commentary on Aristotle's "Nicomachean Ethics,"* 236–43; and ST I–II 24,4, 56,4, and 66,1. For a helpful review of the plethora of texts throughout Aquinas's corpus on the passions' participation in reason, see Kahm, *Aquinas on Emotion's Participation in Reason*, 202–19.
49. This is not to say that eating disorders, phobias, or alcoholism exist only as sensory disorders. When "full-blown" habits, they can (tragically) stably rationally specify a person. Yet granting that this is perhaps not the case in a situation of recovery (since we are talking about a person possessing infused virtue), even powerful and persistent contrary disposition can conceivably be compatible with virtue. See Hursthouse's claim on the possibility of possessing virtue with even strong contrary inclinations, depending on "what makes it hard" to act virtuously, in *On Virtue Ethics*, 98. This line of thought would have helped Sherwin's treatment of Matthew Talbot as to the "relationship between the infused virtues and the remaining effects of his acquired vices" ("Infused Virtue and the Effects of Acquired Vice," 49), removing a prompt for him to posit acquired moral virtues to grant facility.
50. This is a rampant assumption in the literature supporting the coexistence of the acquired and infused virtues. For an article whose very point is this claim, including its support in the Thomistic tradition (e.g., Suarez), see Mirkes, "Aquinas's Doctrine of Moral Virtue." See the appendix, obj. 13.
51. Though she herself does not endorse this view, Knobel addresses it (*Aquinas on the Infused Moral Virtues*, 118).
52. Dell'Olio, *Foundations of Moral Selfhood*, 138. For a more careful account of how the infused virtues are true virtues despite their important differences, see Porter, "The Subversion of Virtue," 32–33.
53. *De virt.* a. 10 ad 14.
54. *De virt.* a. 10 ad 15.
55. For an even more critical view of the importance of pleasure as an indicator of virtue, notably regarding acquired not infused virtue, see Curzer, *Aristotle and the Virtues*, 321–31.
56. Such as martyrdom. See ST II–II 123,8 for Aquinas's recognition that this virtue is compatible with physical pain and even sorrow. For more on this subject, see Clark, "Is Martyrdom Virtuous?," 146.

57. For Aquinas's claim that dispositions on the way to corruption do not preclude the possibility of virtue, see *De virt.* a. 10 ad 16.
58. *De virt.* a. 11 ad 13. See also ST I–II 53,2.
59. *De virt.* a. 11.
60. *De virt.* a. 11.
61. The three texts relied on here are ST I–II 52 on habits in general; *De virt.* a. 11 on infused virtues; and, ST II–II 24 on charity, including its growth.
62. For the former, see *De virt.* a. 11. For the latter, where such growth is explicitly denied, see *De virt.* a. 11 ad 10; and ST II–II 24,5. For a suggestion of growth in infused virtue that is extensive to a greater number of objects, see ST II–II 24,4 ad 1.
63. For greater "rootedness," see *De virt.* a. 11. See also ST II–II 24,5 ad 3: "The infusion of charity implies a change with respect to having charity and not having charity, and so it must be the case that something arrives that had previously not existed in the subject. By contrast, an increase of charity implies a change with respect to having less and having more. And so it does not have to be the case that something now exists that previously had not been infused; rather, it has to be the case that what had previously existed in the subject to a lesser degree now exists to a greater degree. And this is what God effects by increasing charity, viz., that it now exists [in the subject] to a greater degree, and that the likeness of the Holy Spirit is participated in more fully in the soul" (Freddoso trans.). The English Dominicans' translation unfortunately makes charity an agent: "This is what God does when He increases charity, that is, He makes it to have a greater hold on the soul." I am grateful to Patrick Clark for alerting me to this flaw.
64. For "fervent," see *De virt.* a. 11 and ST II–II 24,4 ad 3. For "vehement," see *De virt.* a. 11, where it is equated to a person participating more in the virtue.
65. ST II–II 24,4 ad 1.
66. ST I–II 52,2: "*Augetur etiam nihilominus motus per intensionem, secundum participationem subiecti.*"
67. In that sense it echoes the Aristotelian description of virtue as the "furthest reach" of a power, as Aquinas describes it in ST I–II 66,1 ad 2.
68. See *De car.* a. 12: "The habit of virtue inclines man to act rightly according as through it man has the right estimation of the end."
69. ST I–II 63,4.
70. Determining whether "prayerfulness" is a virtue of infused justice or charity must be bracketed here: if it is part of charity-informed justice, and in my view it is indeed an act of rendering God His due but also an act of charity as friendship with God, it is *not* my view that charity is only a formal virtue without its own distinctive acts.
71. In Porter, *Nature as Reason*, one consistent theme on the natural law is that the natural law is preconventional yet never lived without some particular instantiation, including conventionality. Porter calls this a Ciceronian (rather than Aristotelian) claim regarding nature (266–67). Something similar occurs here. Though the appetitive inclination is not simply toward Ignatian meditation (which would be, akin to "ham and eggs," overly specified), the growth in virtue does not take place without some such specific activity (level three).
72. For example, it could seem that charity is incapable of increase, since its object is God, Who is infinite (*De virt.* a. 10 obj. 17). However, since charity disposes the finite creature, whose activities are created not uncreated, it is capable of growth (*De virt.* a. 10 ad 17; see also ST I–II 3,1).

73. Aquinas explicitly connects this treatment of perfection in charity to growth in charity. See *De car*. a. 10 ad 8 on *intensio*.
74. See *De car*. aa. 10 and 11. Far more commonly treated is Aquinas's parallel (shorter) treatment in the *Summa Theologiae*, at II–II 24, particularly 24,9, with its three stages of charity. For treatments of growth in virtue based on this text, see Pinckaers, *La vie selon l'Esprit*, 195–200; Sherwin, "Infused Virtue," 48–49; and Titus, "Moral Development and Making All Things New in Christ," 246–58. Sherwin addresses the three levels in a manner attuned to relationship between infused virtue and residual effects of previously acquired vice.
75. *De car*. a. 11 and a. 10, respectively (translation slightly modified by author). For more on whether or not it is possible to turn oneself away from mortal sin, see ST I–II 109,8.
76. *De car*. a. 10 ad 2.
77. For a fuller treatment of habitual ordering, see Mattison, "Habitual Ordering in Aquinas."
78. Though the language of habitual and actual here suggests the earlier discussion of possessing infused virtue in habit but not in act, that is a different topic. The prior distinction referred to what is called here level two (in habit) and level three (in act). This topic is habitual ordering of activity, where both actual ordering and habitual ordering reference activity (level three) and in what sense that activity is (and/or is not) referred to the end supplied by a habit.
79. The texts are: I *Sent*. d. 1 q. 3 a. 1 ad 4; II *Sent*. d. 42 q. 1 a. 3 ad 5; *De malo* VII.1 ad 4 and ad 9; *De malo* VII.9; ST I–II 88,1 ad 2 and 3; ST II–II 24,10 ad 2; ST II–II 44,4 ad 2; *De Perf. Spirit*. V; *De car*. 11 ad. 3; and *Super Col*. Cap. 3, lect. 3 (170).
80. For Aquinas's claim that one can act *with* a habit but not *out* of it, see *De car*. a. 6 ad 12.
81. See *Super Col* c. 3, l. 3, 170. This text says "all things" to God, which clearly includes the venial sin, since the subject of the sentence is "the one sinning venially" (*venialiter peccans*).
82. ST I–II 88,1 ad 3 (emphasis added). This claim is found nearly verbatim at *De malo*. 7.1 ad 4. See also ST II–II 24,10 ad 2: "That which we love in venial sin is loved for God's sake habitually though not actually."
83. Note how the meaning of actual as distinguished from habitual is different than the meaning of actual as distinguished from virtual. As noted earlier, an act is virtually ordered toward an end when that further end is not "on one's mind" and is distinguished from "actually" ordered activity, which is indeed consciously so ordered. Such "automaticity" of activity without conscious deliberation of the further end is one way a virtue supplies promptness. Aquinas uses examples of a doctor picking herbs for a potion even though not always thinking of the end of health, or walking on a journey and not always thinking of the destination. See *De car*. a. 11 ad 2 and ST I–II 1,6 ad 3, respectively. See also *Sent*. l. 2 d. 40 q. 1 a. 5 ad 7; and *De Perf. Spirit*. 5. Note that since "actual" means something different when distinguished from virtual or from habitual, the three terms should not be regarded along one and the same continuum. See Mattison, "Habitual Ordering in Aquinas," 1314–21. For an excellent and historically attuned treatment of these distinctions (despite its assumption of one such continuum) see Osborne, "The Threefold Referral of Acts to the Ultimate End," 715–36. See also Jensen, *Sin*, 17–24; as well as Jensen, "Venial Sin and the Ultimate End."
84. This is exactly the problem with Jensen's otherwise excellent treatment of this topic (*Sin*, 19–23). For more on this, see Mattison, "Habitual Ordering in Aquinas," 1302–8.
85. Note that when one only habitually and not actually orders activity to God, presumably it is possible, and indeed more common, to habitually *and* actually order one's activity to God. See Mattison, "Habitual Ordering in Aquinas," 1318–21.

86. See Mattison, 1297n34.
87. See Burnyeat, "Aristotle on Learning to Be Good," 80.
88. See Millgram, *Practical Induction*, 53.
89. Elsewhere I explore whether or not habitual ordering may be applied more extensively, including with reference to the ends of individual virtues and not simply one's last end. See "Habitual Ordering," 1320–21.
90. Jensen, *Sin*, 38–39.
91. See ST II–II 24,11; and *De car.* a. 12.
92. *De car.* a. 12.
93. *De car.* a. 12 ad 23.
94. *De car.* a. 12 ad 9.
95. *De car.* a. 6 ad 12.
96. *De car.* a. 12 ad 11.
97. *De car.* a. 12.
98. This is not to say that it is impossible to act "out of" a virtue and yet in a manner that decreases that virtue (see chap. 5).
99. *De car.* a. 12.
100. For these causes of sin, see ST I–II 75,2; and, in more detail, ST I–II 76–78. See also *De malo.* III.
101. See *De car.* a. 13; and ST II–II 24,12.
102. *De car.* a. 6 (also ad 9).
103. *De car.* a. 13 ad 5.
104. See *De car.* a. 13, where Aquinas claims the cause of charity in a person "depends entirely" on an extrinsic cause. This is dissimilar to acquired virtue, whose "cause is in the subject and not entirely extrinsic" (a. 13 ad 4).
105. *De car.* a. 13.
106. *De car.* a. 6. See also *De car.* a. 13.
107. See *De car.* 6 (also ad 14).
108. See *De car.* a. 6 ad 1. Aquinas also makes this claim about venial sin disposing to mortal sin by saying that charity cannot decrease due to the fact that it is caused by God and God causes no such decrease. On our side it is lost (not decreased) by mortal sin. As for venial sin, "Charity can by no means be diminished, if we speak of direct causality, yet whatever disposes to its corruption may be said to conduce indirectly to its diminution, and such are venial sins, or even the cessation from the practice of works of charity" (ST II–II 24,10). See also Sent l. 1 d. 17 q. 2 a. 5; and *De car.* a. 12 ad 21.
109. *De car.* a. 13 ad 5.
110. See *De car.* a. 13 ad 1: "One loses charity through one act of mortal sin, but some [*aliquae reliquiae*] of the previous perfection remains if he has not lost charity out of malice" *Relicta*[*e*] (which comes from 65,3 ad 2) appears with this meaning in *De virt card.* a. 2 ad 2, though in the opposite case, in the description of a new convert's possession of charity as compatible with *relictae* from prior sins.
111. See appendix, obj. 15.
112. Knobel does not use the term "contrary dispositions" to describe these *relictae.* For her description of how they function in this way, see Knobel, *Aquinas on the Infused Moral Virtues*, 180–82, 212–29.
113. ST I–II 63,4. Aquinas often claims that acts of the cardinal virtues do not cease to have their proximate end even as they are further ordered to supernatural happiness. (See,

e.g., *De car*. a. 3, esp. ad 1, 9, and 10 and a. 5.) This is correct. Acts of, say, infused temperance do not become acts of charity but remain acts of temperance. Yet they are acts of infused temperance, that is, they differ from acquired temperance in formal object and thus achieve a proximate end differently.

114. For a helpful examination of how grace perfects nature yet the natural still parameters the graced life, see Porter, *Nature as Reason*, 378–400.
115. ST I–II 63,4.
116. I am grateful to Patrick Clark for pressing me on this point.
117. See ST I–II 65,4 on both hope and faith without charity. For the key texts on "unformed faith" or "dead faith," see ST II–II 4,4–5; ST II–II 6,2; and *De ver*. XIV.6–7. See also *Sent*. l. 3 d. 23 q. 3 a. 1 qae. 2–3.
118. See ST II–II 2,1.
119. See *Sent* l. 3 d. 23, q. 3, a. 1, qa. 2; *De ver*. XIV.6; ST II–II 4,5; and ST II–II 6,2 ad 1.
120. See *De virt*. a. 7.
121. For a more extended version of this argument, see Mattison III, "Revisiting the Relationship between Infused and Acquired Cardinal Virtues," 3–16.
122. Aquinas calls dead faith a disposition at *Sent*. l. 3 d. 23 q. 3 a. 1 qa. 3. (See also qa. 2 ad 1 and 3.)
123. See ST I–II 49, 2 ad 3, where both are referenced.
124. See *De veritate* XIV.7; and ST II–II 4,5 ad. 3.
125. See ST II–II 4,4 ad 1.
126. See *Sent*. l. 3 d. 23 q. 3 a. 4 qa. 1 and 2; *De ver*. XIV.7; and ST II–II 4,4.
127. See *Sent*. l. 3 d. 23 q. 3 a. 1 qa. 2 ad 1 and 3, esp. qa. 3.
128. See *De car*. a. 13 ad 6. Aquinas seems to be groping for a different sort of appetitive involvement in dead faith, though positing opinion as that involvement appears to deprive even dead faith of the act of belief.
129. *De ver*. XIV.7. Though Aquinas most frequently addresses the case of a change from dead to living faith, he also addresses this case.
130. See ST II–II 6,2 (and also II–II 5,2 ad 2); and *Sent*. l. 3 d. 23, q. 3, a. 2.
131. See *Sent*. l. 3 d. 23, q. 3, a. 2.
132. See III *Sent*. d. 23 q. 3 a. 2 ad 6, where Aquinas claims the act of dead faith comes from God, but not its defect (compare ad 5). See also ST II–II 6,2 ad 2.
133. Based on this analysis, it could be possible to possess "dead cardinal virtues" as *relictae* from previously possessed infused cardinal virtue, though given the possibility of acquired cardinal virtue and of natural dispositions to cardinal virtue without accustomization, such an account would have to carefully delineate dead cardinal virtues as more than simply dead faith or dead hope.

APPENDIX

Disputed Question on the Possibility of Acquired Virtue in the Person with Infused Virtue

This appendix is unusual for a variety of reasons, and therefore warrants introductory remarks. Given the focus on the continuities and differences between the acquired and infused virtues, the relationship between infused and acquired virtues in an individual person's life is squarely within the purview of this project. The precise question is whether or not a person can simultaneously possess both the infused (theological and cardinal) virtues *and* the acquired (cardinal) virtues. Stated differently: Since it is granted here that one can possess acquired virtues without infused virtues, is it possible for a person who possesses infused virtues to also possess acquired virtues? This is commonly called the "coexistence" debate, with some scholars maintaining that the acquired and infused virtues *can* coexist in the same person at the same time. Others disagree.

There has been extensive scholarly debate on this question, particularly in the recent past.[1] The topic is akin to other recent scholarly debates touched on in earlier sections of the book, including the spontaneity of the passions, the role of the gifts of the Holy Spirit, and the function of a person's last end. However, given the extent of debate over the possibility of coexistence and the number of arguments in that debate directly pertaining to growing in virtue, the coexistence debate warrants more extensive treatment.

Why an appendix rather than an additional chapter? Certain features distinguish this appendix rather sharply from the main chapters. First, while the chapters offer a constructive account of habit, the attainment of virtue, and growth in virtue "from the ground up," the appendix focuses squarely on the foray of recent scholarship and delineates the various lines of argument within that debate. Second, this task is appendicular since it is separable from the constructive argument on growth in virtue. Though closely related to the host of arguments on habit and virtue in this project, the position articulated in this appendix is not inextricably bound to that constructive account. One might hold a different position on this debate yet still affirm the account of growth in virtue argued here. The constructive account does not stand or fall based on my position in the debate in this concluding section. Third, and finally, the genre here is the medieval "disputed question." Readers of Aquinas's various works called "Disputed Questions," including *Disputed Questions on the Virtues,* will recognize this format. So, too, will readers of his *Summa Theologiae* (and others of his *Summae*), which are shorter versions of the disputed question genre. The disputed question genre displays some of the greatest assets of Scholastic texts: precisely worded and differentiated questions; clearly delineated arguments and responses; and serious engagement with contrary positions in humble search for truth and charitable trust that contrary positions generally contain some kernel of truth that must be acknowledged.[2] This genre is especially useful for addressing a precise question and for delineating precise arguments and counterarguments.

Aquinas's disputed questions commonly addressed one topic with a variety of subquestions, called articles. Only one question, with no articles, is under review here: Can the person who possesses the infused virtues also possess the acquired virtues? As is standard for the genre, the question begins with a set of "objections" (labeled *obj.*), which in most cases (and certainly in this one) are contrary to the position endorsed. Following that is a brief claim, called "on the contrary" (labeled *sed contra*), which, as is also usually the case, is based on an appeal to a respected authority. Next comes the "response" (labeled *respondeo*), where the author gives an answer to the title question. (Some find it helpful to read the response before reading the objections and replies.) Finally comes a set of "replies to objections" (labeled *rep.*), presented in numerical order corresponding to the opening objections. Though a response contains the author's answer to the question, it is often within the replies to objections that refined arguments are found. This is the case here: replies are best read alongside their corresponding objections rather than reading all the objections or replies in succession.

One cautionary note on the genre is in order. Since disputed questions are generally phrased as a binary yes-or-no choice, one can wrongly assume that there are only two positions regarding the question at hand, namely, yes or no. In a sense this is true. But in another sense it is misleading, since different readers can affirm a yes or no answer to the question at hand yet have importantly different reasons for supporting their answers. This is also certainly the case here. The disputed question format should *not* be taken to suggest that all the objections together articulate one unified position. For instance, there may be a variety of ways to support the claim that a person can possess both infused and acquired virtues even if those ways do not all cohere with one another. The same may be said of the rival position. Furthermore, on occasion the work of one scholar may be cited in a reply against an argument in that objection even though two scholars who hold the same yes-or-no answer may do so for very different reasons. Why, then, employ this format? Because, in addition to the reasons already noted, the format provides a mental map of various relevant scholarly claims on the topic.

The question at hand is this: Can a person with infused virtues possess the acquired virtues? My own answer is no, a person cannot. Before noting the various groups of arguments pertinent to this question, allow me to address a more fundamental issue, namely, whether the question here concerns Aquinas's position on this issue or the answer to the question itself regardless of whether Aquinas says so or not. Obviously scholars find in Aquinas's work an enormous resource for an accurate grasp of matters of moral theology, including the topics of virtue and grace. That said, the two questions are not the same and they should be distinguished. The immediate concern is finding the accurate answer to the question rather than presenting what Aquinas says directly on the question. Yet, given the importance of Aquinas's work for the subject at hand, a pause is taken to assess Aquinas's texts on the topic as a whole.

My view is that the claim that a person with infused virtue *cannot* possess acquired virtue is in line with Aquinas's central commitments on grace and virtue. Indeed, texts in Aquinas's mature works commonly cited in support of the coexistence of infused and acquired virtue in the same person are misinterpreted, and in context they are as likely to support the opposite claim. Extended engagement with these texts is not offered here, as that task has been taken up elsewhere.[3]

There are two early texts from *Commentary on the Sentences* that seem to affirm the coexistence of infused and acquired virtue in the same person.[4] Some scholars treat these two texts as definitive.[5] I do not. Though Aquinas never repudiates these writings, he never repeats those direct claims in his later work. I offer no argument here as to whether these early texts do not say what they seem to say or whether Aquinas later changed or developed his position. It is conceivable that Aquinas was inconsistent throughout his corpus or even was inconsistent within his earlier work. The focus here is not primarily on an interpretation of the texts in Aquinas that most closely address this question. Rather, the focus is on answering accurately the question at hand, drawing on the extraordinary resources in Aquinas for an account of grace and virtue. However, I do endorse two claims on this matter with regard to Aquinas's texts: first, as recognized by scholars on opposite sides of this contemporary debate, Aquinas's work on the relationship between the acquired and the infused virtues in the same person is not clear; and second, that the acquired virtues *cannot* exist in the person with infused virtue is far more consistent with Aquinas's clear claims about grace and virtue.

I have grouped the sixteen objections and their replies in this way: the first two address the existence of the infused theological and cardinal virtues, an important prolegomenous point not contested by scholars who affirm coexistence. The next group concerns the relationship between nature and grace and the singularity of the last end. The next set addresses how higher acts and virtues can order lower acts and virtues. The penultimate group addresses the possibility and manner of growth in virtue, with attention to acts necessary for salvation and facility of virtuous action. The final set addresses the attainment of or loss of infused virtue. How one understands each topic has ramifications for the possibility of the coexistence of the infused and acquired virtues in the same person.

CAN THE PERSON WITH INFUSED VIRTUES ALSO POSSESS ACQUIRED VIRTUES?

It seems that the person living the graced life of discipleship *can* have the acquired virtues.

[The following objections concern the need for infused virtues in general and for infused cardinal virtues in particular.]

Obj. 1. In the life of grace, the natural acquired virtues remain unchanged, but the person changes.[6] Therefore, there is no need for graced virtues where natural virtues can exist.

Obj. 2. The Christian possesses infused theological virtues to incline her toward her supernatural end. Given the supernatural object of the theological virtues, they cannot be acquired and therefore must be infused. However, in activities that can be accessible to unaided natural reason, such as those of the cardinal virtues, the person can attain on her own the acquired virtues. Hence the Christian requires infused theological virtues but not infused cardinal virtues. Therefore, the acquired virtues can exist in the Christian with infused theological virtues.[7]

[The following objections address the relationship between the natural and supernatural end.]

Obj. 3. According to the Scholastic dictum, grace "perfects" (rather than destroys or leaves untouched) nature. The acquired virtues are natural virtues, and the natural is not eliminated in the life of grace. Therefore, the acquired virtues exist in the Christian in a state of grace.[8]

Obj 4. The graced life does not simply perfect a person's grace-enabled supernatural life but also her natural life. In other words, the human person retains a natural end even in the life of grace.[9] Acquired virtues orient a person toward activity constitutive of the natural end of human flourishing.[10] Therefore, the acquired virtues are necessary for the fully virtuous graced life.[11]

Obj. 5. If there is only one ultimate end for a human person, to which she directs all her activity, it is quite plausible that a person in a state of grace possesses only the infused virtues whereby she directs all her activity to supernatural happiness. However, it is not true that Christians have only one last end.[12] "The term 'final' does not mean simply one and only."[13] An example of this dynamic is the "different" souls of the human person: living, sentient, and rational. The ends of each of these souls are last ends in that they are not mere means to an end, even as they are further ordered. A human person remains living and sentient even as she is rational. Something comparable happens with the new ends supplied by God's grace and the infused virtues. Since the "lower ends" remain, so do the acquired virtues. Therefore, a person in a state of grace with the infused virtues can possess the acquired virtues.

Obj. 6. When a person possesses the infused moral virtues, the person still possesses the acquired moral virtues, albeit virtually. There are different ways to understand virtual presence. It can be used to explain how the finality of acquired virtue is still achieved in infused virtue.[14] Or it can be used to describe the dynamic whereby acquired virtues are not present in the life of grace "in their full actuality or essentially," although "some of their accidental features remain."[15] Either way, the person in a state of grace can possess the acquired virtues, albeit virtually.

[The following objections address whether or how the infused virtues and/or their acts can order the acquired virtues and/or their acts.]

Obj. 7. Though the person in a state of grace is ordered toward her supernatural end as last end, the natural end of human flourishing is fulfilled in the life of grace, even though not as last end. This occurs because the virtues operate in concert, with the acquired virtues being ordered by the infused moral virtues extrinsically, so to speak, and the immediate end of the acquired virtues is maintained even as the further supernatural end of the infused virtues is supplied by infused virtues.[16] When this occurs, the acquired virtues are "made meritorious" by the infused virtues.[17] Therefore, the acquired virtues can be possessed by one with the infused virtues.[18]

Obj 8. It is quite common for one virtue to order another virtue. For instance, a musician may attain the habit of knowledge in mathematics or a ship captain may attain the habit of sail-rigging.[19] In both cases the lower habit is ordered by the higher one and yet is not included into the higher habit. "Subordination is not inclusion."[20] Similarly, the infused virtues can "use" the acquired virtues. When this occurs, the acquired virtues persist. Therefore, the acquired virtues can coexist with the infused virtues.

Obj. 9. At times a "higher virtue" can order a lower virtue. Aristotle and Aquinas describe this dynamic in regard to prudence, as when an individual's prudential activity in her own life is ordered by civic prudence. In this case the person is a leader in the community and makes prudential decisions in her own life in a manner informed by her role as a leader in that community. When this occurs, she is said to possess individual prudence and civic prudence, with the former ordered by the latter.[21] One could imagine other examples of such ordering, as when a married couple has a child and the new end of their family orders their marital love with each other.[22] Similarly, a person in the graced life of discipleship is ordered toward participation in the earthly (natural) city and toward participation in the heavenly (supernatural) city. Thus she can simultaneously possess acquired virtue to incline her toward good activity constitutive of the earthly city and infused virtue inclining her toward activity constitutive of the heavenly city. In this case the higher (infused) virtue orders the lower (acquired) virtue.[23] Therefore, the person with infused virtues can possess acquired virtues.

Obj. 10. In the life of grace, charity commands the acts of the infused moral virtues. Yet even when this occurs, elicited acts are still the result of the infused moral virtues, not charity. Charity does not replace the infused moral virtues, even as it commands them.[24] The same is true for how the infused moral virtues command the acquired moral virtues.[25] When this occurs, a person with infused virtue (including infused moral virtue) undertakes an act measured by human reason (and thus acquired virtue) and yet commanded by infused virtue.[26] In such a case, there is a single act of both acquired and infused virtue.[27] Therefore, the person with the infused virtues can possess the acquired virtues.

[The following set of objections concern the possibility and manner of growth in infused virtue.]

Obj. 11. The infused moral virtues are bestowed at once, as a gratuitous gift, through God's grace. However, it is possible (indeed necessary) to continue to grow more virtuous in the graced life of discipleship even with possession of the infused virtues, whether they be bestowed in infancy or to an adult convert. Since the infused virtues are already possessed, this growth must consist in the attainment of acquired virtue. Therefore the person in a state of grace can and must attain the acquired virtues.[28]

Obj. 12. It is possible for a person in a state of grace to possess the infused virtues and yet not act consistently well in certain arenas of activity that are not necessary for salvation. Therefore, the inclination to act well in those areas of life is not supplied by the infused virtues. When a person does become virtuous in those areas of life, it is through the attainment of acquired virtues. Therefore, the person in a state of grace who possesses the infused virtues can and should develop the acquired virtues to incline her to act well in those arenas of activity.[29]

Obj. 13. A person who possess the infused virtues more commonly experiences a lack of facility in acting virtuously than a person who possesses the acquired virtues. This more common lack of facility, or ease in acting well, is caused by the greater possibility of contrary dispositions and is due in significant part to the distinct manner of attainment of infused virtue. Yet the person with the infused virtues can grow in virtue to act with greater facility, or ease, such that the virtuous act is pleasant. Since the person possesses infused virtue without facility, it is not provided by that infused virtue. When such growth occurs, it is through the attainment of acquired virtue to support activity of infused virtue. Therefore, the person in a state of grace who possesses infused virtues can develop acquired virtues to facilitate acting well in those arenas of activity.[30]

[The following objections concern the gain or loss of infused virtue.]

Obj. 14. It does not seem fitting that mortal sin (and the resulting loss of infused virtue) be an occasion for the gain of a good thing, namely, acquired virtue. Yet it is possible that the person who sins mortally perform consistently good actions after that mortal sin. If these good actions are caused by acquired virtues, the acquired virtues could not be attained through the performance of mortal sin. Therefore the acquired virtues must have coexisted with the infused virtues before the loss of the latter. Therefore, the acquired virtues can coexist with the infused virtues in the graced life of discipleship.[31]

Obj. 15. When a person sins mortally and loses the infused virtues, she commonly continues to perform consistently good acts. Yet these can no longer be acts of infused virtue since the infused virtues have been lost. Hence they must be acts of acquired virtue.[32] There must have been acquired virtues present alongside infused virtues, since it must be acquired virtue that inclines the person to act well upon the loss of the infused virtues (acquired virtues cannot be attained via mortal sin). Therefore, the person in a state of grace who possesses the infused virtues can also possess the acquired virtues.

Obj. 16. It does not seem fitting that a good thing be lost due to the bestowal of God's grace. The acquired virtues are a good thing, ultimately received from God (albeit through God's creative/common grace rather than through God's healing and elevating sanctifying grace). Therefore, if a person who possesses the acquired virtues converts and is bestowed the infused virtues, she would lose the acquired virtues if the two could not coexist, which is unseemly.[33] Therefore, the person in a state of grace possessing the infused virtues can possess the acquired virtues, assuming they were possessed before conversion.

Sed contra. Thomas Aquinas claims that each person has one last end and does all for the sake of that last end.[34] The infused virtues and the acquired virtues order a person to act toward different last ends, engendering distinct rules or measures for all of one's acts and concomitantly for acts that differ in species or formal object from one another.[35] Therefore, one and the same person cannot possess both infused virtues and acquired virtues.

Respondeo. Many misunderstandings come about when people regard the virtues as substantial forms rather than qualities. Habits and dispositions are qualities; they qualify natural powers by further specifying their ends in a more or less stable manner. When this occurs stably, in a manner where the specification is supplied rationally, a habit in the properly human sense is possessed. Virtues as habits provide stable specification of natural human powers toward good activity, constitutive of flourishing, in a manner whereby the stable specification is supplied rationally. This account of virtue has various ramifications for the possibility of acquired and infused virtues being possessed by the same person.

Possession of a habit neither necessitates action nor ensures action that does ensue is in conformity with one's habit. The activation of the habituated power requires further specification that is aided and causally impacted by the possession of the habit. To have a power qualified by stable rational specification (i.e., to be habituated) is to have the object of the natural power specified in a more particular manner than the manner supplied by nature. This more particular end of the power as rationally supplied by habit is specified in relation to other various ends, circumstances, and so forth, in relation to the whole. It is for this reason that the virtues are said to be connected to one another and to be ordered toward a person's last end. This last end provides a coherence and unity (albeit not perfect in this life) to a person's various habits and activities.

Therefore it is not possible to possess acquired virtues, *qua* habits, whose stable rational specification is ordered to the natural end as last end, along with infused virtues, since infused virtues stably (supra-)rationally order the person to supernatural happiness as the last end. In a person with the infused virtues, "the whole" or "overall good" is supernatural, such that orientation toward the natural end as last end will dislodge the supernatural end as last end in supplying a different overall good of the person's life.

This does not of course mean the natural end cannot be achieved or fulfilled in the person with infused virtues. It can, indeed, but not as last end. In other words, it is fulfilled but as part of a supernatural overall good that is beyond the natural even as it includes it. Even good acts that are observably the same (e.g., eating well) are ordered to attaining the natural end as further ordered toward the supernatural end and result in a formally different (even if observably similar) action.

This does not mean that a person possessing infused virtues attains and acts in a manner constitutive of the supernatural end perfectly or, for that matter, perfectly achieves the natural end (in the broader context of the supernatural). Just as there is "room for growth" in the person with the acquired virtues oriented toward the natural end as last end, there is room for growth (in this life) in the person with infused virtues oriented toward the supernatural end, and even room for growth in the extent to which they fulfill the natural end, not as last end but as part of the broader supernatural last end. Hence a person with the infused virtues may grow in how fully she attains natural flourishing. Yet, granting the possession of the infused virtues, greater achievement of natural human flourishing always occurs in the context of a person's overall good as supernatural flourishing, and thus the growth is in infused virtue, rather than just added possession of (or growth in) acquired virtue. This is also true in the elimination of contrary dispositions, which is not the primary manner of growth in (any) virtue. But when it does occur, it is a fuller integration of the person's sensory dispositions toward activities ordered ultimately toward the supernatural end, even as those activities attain readily observable natural ends.

Therefore not only is it not possible for a person to possess acquired virtues along with infused virtues but the reasons commonly offered in support of that coexistence are readily (and less problematically) explained by growth in infused virtue.

[The following replies concern the need for infused virtues in general and infused cardinal virtues in particular.]

Rep. 1. God's grace does indeed change a person, qualifying the essence of the soul, whereas virtues qualify the soul's powers. Nevertheless, in order to possess virtues inclining one to actions toward the supernatural end, God's grace is necessary to possess such virtues, which are therefore called infused virtues. God does not give more stingily in the life of grace than in the naturally virtuous life. Since God provides natural virtue (by common, created grace) to enable one to act well out of the seeds of virtue (supplied by nature, God's "first gift"), God also provides infused virtues to enable a person to act well toward the supernatural end once the person is "born again" and ordered toward supernatural happiness. Therefore, infused virtues are necessary in the Christian life.

Rep. 2. The theological virtues incline a person to act well toward God directly, in faith, hope, and love. Nevertheless, other virtues, the moral virtues, enable a person to act well in matters that can be accessible to unaided reason. Yet when these latter are done in further relation to God and supernatural happiness, they are done according to a supernatural rule or measure.[36] As such they cannot be attained by a person's own powers, but rather require God's grace. Virtues that require God's grace and ultimately direct a person toward supernatural happiness are called infused virtues. Moral virtues incline a person toward arenas of activity that are in principle accessible to unaided reason, yet when done in further reference to supernatural happiness, require God's grace and are thus infused. Therefore, the infused moral virtues are necessary in the Christian life.

[The following replies address the relationship between the natural and the supernatural end.]

Rep. 3. Grace perfects rather than destroys or leaves untouched human nature in the life of infused virtue. However, what is "natural" in the life of virtue is not "second nature" habits such as the natural (acquired) virtues, but rather the natural human powers that are qualified by habits such as the natural virtues.[37] These natural human powers persist in the graced life, and they are rendered capable of supernatural activity by the infusion of grace in the essence of the soul (which persists, with its powers) and graced virtues qualifying that nature (or really its powers). Hence in the graced life, grace does indeed perfect nature, but this entails the persistence of natural human powers, not "second nature" acquired virtues.

Rep 4. It is true that the natural end of a person is fulfilled in the life of grace. The supernatural life toward which the person of grace is ordered fulfills, even as it surpasses, the natural end. Indeed, one reason for God's gift of the infused moral virtues is so that the human person can act well in matters that, while in principle are accessible to unaided reason, can also be done in a manner that is reflective of the Divine rule of supernatural beatitude. When this latter occurs, the natural end of human flourishing is attained by the infused moral virtues even though it is no longer the last end of the person in the graced life of discipleship, the last of which is supernatural happiness.[38] Therefore, the natural end is fulfilled by the infused cardinal virtues and additional acquired cardinal virtues are not needed.

Rep. 5. Much of what is said here is true, but it betrays an inadequate grasp of the last end. A person can have only one last end, even as lower ends are retained though not as last ends. As noted earlier, the supernatural end includes the natural end. Yet, when any persisting end of a person is further ordered toward new ends, that persisting end is no longer rightly called a last end, since its formality is shaped by its reference to that further end. This is true not only of particular acts (as described later) but also with regard to powers of the soul, which is the rationale for taking the unicity of forms position in debates about the plurality of forms.[39] Even supporters of multiple last ends seem to recognize this when they say, "The newer end always subtly transforms the lower ends even as it preserves them."[40] Since any virtue "further ordered" toward the supernatural end is "transformed" in a manner only possible with God's grace, such virtues are rightly called infused. Therefore, the person with the infused virtues does not possess the acquired virtues.

Rep. 6. Both uses of virtual presence capture something true, but in neither case is it correct to say that the acquired virtues remain present in the person possessing infused virtues, even virtually. The way in which natural finality is attained in a person with infused virtue is described in Rep. 4. As to "accidental features" of acquired virtues remaining, it is true that residual dispositions from prior possession of acquired virtue can remain in a person with infused virtue. But even supporters of this view recognize those features to be "dispositions" that are "less than a settled habit."[41] Since those causal influences, though real, are not settled habits, they cannot be acquired virtues. It is better to call them dispositions. Therefore, the acquired virtues are not even virtually present in the person with infused virtue.

[The following replies address whether and how the infused virtues and/or their acts can order the acquired virtues and/or their acts.]

Rep. 7. It is true that the natural end persists and is fulfilled in the life of grace. However, the acquired virtues cannot be ordered to supernatural happiness, even extrinsically by infused virtue.[42] The acquired virtues are by definition caused by a person's actions, not (healed and) elevated by grace. To claim that they can be meritorious renders God's grace unnecessary for salvation. Concomitantly, the acquired virtues are ordered to the natural, civil, earthly good as last end.[43] If virtues are further ordered toward a person's supernatural end, those virtues are governed by the measure of the Divine law. They are thus, by definition, caused by God's grace and therefore infused. Therefore, the acquired moral virtues cannot be further ordered, even extrinsically, toward supernatural happiness.

Rep. 8. It is true that higher virtues can use lower ones in the manner described here. But in these cases, the "lower virtues" are not virtues in the most proper human sense. They are either skills or habits of the speculative intellect. The perfection of a skill occurs not in the agent but in the product, such as when a sail is rigged well.[44] This can occur for a good or bad end, so the habit does not engage the person's will in the specification of its object and thus it does not connect to a person's last end and concomitant rule or measure in the same way that a virtue in the proper sense does. Similarly, intellectual virtues such as knowledge of math can be used for good or ill, and specification of their objects does not involve the will in a manner connected to a person's last end and its concomitant rule. Hence these are not virtues in the properly human sense, and given their lack of involvement of the will in specification of the object, they can be possessed by the person possessing moral virtues or vices. This is not true of the acquired and infused moral virtues. Therefore, the examples here do not support the coexistence of the infused and acquired moral virtues.

Rep. 9. The person in a state of grace does indeed participate in the earthly city even as she participates in the heavenly city. However, regarding the example of prudence, both types of prudence retain the same last end (e.g., natural human flourishing) even as they concern different arenas of activity (e.g., decisions for an individual's life and decisions for a community by its leader). Thus, two distinct types of virtue can be operative in concert. However, the comparison to the acquired and infused virtue fails since these virtues concern the *same* arena of activity (e.g., prudence) though in relation to different last ends (natural as distinct from supernatural flourishing).[45] It is the further end that supplies the rule or measure of virtue even as more proximate ends are achieved. Hence the same person cannot in one and the same arena of activity act in a manner informed by two different last ends and their respective measures. Therefore, the person with infused virtues cannot possess acquired virtues.

Rep. 10. It is true that one virtue can order another virtue toward a higher end, and both can be virtues in the properly human sense (involving the will in specification of activity). However, this only occurs when the arena of activity of the higher-order virtue is broader than the arena of the subordinate virtue. So, for instance, through charity, whose "object" is God, a person can order the acts of other subordinate virtues toward God as final end. Commanding and referring is indeed part of charity's activity as a virtue, with God as object. When this occurs, the infused moral virtue is indeed subordinated, not excluded, and retains its own proximate object even as it is commanded by charity. When this occurs, the subordinate virtue has the same last end as the commanding virtue, in this case God.

Yet in the purported case of infused moral virtues ordering acquired moral virtues, both have the same immediate arena of activity. Whereas when charity refers the infused virtues toward God as last end, its act can simply be that command; the infused moral virtues have as their arenas of activity not God as last end but the very sorts of activities that the acquired virtues concern as well.[46] Thus their very act cannot be to command the acquired virtues toward a further end.[47] For instance, a person's infused temperance does not order her acts of eating moderately through acquired temperance to God, but it does supply the particular end of eating moderately in light of her relationship to God, an act that is commanded by charity to be done for the sake of love of God.[48]

Furthermore, since habits qualify human powers by particularizing their ends as supplied by nature, possessing two different types of virtue with different formal objects according to different rules yet which nonetheless qualify one and the same natural powers with particular ends in light of those rules, is not possible in the same person.[49] The acquired and infused moral virtues have different last ends and thus different rules or measures. So while they supply more particular ends for the same arena of activity (e.g., eating for temperance), those particular ends are specified differently.[50] Therefore, the infused moral virtues cannot order and command the acquired moral virtues.

[The following replies concern the possibility and the manner of growth in infused virtue.]

Rep. 11. It is true that the person with the infused virtues in the graced life of discipleship can and should continue to grow in virtue. However, the fact that infused virtues are bestowed all at once does not mean that further growth in infused virtue is not possible. In fact, due to the connectivity of the virtues it is also true that the acquired virtues are attained all at once as well, even if it is more difficult to discern when the person has crossed the line to possess the acquired virtues. Further growth in even acquired virtue is possible and indeed necessary after their possession.[51] It is not necessary to posit an additional or other set of virtues (the acquired virtues) to explain the possibility and necessity of further growth in the infused virtues once possessed. Even those who claim people with infused virtues need also acquired virtue for growth recognize the possibility and necessity of ongoing growth in the theological virtues of faith, hope, and love, yet they do not posit the need to attain "acquired theological virtues" to explain such growth. Therefore, it is not necessary to attain acquired virtue in order to continue to grow in infused virtue once the infused virtues are possessed.

Rep. 12. It is true that a person with infused virtue may not consistently act well in arenas of activity not necessary for salvation. However, when this occurs, it does not mean the activity in this arena constitutes a realm that is not related to salvation, to one's last end of supernatural happiness. It is, rather, an arena of activity that, even though "covered" by the possessed infused virtue, constitutes an arena for growth in that virtue. Since the activity is not necessary for salvation, a lack in this area does not preclude the possession of the relevant infused virtue. When growth in that arena of activity occurs, it is not the attainment of acquired virtue alongside infused virtue but rather growth in the relevant infused virtue and a greater integration of all of the person's activity toward her last end.

There are two reasons why it is important that such growth be growth in the pertinent infused moral virtue and not through a parallel acquired virtue. First, if this were not the case, there would be arenas of a person's life that are "covered" by acquired virtue rather than the parallel infused virtue, unrelated to the person's last end of supernatural happiness.[52] Second, and relatedly, since acquired and infused virtues (say, temperance) concern the same matter or types of activity, it is not clear how to distinguish realms of activity (rather than particular acts) that differ in terms of necessity for salvation and yet rightly call both the same virtue.[53] Therefore, it is not necessary to attain acquired virtue in order to grow in activities not necessary for salvation.

Rep. 13. It is true, although not always the case, that those who have been gifted the infused virtues may act without facility in certain types of activity. A virtue is a stable disposition to act well in a certain area of life, and though facility is a common feature of the possession of virtue, it is not essential to that possession for infused virtue or even acquired virtue. Sometimes facility is impeded by external circumstances (e.g., poverty, victimization). Sometimes facility is even impeded by internal causes. There may persist contrary dispositions from nature or custom in the person who possesses virtue. Though such contrary dispositions cannot be stably specified at the rational level of a person's powers—lest the person not possess that virtue—they can exert a real causal influence and impede facility of action. When such contrary dispositions are lessened or eliminated in the person with infused virtue, it is not due to the attainment of acquired virtue alongside infused virtue, but rather through growth in the infused virtue itself. Such growth occurs by the infused virtue taking greater root in the person, commonly through changes in sensory dispositions as they participate more fully in—become more fully integrated with—the person's infused virtue. Thus, while proponents of coexistence on the basis of facility do accurately describe a possible area for growth in infused virtue, that growth does not occur by the possession of a parallel acquired virtue.

[The following replies concern the gain or loss of infused virtue.]

Rep. 14. Though it is possible for acquired virtue to be possessed after the loss of infused virtue, it does not happen in the way described here and thus this is not evidence that the acquired virtues coexisted with the infused virtues before mortal sin and the loss of the latter. There is a coherence to both infused and acquired virtue such that they are specified rationally and therefore are connected with other virtues and have a coherent orientation toward a person's last end.

When the basis of the coherence of infused virtue is lost in mortal sin, the infused virtues are lost as virtues in the proper sense. What is left behind is not immediately a new coherence toward natural human flourishing (or certainly a vicious coherence, since vices are rationally specified but not comparably connected or coherent), for two reasons. First, mortal sin is usually against both supernatural flourishing and natural flourishing, so a mortal sin could not engender acquired virtue. Second, acquired virtues are caused by repeated acts until the rational specification of the acts of virtue is impressed on the person's appetites to engender an acquired virtue. So the objection is correct that a mortal sin cannot cause the attainment of acquired virtue. But, similarly, acts of infused virtue that reflect and (through God's grace) sustain (even increase) the infused virtue cannot have also sustained coherent acquired virtues. The coherence entailed in either the acquired or the infused virtues is due to the measure of each type of virtue, to the rule of human reason or to the rule of Divine law, respectively. As noted earlier, that different measure is one reason the acquired and infused virtues cannot coexist.

Thus, it is true that mortal sin cannot cause the acquired virtues. It is also true that the loss of infused virtue cannot leave behind a coherent set of acquired virtues that had merely lost their "topping off" or extension to the supernatural end. For a person to possess acquired virtue after mortal sin, it would take some degree of repeated action toward natural flourishing as last end that would impress that rational specification on the person's powers and engender concomitant connectivity and orientation toward a new coherent last end.

Rep. 15. It is true that those who lose the infused virtues through mortal sin can continue to perform good acts consistently in the manner of a habit. Yet consistent good acts performed after the loss of infused virtue do not necessarily indicate the possession of a habit (in this case a virtue) in the proper sense. They may be caused by a disposition (which may even be quite stable) that persists residually from previously possessed virtue. Custom dispositions to even relatively complex acts can be caused by repeated actions that lack requisite rational specification, and thus without connection to other virtues and orientation toward a person's last end.[54] Therefore, the continuation of even persistent observably good acts after the loss of infused virtue is not necessarily evidence of the presence of acquired virtue, let alone the coexistence of acquired virtue with the infused virtues before the loss of the latter.

Rep. 16. It is true that it would be unfitting for the bestowal of God's grace to result in a loss to the recipient. However, with grace bestowed the recipient does not lose her natural capacities, which are requalified by the infused virtue. Furthermore, the "loss" of a lesser state of something in favor of a better state is not truly a loss. For instance, when one has a rudimentary understanding of math and studies diligently, the prior mediocre disposition of knowledge is lost in favor of a strengthened habit. A continent person possesses the good habit of continence but becomes temperate in growing more virtuous. Childhood is lost when one becomes an adult. These are not trade-offs. Rather, they are examples of a better qualification of the same thing that is attained (in the case of virtue it is natural potency, the "matter" of the virtue), not the loss of one good thing for a different sort of better thing. In all these cases the underlying potency remains, but the end toward which it is naturally oriented is fulfilled to a greater degree. The bestowal of infused virtue is an improvement, not in the sense of a tradeoff but in terms of the greater fulfillment of the ends of the same thing (or, in this case, the same nature now qualified by God's grace), and though a person can no longer possess the acquired virtues after the bestowal of infused virtue, the change is not properly understood as a loss but an improvement, especially since the goods of natural flourishing are attained in the life of grace even as they are surpassed (see Rep. 4). Furthermore, though acquired virtue *qua* habit does not remain after the bestowal of infused virtue, it is true that residual effects of such prior habits (*relictae*) can remain, which explains possible ongoing causal influence of prior habituation even without possession of the prior habit.[55] Therefore, there is no true "loss" caused by bestowal of infused virtue and thus no need to posit acquired virtue as persisting once infused virtue is bestowed.

NOTES

1. Though there are also historical precedents for this debate, they are not the focus here. For examination of this issue in the mid-twentieth century and before, see Coerver, "The Quality of Facility in the Moral Virtues."
2. For more on the historical context of the disputed question, see Torrell, *Thomas Aquinas, Vol. I*, 59–63; as well as Weisheippl, *Friar Thomas D'Aquino*, 123–26.
3. These texts are: ST I–II 51,4 ad 3; ST I–II 65,3 ad 2; ST II–II 47,14 ad 1; and, *De virt.* a. 10 ad 4. For extended treatments of these texts see Mattison, "Can Christians Posses the Acquired Cardinal Virtues?," 566–69, 576–84; Knobel, *Aquinas and the Infused Moral Virtues*, 81–106; and Knobel, "Relating Aquinas's Infused and Acquired Virtues," 411–31.
4. These two texts are *Sent.* l. 3 d. 23 q. 3 a. 4 qa. 1; and *Sent.* l. 3 d. 33 q. 1 a. 2 qa. 4.
5. For instance, on the former text from *Sentences*, see Decosimo, "More to Love," 55. On the latter, see Newton, "The Virtual Presence of the Cardinal Virtues," 17.
6. Gilson, *Christian Philosophy*: "Natural virtues remain what they were; it is the one who possesses them who has changed" (349). See also Dell'Olio, *Foundations*, 134: "The natural virtues are now put to the service of a new end by their existence in a new kind of person."
7. See Bowlin, "Elevating and Healing": "Acts of acquired virtue can be elevated beyond their natural, temporal ends and ordained to the ends of supernatural charity" (40); Lottin, *Principes*: "The acquired moral virtues . . . as penetrated by the intention of charity fit the appetite for the supernatural end" (2: 221–22); and Dell'Olio, *Foundations*: "The naturally acquired moral virtues of the Christian are not lost with the infusion of the moral virtues with charity. Rather, they continue to do their own work, although now that work serves the end of charity" (135).
8. See Mirkes, who describes the acquired virtues as the "matter" on which the formal principle, i.e., infused virtue, operates ("Aquinas's Doctrine of Moral Virtue," 195, 204, 212, 218). Dell'Olio claims: "The natural end remains a partial and limited participation of the human being *qua* human in the divine goodness, and the natural virtues that allow us to realize this end remain true goods, in the new contour of the life of grace" (137). In a slightly different point, Newton claims that there are innate virtues, and since they must be natural, not supernatural, they persist in the life of grace ("Virtual Presence," 24). But,

though Aquinas affirms the existence of "innate virtues," they are more properly called innate dispositions, not virtues.

9. Osborne claims that Mattison and Knobel both assume that the "supernatural and natural ends are in some way incompatible" ("What Is at Stake?," 126) and therefore "the operation of a natural virtue is entirely suppressed by the presence of charity" (125). Kent claims that "having as one's ultimate end the complete happiness possible only in the presence of God does not prevent one from regarding the happiness of this life as an intrinsic good. A good can be loved both for its own sake and yet as subordinate to a higher end" ("Habits and Virtues," 125).
10. See Decosimo, "More to Love," 55, for the claim that "infused virtue cannot apply right reason to some matter any more than acquired virtue can apply New Law." The latter claim is correct; the former is not.
11. Decosimo claims that to live "exclusively in immediate view of the gospel" is to live "to the *exclusion* of acts and virtues ordered immediately to subordinate goods" ("More to Love," 68, [emphasis added]). If by "immediate" Decosimo means the arena of activity, in the sense that the theological virtues have God as their object and moral virtues do not, then both acquired and cardinal virtues share the same "immediate" activities. If "in immediate view of the gospel" he means activity specified according to Divine rule, then his argument assumes that rule does not fulfill the "subordinate goods" of nature, which in fact it does. Though Decosimo indicates recognition that the supernatural good is "all-encompassing," he perplexingly thinks that any fulfillment of the natural good in supernatural activity would be merely "incidental and indirect, a mere side effect" ("More to Love," 69). Decosimo offers three different visions of the understanding of natural goods to the supernatural beatitude in the course of a single page. In addition to describing the supernatural good as "all encompassing" in character but with mere "incidental and indirect" relation to natural goods, he at times describes the Divine rule "to the exclusion of subordinate good" (69).
12. Newton, in "The Virtual Presence of the Cardinal Virtues," claims, "Aquinas does not say what Mattison interprets him as saying—namely that Christians have only one ultimate end" (26). See also Ryan, "Must an Acting Person," for an extended attack on the claim that a person must have only one final end at any one time (334, 354). See McInerny, *The Difficult Good*, for the claim that there are multiple "last ends" (52), though even he recognizes they are referred to as an "absolutely ultimate end" (42).
13. See Newton, "The Virtual Presence of the Cardinal Virtues," 34. See also Newton's claims that when "new goals come," the prior ends are "not replaced" but are "elevated" (29) and that a person's "new end does not mean that they no longer have the lower ends" (33).
14. Decosimo claims "virtual presence is not actual presence," a phrase he understands as equivalent to "subordination is not exclusion" ("More to Love," 56). See also Newton, "Virtual Presence of the Cardinal Virtues."
15. Cleveland and Dahm, "The Virtual Presence of the Acquired Virtues," 95.
16. See Decosimo, "More to Love," 54–57. He claims that acquired virtue is concerned "immediately" with the rule of reason and "sometimes the best way to [act in accord with the new law] may be to undertake an act in immediate accord with right reason, an act of acquired virtue. In such cases, infused virtue is also at work" (57). Of course, an act in accord with the new law will also accord with right reason. But his claim is that an act of acquired virtue can be ordered by infused virtue, "ordering that act to its own higher end" (57).

17. Kent claims that "with the virtue of charity . . . the acts of these naturally acquired virtues are made meritorious" ("Habits and Virtues," 125); Bowlin claims that "an act that stems from an acquired virtue . . . can be meritorious" ("Elevating and Healing," 42); Decosimo claims that "acquired virtue can be made perfect by remote reference to beatitude" (*Ethics as a Work of Charity*, 195) and "true acquired virtues [are] informed by charity" (196); Austin speaks of "charity making the act of acquired virtue meritorious" (*Aquinas on Virtue*, 183); and Mirkes claims that an infused moral virtue "is able to effect, produce, or create its own form or perfection in its acquired counterpart, enabling the acquired virtue to function just like the infused" ("Aquinas's Doctrine of Moral Virtue," 196–97).
18. Decosimo, "More to Love": "Acquired and infused virtues are compatible. . . . They can be had and used together by a Christian. More than that, they should be. . . . To fail to do so is a failure of discipleship" (47).
19. These examples are taken from Decosimo, "More to Love," 56–57. See also his treatment of subalternate sciences in *Ethics as a Work of Charity*, 194.
20. Decosimo, "More to Love," 56.
21. For reliance on Aristotle's and Aquinas's thoughts on the relationship between different types of prudence (or courage), see Decosimo, "More to Love," 51–52, where he not only describes levels of prudence but also the virtue of religion. See also Austin, *Aquinas on Virtue*, 182; and Sherwin, "Infused Virtue," 50.
22. For a beautiful example of this, see Decosimo's treatment of how his and his wife's relationship was changed upon having a child, not simply in having the additional end of child-raising but in how that end changed how they relate to one another as spouses ("More to Love," 70). Bowlin offers another such example, namely, having his son in his class as a college professor and how his treatment of his son as student is further ordered toward his relationship with him as son ("Elevating and Healing," 41).
23. For examples of this claim, see Garrigou-Lagrange, who claims: "Infused chastity. . . . makes use of acquired chastity. . . . They are exercised together; acquired chastity is thus at the service of infused chastity" (*The Three Ages of the Interior Life*, 2:133–34). Sherwin claims the acquired virtues are elicited and then commanded by the infused moral virtues ("Infused Virtue," 50).
24. As Decosimo is fond of stating, "Subordination is not inclusion." This is indeed true with regard to charity and the infused moral virtues (Decosimo, "More to Love," 56).
25. Decosimo claims: "It is mistaken to think that having its act ordered to a remote end by a higher virtue changes the operation or end of the virtue so ordered" ("More to Love," 64).
26. See Decosimo, "More to Love": "There are myriad ways to fulfill the New Law, to act according to its rule. And sometimes the best way to do so may be to undertake an act in immediate accord with right reason, an act of acquired virtue" (56–57). See also: "Infused moral virtue can command acquired virtue to act and refer that act to beatitude, while acquired virtue's act remains its self-same ordinary act" (59). This seems to be what Sherwin means when he claims that "the (elicited) acts of the acquired moral virtues are commanded by the infused moral virtues" ("Infused Virtues," 50). See also Bowlin's claim that "every moral virtue, perfected by grace and transformed by charity, . . . is ordered to two ends, one proximate and determined by reason and another that is 'remote and excelling, namely God'" (*Contingency and Fortune*, 217–18).
27. As to how the act is one of infused virtue (as well as acquired virtue), Decosimo claims: "The act of infused virtue just is commanding and referring—commanding and referring

a subordinate act that is itself in immediate accord with right reason" ("More to Love," 57). This quote hints at a different problem, namely, assuming virtues as agent rather than qualifications of powers of the person who is an agent. Speaking as if virtues are agents disintegrates the person. Decosimo attempts to guard the priority of infused virtue while maintaining the existence of acquired virtue, yet does so by speaking of them as agents and thus threatening the unity of the person. In describing how they operate together, he says infused prudence "has determined that deploying an act in immediate accord with right reason," and it is only then that "acquired virtue begins to speak" ("More to Love," 66).

28. Decosimo claims the acquired virtues are necessary to complete the infused virtues when he says: "Acquired and infused virtues are compatible. . . . They can be had and used together by a Christian. More than that, they should be. . . . To fail to do so is a failure of discipleship" ("More to Love," 47). In fact, each of the citations in the next two objections suggest the need for acquired virtue to complete infused virtue, though in different ways as addressed in each of those two objections.

29. This is arguably the most frequent argument in support of the need for the acquired virtues in the life of grace. The claim is that infused prudence concerns only a "narrow band" of activities (Sherwin, "Infused Virtue," 42). Kent claims: "Infused prudence does not enable one to deliberate well about everything under the sun, but only about things related to salvation" (125). Anderson claims: "The infused cardinal virtues, then, are not brought to bear on every end of human life" (*Virtue and Grace,* 24). Decosimo affirms the same when he says the possession of acquired virtues for one with infused virtues gives her "more to love" ("More to Love," 70). Scholars commonly make a further claim, that the most fully virtuous life requires possession of both infused and acquired virtue. Decosimo: "By them [acquired virtues] Christians [i.e., those with infused virtues] come to behold and love goods to which they are otherwise blind and indifferent" (70); And Anderson: "Not only can the acquired and infused cardinal virtue be had simultaneously, but they both must be possessed if one is to reach the ultimate end" (24). Pieper claims that infused prudence is "limited solely to what is necessary for eternal salvation" and thus a "fuller prudence" is constituted by infused and acquired prudence "combined" in a "literally graced unity" (*The Four Cardinal Virtues,* 14). Dell'Olio similarly claims "fuller prudence," the "working together . . . of naturally acquired prudence and supernaturally infused prudence, constitutes the fullest, most complete, indeed 'perfect' expression of prudence in the human being. Without it, there is no connection of the natural and supernatural virtues and no harmonious development of the human being" (*Foundations of Moral Selfhood,* 137). Herdt also makes this claim, citing Pieper as Dell-Olio does (*Putting on Virtue,* 87–88).

30. The claim that acquired virtue supplies facility of action to infused virtue is rather common. See Inglis's claim that the acquired virtues enable one with infused virtue to "move more easily" ("Aquinas's Replication of the Acquired Moral Virtues," 22). See also Sherwin, "Infused Virtue," 51; and Miner, "Non-Aristotelian Prudence in the *Prima Secundae,*" 421. What is more surprising is the not-uncommon claim that infused virtues need the acquired virtues to even be virtues. Herdt claims: "On their own, the infused virtues do not make it easy or pleasant to act virtuously." Yet she further claims, "The infused virtues alone seem to render a person continent rather than virtuous" and "The infused virtues . . . are incomplete without the acquired virtues" (*Putting on Virtue,* 87). Dell'Olio, whom Herdt cites, claims "The infused virtues, without the facility or ability that comes

with acquired virtues, are habits only in an analogous sense. For they lack the ease or facility of operation that characterize a habit in the strict sense" (*Foundations of Moral Selfhood*, 137–38). He even says, "The naturally acquired virtues aid the infused virtues by enabling them to exist in the person in the condition of full virtues, that is, as good *habits* abiding in one's character, rather than mere dispositions" (138) (emphasis added). While Dell'Olio should be commended for recognizing the disposition/habit distinction, the claim that grace-bestowed infused virtues require acquired virtues to be virtues is enormously problematic, not only on a moral theological level but also on a soteriological one. A yet even more extraordinary claim in the context of facility is that the acquired virtues can displace "vices" that can be possessed with infused virtue: "Until the person [with infused virtue] is able to replace the acquired vice with an acquired virtue, ease in performing the infused virtue cannot occur" (Mirkes, "Aquinas' Doctrine of Moral Virtue," 205–6).

31. For an example of this argument, see Cleveland and Dahm, "The Virtual Presence of the Acquired Virtues," 79, esp. the discussion of "Timothy."
32. See Cleveland and Dahm, "The Virtual Presence of the Acquired Virtues," for a clear expression of this position, which they term "recoverability": "The acquired virtues need to be present in some sense due to their recoverability, due to the explanatory work they are doing" (80). They also say that if someone "were to receive infused temperance and have it increase greatly over time, he would then have something like acquired temperance were he to lose infused temperance" (97). Note this latter claim also suggests that growth in infused virtue comes through possession of acquired virtue (or what they call the "virtual presence" of acquired virtue).
33. Cleveland and Dahm, in "The Virtual Presence of the Acquired Virtues," call this the "unsuitability of goods being eliminated rather than perfected by grace" (84) or the "unseemly elimination of the acquired virtues" (96).
34. See ST I–II 1, 4–6.
35. The claims that the acquired virtues are ordered to the earthly city and natural happiness and that infused virtues are ordered toward the heavenly city and supernatural happiness are rampant throughout Aquinas's corpus. More particularly relevant here is Aquinas's claim that that the acquired virtues cannot be ordered toward supernatural happiness (ST I–II 63,2) and that they are ordered toward the civil good last end (*De virt. card.* a. 4 ad 3). The infused virtues, however, are not ordered to the civil good as last end but to the heavenly city (*De virt. card.* a. 4 ad 3). See *Sent.* l. 3 d. 33 q. 1 a. 2 qa. 3 and 4; ST I–II 63,2 and 63,4; and, *De virt.* a. 10 ad 8–10.
36. Cessario, *The Moral Virtues and Theological Ethics*: "This conception [that the life of grace entails only infused theological virtues and acquired moral virtues] leaves the acquired virtues touched only from the outside, as it were, by divine grace. For his part, Aquinas holds out for a bolder and more reassuring explanation than this: divine grace creates a new virtue. The infused virtues imply a relation to activity since they shape the proximate sources of activity in the human person, what the scholastics call the operative powers or capacities" (170).
37. Cates helpfully describes how virtues qualify natural powers (not natural virtues) when she speaks of charity "transforming the will itself" (*Choosing to Feel*, 39). See also Porter: "Grace is a quality of the whole soul, comprehensively transforming all its distinctively human potencies in accordance with a participation in divine nature. This comprehensive transformation comes about through the perfection and actualization of these

potencies." ("Moral Virtues, Charity, and Grace," 62). It is noteworthy when a scholar claims the persistence of acquired virtue is necessary to honor the idea that "grace perfects nature" yet admits the acquired virtues are not present in the lives of the blessed in heaven (e.g., Dell'Olio, *Foundations,* 142). As to the matter/form point, see Cleveland and Dahm, "The Virtual Presence of the Acquired Virtues," for a more precise usage of these terms with regard to infused virtue (82).

38. See Goris, "Acquired and Infused Moral Virtues": "Aquinas thinks that the supernatural end does not exclude man's natural goods and that the rule of divine law includes the rule of reason" (38). Knobel describes how this is true even with infused theological virtue when she claims: "When we reason in the light of faith, we still make use of the truths that unaided reason can grasp" yet "see those truths in their fullness" (*Aquinas and the Infused Moral Virtues,* 147). See Irwin: "continuity of the infused with the acquired virtues affects the plausibility of Aquinas' theory as a whole. If he could not show that the infused virtues express more fully the outlook of the acquired virtues, it would be difficult for him to show that they are the exercise of the same free will that is moved by deliberation about the final good to form the states of character that constitute the acquired virtues" (*Development of Ethics,* 647–48). This fact, that infused cardinal virtues qualify the same powers of the person toward the same activities (in matter, not formal object), is captured well by Cates: "The infusion of charity transforms the whole of the person, such that she becomes oriented fundamentally toward the attainment of supernatural happiness. Even when she chooses to act and to feel in such a way that she will attain to natural human happiness, she necessarily sees natural human happiness as subordinate to (and thus qualified by) her vision of supernatural human happiness" (*Choosing to Feel,* 39). This leads Cates to conclude that the life of grace "does not require, and technically speaking does not even allow, the acquisition of merely acquired virtue" (38, 45). Gilleman describes this well: "The ideal of action proper to the infused virtue includes and surpasses that of the corresponding acquired virtue, for supernatural finality does not suppress natural finality, but rather deepens it and leads it into contact with God" (*The Primacy of Charity in Moral Theology,* 184). Christoph also notes the inclusion of natural finality in infused virtue: "the formal object of acquired virtue is inclusively present in infused virtue, granted that the object of the natural virtue is elevated to conform to the divine rule" ("Justice as an Infused Virtue in the *Secunda secundae,*" 211; see also Huetter, *Bound for Beatitude,* 306n21). However, Christoph's language, of the "formal object" of acquired virtue remaining present in infused virtue but "elevated to conform to the divine rule," is not accurate. That new rule renders the virtue infused, with a new formal object, even as the natural finality is attained under that new formality.

39. See Porter, "Moral Virtue," which addresses the relationship between the various souls of the human person. There she quotes Aquinas: "When a more perfect form comes to be, the prior form decays, yet in such a way that the subsequent form has whatever the first form had, and has it more fully . . . (*ST* I 118, 2 ad 2)" (64).

40. Newton, "Virtual Presence," 34. It should be noted that there are varying ways to deny that a person has one last end. Newton labels as last ends those ends that persist even as they are further ordered. The dynamic he describes is correct, but the further ordered ends are not properly called last ends. Others adopt a more "aggregate" view of the last end, describing different human actions as ordered toward various "portions" of one's last end. See Decosimo, *Ethics as Work of Charity,* 211–13; and for a critique of this, Mattison, "Habitual Ordering in Aquinas," 1301. Others simply deny the existence of

one last end due to various ways a human life (in this life) lacks coherence. See Ryan, "Must an Acting Person Have a Single Ultimate End?," 334. For attempts to address this lack of integration in human activity and yet guard the claim that a person does all for the sake of the last end, see Mattison, "A New Look at the Last End" and "Habitual Ordering in Aquinas."

41. See Cleveland and Dahm, "The Virtual Presence of the Acquired Virtues," 95. Later they accurately claim: "When an infused virtue is given, the acquired habit (if one is present) is unsettled such that it is not longer a full habit but now remains virtually in a less-than-habit disposition of a power" (96). This perfectly describes what happens (addressed in later replies). For now it suffices to note that "less-than-habit" dispositions cannot be acquired virtues.
42. See Porter: "Orientation toward connatural happiness is constitutive of the acquired virtues. . . . That is why the acquired virtues do not have the capacity, as it were, to be perfected through the commanding operations of the theological virtues" (Moral Virtues, Charity, and Grace," 48–49). Cleveland and Dahm state: "The main problem for the coexistence view is that the proximate ends of the acquired virtues are not able to be ordered toward supernatural beatitude" ("The Virtual Presence of the Acquired Virtues," 81). Christoph claims: "The graced agent is directed to supernatural union with God by charity and the infused virtues, and this new orientation becomes the first principle of all of his acts. Consequently, if such a person fulfills any virtuous deed that is determined superficially by natural standards, it will finally be directed to that supernatural end, i.e. it will be always a supernatural act since every moral act is measured in respect to the final end" ("Justice as an Infused Virtue," 213). See also Huetter, *Bound for Beatitude,* 306. Bradley claims that "no natural or humanly acquired virtue can set such a supernatural end for man or enable him to attain it by the appropriate supernatural means," and "humanly acquired prudence . . . cannot, by definition, direct men to a supernatural end" (*Aquinas on the Twofold Human Good,* 15–16).
43. Goris claims that acts of acquired virtues "intend only a civil or political end and are indifferent to merit or demerit" ("Acquired and Infused Moral Virtues," 40). Even Gilson recognizes this: "The end of natural moral virtues is the welfare of the city or state which is the highest human good because it embraces and rules all others" (*The Christian Philosophy of St. Thomas Aquinas,* 337); and further, "it is essential to purely natural moral virtues that they have ends that fall short of man's supernatural end" (Gilson, 340).
44. See Knobel, *Aquinas and the Infused Moral Virtues,* 144–45, for discussion of these habits as skills.
45. Knobel claims that one virtue can order another when they "operate in distinct arenas of life" and "are subordinate to the same ultimate end" (*Aquinas and the Infused Moral Virtues,* 112). Contrary to this, Bowlin (like Decosimo) wrongly assumes acquired and infused justice "regard distinct social relationships" ("Elevating and Healing," 43), whereas they actually have the same arena of activity. He claims operating according to infused justice alone would render one "without attention to the norms and requirements of the temporal relationships they would ordinarily set aright" (43). Yet such is the "matter" of infused justice, not only acquired justice. See also Porter: "A higher virtue can be said to perfect a lower virtue by actualizing it, in the sense of commanding its proper act and ordering it toward a higher or more comprehensive good. This can only work if the higher and lower virtue are already oriented in some way toward the same overarching aim, the latter presumably in a more limited way; otherwise, the commanding activity

of the higher virtue would distort the innate orientation of the lower virtue, rather than perfecting it" ("Moral Virtues, Charity, and Grace," 48). On the problems caused by two habits residing in the same power toward the same sort of activity yet according to different measures, Porter goes on to say: "Decosimo claims that habits can co-exist in the same faculty, if they are different in species from one another ["More to Love," 55]. But this is too sweeping. Aquinas says that specifically distinct habits can co-exist in one faculty because the faculties of the human person are oriented to more than one kind of action, each of which is informed by an appropriate habit (ST I–II q. 54, a. 1). But this does not mean that any two specifically distinct habits [due to different measures] can co-exist—otherwise, someone could simultaneously have a virtue and its contrary vice (cf. ST I–II q. 71, a. 3)" ("Moral Virtues, Charity, and Grace," 52n15). Despite his own position, Sherwin also recognizes the problem of having different measures for the same type of activity ("Infused Virtue," 50).

46. For an example of wrongly assuming the infused moral virtues concern beatitude directly, rather than activities accessible to unaided reason performed in light of supernatural beatitude, see Austin: "The acquired virtues are intrinsically oriented toward particular goods, the infused moral virtues to perfect beatitude" (*Aquinas on Virtue*, 183).
47. Decosimo claims that virtues can be "immediately ordered to beatitude" or "remotely ordered" and that "it is not by acquired virtues own power but through its use by infused [presumably moral] virtue" that acquired virtue is directed to supernatural beatitude" (*Ethics as a Work of Charity*, 192). Yet this wrongly applies aspects of charity's command of infused moral virtues to a purported dynamic of infused moral virtues ordering acquired moral virtues. Decosimo elsewhere aligns acquired virtue with the proximate end of an act, and infused *moral* (rather than theological) virtue with the remote end ("More to Love," 65).
48. For recognition that the dynamic of virtues commanding virtues must occur at different levels (e.g., theological and moral), see Huetter, *Bound for Beatitude*, 310, 314.
49. Those who affirm coexistence commonly recognize this problem of differently specified actions of infused and acquired moral virtue toward the same activity. The standard response is that there must not be any conflict when infused moral virtues command acquired moral virtues (and if there is such conflict, there can be no command). Recall Sherwin on this point ("Infused Virtue," 50). See also Austin, who grants the formal object of acquired moral virtue differs from infused moral virtue in one who does not possess grace, but claims: "When an acquired virtue is under the command of infused virtue, there is no conflict in rule or mean" (*Aquinas on Virtue*, 184).
50. Porter describes this well: "Those who defend the compatibility of acquired and infused virtues presuppose that the acquired virtues are defined by an orientation towards some kind of finite good, which can be directed towards either natural or supernatural ends. But this is not Aquinas's view. Rather, he holds that acquired and infused virtues are both defined by reference to a formally distinctive kind of action, which pursues its end in a characteristic way, in accordance with some rule. This point is worth underscoring: These two kinds of virtue are distinguished both by their orientation towards two different kinds of perfection, but also, and correlatively, by two formally distinctive kinds of objects (I–II 63,4 ad 1)" ("Moral Virtue, Charity, and Grace," 51–52). See also Cleveland and Dahm, "The Virtual Presence of the Acquired Virtues," on how infused and acquired virtues "differ formally in three ways: final end, formal object, and rule" (85).

51. As Porter notes in "Moral Virtues, Charity, and Grace," Aquinas claims growth in a virtue, that is, a virtue's extension or being rendered more effective, does not happen by the addition of a new form (similar to what happens for an acquired virtue to an infused virtue) (43, which cites ST I–II 52,2). For a helpful treatment of growth in both acquired and infused virtue (though not coexisting), see Brandt, "Growth in Infused Virtue." Brandt accurately explains how all virtues in the fullest sense grow by the subject's greater participation in them, yet intellectual virtues like faith and prudence can also grow by extension (132–35).
52. Though he affirms coexistence, Cessario rightly recognizes this point: "The infused moral virtues illustrate how divine grace informs the whole of human life" (*The Moral Virtues and Theological Ethics*, 163). See also Goris, who claims: "Aquinas refuses to divide the life of those who are in grace into a secular and a religious domain" ("Acquired and Infused Moral Virtues," 39). See Knobel on how the infused virtues do not concern "some kind of separate sphere of action" (*Aquinas and the Infused Moral Virtues*, 147). Elsewhere she examines scholars who posit arenas of activity purportedly not necessary for salvation to show that it is "manifestly incorrect" that these arenas can be cleaved off in such a way (122).
53. As evidence of the difficulty of separating infused and acquired virtues as to arenas of actions necessary for salvation, see Hall, *Narrative and the Natural Law*: "Infused prudence is sufficient for the end of salvation. . . . But it does not confer ability and experience for directing matters with regard to this life, even as it is subordinated to God" (82). Yet "directing matters with regard to this life" is exactly what infused prudence does, lest it would not be prudence. The fact that it does so in a manner "subordinated to God" is what makes it infused prudence.
54. Cleveland and Dahm actually describe the "virtual presence" of acquired virtue as akin to just such a disposition, rather than a habit. ("The Virtual Presence of the Acquired Virtues," 96–97). See Rep. 6. For an argument that such a dynamic is best explained through custom dispositions, see Mattison, "Aquinas, Custom, and the Coexistence of Infused and Acquired Cardinal Virtues."
55. Cleveland and Dahm rightly note that residual effects of prior habit are not necessarily all eliminated ("The Virtual Presence of the Acquired Virtues," 96–97). They state: "Dispositional properties remaining from" previous acquired virtue may exert causal influence, "without their constituting a full habit" (97).

BIBLIOGRAPHY

WORKS BY AQUINAS

Commentary on Colossians. Translated by Fabian Larcher, OP. https://isidore.co/aquinas/SSColossians.htm.

Commentary on the Gospel of John, Part 1, Chap. 1–7. Translated by James Weisheippl, OP. https://isidore.co/aquinas/SSJohn.htm.

Commentary on the Nicomachean Ethics. Translated by C. I. Litzinger, OP. https://isidore.co/aquinas/Ethics.htm.

Commentary on Romans, https://aquinas.cc/la/en/~Rom.

Commentary on the Sentences. https://isidore.co/aquinas/.

Disputed Questions on the Virtues. Translated by E. M. Atkins. Cambridge: Cambridge University Press, 2012.

Disputed Questions on Truth. https://isidore.co/aquinas/QDdeVer.htm.

Disputed Questions on Virtue. Translated by Ralph McInerny. https://isidore.co/aquinas/QDdeVirtutibus.htm.

On Evil. Translated by Jean and John Oesterle. Notre Dame, IN: University of Notre Dame Press, 1995.

On Love and Charity: Readings from the "Commentary on the Sentences" of Peter Lombard. Translated by Peter Kwasniewski. Washington, DC: Catholic University of America Press, 2008.

On the Perfection of the Spiritual Life. Translated by John Procter, OP. https://isidore.co/aquinas/PerfectVitaeSpir.htm.

Summa Theologiae. Leonine Commission Critical Edition (Latin and English). https://isidore.co/aquinas/.

Summa Theologiae. Translated by Fred Freddoso. https://www3.nd.edu/~afreddos/summa-translation/TOC.htm.

PUBLISHED WORKS

Ackerill, J. L. "Aristotle on Eudaimonia." In *Essays on Aristotle's Ethics*, edited by Amélie Rorty, 15–33. Berkeley: University of California Press, 1980.

Anderson, Justin. *Virtue and Grace in the Theology of St. Thomas Aquinas.* Cambridge: Cambridge University Press, 2020.

Annas, Julia. *Intelligent Virtue.* Oxford: Oxford University Press, 2011.

———. *The Morality of Happiness.* Oxford: Oxford University Press, 1993.

Aristotle. "Categories." In *The Basic Works of Aristotle,* edited by Richard McKeon, 7–37. New York: Random House, 1941.

———. "On the Heavens." In *The Basic Works of Aristotle,* edited by Richard McKeon, 398–466. New York: Random House, 1941.

Augustine. *Confessions.* Translated by Maria Boulding, OSB. Hyde Park, NY: New City, 1997.

———. *Teaching Christianity.* Translated by Edmund Hill, OP. New York: New City, 2014.

Austin, Nicholas, SJ. *Aquinas on Virtue: A Causal Reading.* Washington, DC: Georgetown University Press, 2017.

Berkman, John, and William C. Mattison III, eds. *Searching for a Universal Ethic: Multidisciplinary, Ecumenical, and Interfaith Responses to the Catholic Natural Law Tradition.* Grand Rapids, MI: William B. Eerdmans, 2014.

Berkman, John, and Craig Steven Titus. *The Pinckaers Reader.* Washington, DC: Catholic University of America Press, 2005.

Bourdieu, Pierre. *Distinction: A Social Critique of the Judgment of Taste.* London: Routledge, 2010.

———. *Outline of a Theory of Practice.* Cambridge: Cambridge University Press, 1977.

Bowlin, John. *Contingency and Fortune in Aquinas's Ethics.* Cambridge: Cambridge University Press, 1999.

———. "Elevating and Healing: Reflections on *Summa Theologiae* I–II 109,2." *Journal of Moral Theology* 3, no. 1 (2014): 39–53.

Bradley, Denis. *Aquinas on the Twofold Human Good.* Washington, DC: Catholic University of America Press, 1999.

Brandt, Jared. "Growth in Infused Virtue in the Thought of Thomas Aquinas." PhD diss., Baylor University, 2018.

Breen, Katharine. *Imagining an English Reading Public, 1150–1400.* Cambridge: Cambridge University Press, 2010.

Broadie, Sarah. *Ethics with Aristotle.* Oxford: Oxford University Press, 1991.

Bullet, Gabriel. *Vertus morales infuses et vertus morales acquises selon Saint Thomas D'Aquin.* Fribourg: Éditions Universitaires, 1958.

Burnyeat, M. F. "Aristotle on Learning to Be Good." In *Essays on Aristotle's Ethics,* edited by Amélie Rorty, 69–92. Berkeley: University of California Press, 1980.

Butera, Giuseppe. "On Reason's Control of the Passions in Aquinas's Theory of Temperance." *Medieval Studies* 68, no. 1 (2006): 133–60.

Casey, John. *Pagan Virtue: An Essay in Ethics.* Oxford: Clarendon, 1990.

Cates, Diana Fritz. *Aquinas on the Emotions.* Washington, DC: Georgetown University Press, 2009.

———. *Choosing to Feel: Virtue, Friendship, and Compassion for Friends.* Notre Dame, IN: University of Notre Dame Press, 1997.

Cessario, Romanus. *Christian Faith and the Theological Life.* Washington, DC: Catholic University of America Press, 1996.

———. *Introduction to Moral Theology.* Washington, DC: Catholic University of America Press, 2001.

———. *The Moral Virtues and Theological Ethics.* 2nd ed. Notre Dame, IN: University of Notre Dame Press, 2008.

Chenu, M. D., OP. "Body and Body Politic in the Creation Spirituality of Thomas Aquinas." *Listening* 13, no. 1 (1978): 214–32.

Christoph, Markus. "Justice as an Infused Virtue in the *Secunda secundae* and Its Implications for Our Understanding of the Moral Life." PhD diss., University of Fribourg, 2010.

Clark, Patrick. "Is Martyrdom Virtuous?: An Occasion for Rethinking the Relation of Christ and Virtue in Aquinas." *Journal of the Society of Christian Ethics* 30, no. 1 (2010): 141–59.

Clear, James. *Atomic Habits: An Easy and Proven Way to Break Bad Habits and Build Good Ones.* New York: Avery, 2018.

Cleveland, W. Scott, and Brandan Dahm. "The Virtual Presence of the Acquired Virtues in the Christian Life." *American Catholic Philosophical Quarterly* 93, no. 1 (2019): 75–100.

Cloutier, David, and William C. Mattison III. "The Resurgence of Virtue in Recent Moral Theology." *Journal of Moral Theology* 3, no. 1 (2014): 228–59.

Coerver, Robert F., CM. "The Quality of Facility in the Moral Virtues." PhD diss., Catholic University of America, 1946.

Curzer, Howard. *Aristotle and the Virtues.* Oxford: Oxford University Press, 2012.

Daly, Daniel. *The Structures of Virtue and Vice.* Washington, DC: Georgetown University Press, 2021.

Decosimo, David. *Ethics as a Work of Charity: Thomas Aquinas and Pagan Virtue.* Stanford, CA: Stanford University Press, 2016.

———. "More to Love: Ends, Ordering, and the Compatibility of Acquired and Infused Virtues." In *The Virtuous Life: Thomas Aquinas on the Theological Nature of Moral Virtues,* edited by Harm Goris and Henk Schoot, 47–72. Leuven, Belgium: Peeters, 2017.

De Haan, Daniel D. "Moral Perception and the Function of the *Vis Cogitativa* in Thomas Aquinas's Doctrine of Antecedent and Consequent Passions." *Documenti e studi sulla tradizione filosofica medivale* 25 (2014): 289–330.

———. "Thomistic Hylomorphism, Self-Determination, Neuroplasticity, and Grace: The Case of Addiction." *Proceedings of the American Catholic Philosophical Association* 85 (2012): 99–120.

Dell'Olio, Andrew. *Foundations of Moral Selfhood: Aquinas on Divine Goodness and the Connectivity of the Virtues.* New York: Peter Lang, 2003.

Dihle, Albrecht. *The Theory of the Will in Classical Antiquity.* Berkeley: University of California Press, 1982.

Doris, John. *Lack of Character: Personality and Moral Behavior.* Cambridge: Cambridge University Press, 2002.

Duhigg, Charles. *The Power of Habit: Why We Do What We Do in Life and Business.* New York: Random House, 2014.

Elder-Vass, Dave. *The Causal Power of Social Structures: Emergence, Structure and Agency.* Cambridge: Cambridge University Press, 2010.

Falanga, Anthony. *Charity: The Form of the Virtues According to Saint Thomas.* Washington, DC: Catholic University of America Press, 1948.

Feingold, Lawrence. *The Natural Desire to See God According to St. Thomas and His Interpreters.* Rome: Apollinare studi, 2001.

Finn, Daniel, ed. *Moral Agency within Social Structures and Culture: A Primer on Critical Realism for Christian Ethics.* Washington, DC: Georgetown University Press, 2020.

Pope Francis. *Lumen Fidei*. Encyclical Letter, 2013. https://www.vatican.va/content/francesco/en/encyclicals/documents/papa-francesco_20130629_enciclica-lumen-fidei.html.

Garrigou-Lagrange, Réginald. *The Three Ages of the Interior Life: Prelude of Eternal Life*. 2 vols. Rockville, IL: Tan, 1989.

Gilleman, Gérard. *The Primacy of Charity in Moral Theology*. Westminister, MD: Newman, 1959.

Gilson, Etienne. *The Christian Philosophy of St. Thomas Aquinas*. Notre Dame, IN: University of Notre Dame Press, 1994.

Gondreau, Paul. "The Passions and the Moral Life: Appreciating the Originality of Aquinas." *The Thomist* 71 (2007): 419–50.

———. *The Passions of Christ's Soul in the Theology of Thomas Aquinas*. Münster, Germany: Aschendorf, 2002.

Goris, Paul. "Acquired and Infused Virtues in Wounded Nature." In *The Virtuous Life: Thomas Aquinas on the Theological Nature of Moral Virtues*, edited by Harm Goris and Henk Schoot, 21–46. Leuven, Belgium: Peeters, 2017.

Grisez, Germain. "The True Ultimate End of Human Beings: The Kingdom, Not God Alone." *Theological Studies* 69 (2008): 38–61.

Hall, Pamela. *Narrative and the Natural Law*. Notre Dame, IN: University of Notre Dame Press, 1994.

Hardie, W. F. R. "The Final Good in Aristotle's Ethics." *Philosophy* 40 (1965): 277–95.

Harman, Gilbert. "Moral Philosophy Meets Social Psychology: Virtue Ethics and the Fundamental Attribution Error." *Proceedings of the Aristotelian Society* 99 (1999): 315–31.

Hauerwas, Stanley. "Habit Matters: The Bodily Character of the Virtues." In *Habits in Mind: Integrating Theology, Philosophy and the Cognitive Science of Virtue, Emotion, and Character Formation*, edited by Gregory R. Peterson, James van Slyke, Michael Spezio, and Kevin Reimer, 24–40. Leiden, Netherlands: Brill, 2017.

Herdt, Jennifer. *Putting on Virtue: The Legacy of the Splendid Vices*. Chicago: University of Chicago Press, 2008.

Hibbs, Thomas. *Virtue's Splendor: Wisdom, Prudence, and the Human Good*. New York: Fordham University Press, 2001.

Hoffman, Tobias. "Aquinas on Moral Progress." In *Aquinas's "Summa Theologiae": A Critical Guide*, edited by Jeffrey Hause, 131–49. Cambridge: Cambridge University Press, 2018.

———. "Aquinas on the Moral Progress of the Weak Willed." In *The Problem of Weakness of Will in Medieval Thought*, edited by Tobias Hoffman, 221–47. Leuven, Belgium: Peeters, 2006.

Houser, R. E. *The Cardinal Virtues: Aquinas, Albert, and Philip the Chancellor*. Toronto: PIMS, 2004.

———. "The Virtue of Courage (IIa–IIae qq. 123–140)." In *The Ethics of Aquinas*, edited by Stephen J. Pope, 304–20. Washington, DC: Georgetown University Press, 2002.

Huetter, Reinhard. *Bound for Beatitude: A Thomistic Study in Eschatology and Ethics*. Washington, DC: Catholic University of America Press, 2019.

———. "Grace and Charity, Participation in the Divine Nature and Union with God: The Surpassing Contemporary Significance of Thomas Aquinas's Doctrine of Divinization." *Espíritu* 65, no. 116 (2016): 173–99.

Hursthouse, Rosalind. *On Virtue Ethics*. Oxford: Oxford University Press, 1999.

Inglis, John. "Aquinas's Replication of the Acquired Moral Virtues: Rethinking the Standard Philosophical Interpretation of Moral Virtue in Aquinas." *Journal of Religious Ethics* 27, no. 1 (1999): 3–27.

International Theological Commission. "In Search of a Universal Ethic: A New Look at the Natural Law." In *In Search of a Universal Ethic: A New Look at the Natural Law,* edited by John Berkman and William C. Mattison, 25–92. Grand Rapids, MI: Eerdmans, 2014.

Irwin, T. H. *Development of Ethics.* 3 vols. Oxford: Oxford University Press, 2011.

———. "Stoic and Aristotelian Conceptions of Happiness." In *The Norms of Nature,* edited by M. Schofield and G. Striker, 205–44. Cambridge: Cambridge University Press, 1986.

Jensen, Steven. *Sin: A Thomistic Psychology.* Washington, DC: Catholic University of America Press, 2018.

———. "Venial Sin and the Ultimate End." In *Aquinas's "Disputed Questions on Evil": A Critical Guide,* edited by M. V. Dougherty, 75–100. Cambridge: Cambridge University Press, 2015.

———. "Virtuous Deliberation and the Passions." *The Thomist* 77 (2013): 193–227.

Pope John Paul II. *Fides et ratio.* Papal Encyclical, 1994. https://www.vatican.va/content/john-paul-ii/en/encyclicals/documents/hf_jp-ii_enc_14091998_fides-et-ratio.html.

———. *Veritatis splendor.* Papal Encyclical, 1993. http://w2.vatican.va/content/john-paul-ii/en/encyclicals/documents/hf_jp-ii_enc_06081993_veritatis-splendor.html. Accessed September 21, 2018.

Johnson, Mark. "St. Thomas and the 'Law of Sin.'" *Recherches de théologie et philosophie médiévales* 67, no. 1 (2000): 80–95.

Kahm, Nicholas. *Aquinas on Emotions' Participation in Reason.* Washington, DC: Catholic University of America Press, 2019.

Kent, Bonnie. "Aquinas and Weakness of Will." *Philosophy and Phenomenological Research* 75, no. 1 (2007): 70–91.

———. "Habits and Virtues (Ia–IIa, qq. 49–70)." In *Ethics of Aquinas,* edited by Stephen Pope, 115–30. Washington, DC: Georgetown University Press, 2002.

———. *Virtues of the Will: The Transformation of Ethics in the Late Thirteenth Century.* Washington, DC: Catholic University of America Press, 1995.

Keys, Mary. "Aquinas's Two Pedagogies: A Reconsideration of the Relation Between Law and Moral Virtue." *American Journal of Political Science* 45, no. 3 (2001): 519–31.

Kim, Andrew. "Progress in the Good: A Defense of the Thomistic Unity Thesis." *Journal of Moral Theology* 3, no. 1 (2014): 147–74.

———. "Thomas Aquinas on the Connection of the Virtues." PhD diss., Catholic University of America, 2012.

Klubertanz, George P., SJ. *Habits and Virtues: A Philosophical Analysis.* New York: Appleton-Century-Crofts, 1965.

Knobel, Angela. "Aquinas and the Pagan Virtues." *International Philosophical Quarterly* 51, no. 3 (2011): 339–54.

———. "Can Aquinas's Infused and Acquired Virtues Coexist in the Christian Life?." *Studies in Christian Ethics* 23 (2010): 381–96.

———. "Elevated Virtue?: A Reply to Bowlin and Aquinas." *Journal of Moral Theology* 8, no. 2 (2019): 25–39.

———. "Intellectual Virtue: Acquiring Understanding," In *The New Cambridge Companion to Aquinas,* edited by Eleanor Stump and Thomas Joseph White, OP, 184–201. Cambridge: Cambridge University Press, 2022.

———. "Relating Aquinas's Acquired and Infused Virtues: Some Problematic Texts." *Nova et Vetera* 9, no. 2 (2011): 411–31.

———. *Thomas Aquinas on the Infused Moral Virtues.* Notre Dame, IN: University of Notre Dame Press, 2021.

———. "Two Theories of Christian Virtue." *American Catholic Philosophical Quarterly* 84 (2010): 599–618.

Knuuttila, Simo. *Emotions in Ancient and Medieval Philosophy.* Oxford: Oxford University Press, 2004.

Korsgaard, Christine. *Self-Constitution: Agency, Identity and Integrity.* Oxford: Oxford University Press, 2009.

Levering, Matthew. "Natural Law and Natural Inclinations: Rhonheimer, Pinckaers, and McAleer." *The Thomist* 70, no. 2 (2006): 155–201.

Lombardo, Nicholas, OP. *The Logic of Desire: Aquinas on Emotion.* Washington, DC: Catholic University of America Press, 2011.

Lottin, Dom, OSB. *Morale fondamontale.* Tournai, Belgium: Desclee and Cie, 1954.

———. *Principes de morale.* 2 vols. Louvain: Editions de Mont-César, 1947.

MacDonald, Scott. "Ultimate Ends in Practical Reasoning: Aquinas's Aristotelian Moral Psychology and Anscombe's Fallacy." *Philosophical Review* 100, no. 1 (1991): 31–66.

MacIntyre, Alasdair. *After Virtue.* 2nd ed. Notre Dame, IN: University of Notre Dame Press, 1984.

———. *Dependent Rational Animals.* Notre Dame, IN: University of Notre Dame Press, 1999.

———. *Ethics in the Conflicts of Modernity.* Cambridge: Cambridge University Press, 2016.

Maritain, Jacques. *The Range of Reason.* New York: Charles Scribner's Sons, 1952.

Martinez, Luis. *The Sanctifier.* Boston: Pauline, 2003.

Mattison, William C., III. "Aquinas, Custom, and the Coexistence of Infused and Acquired Cardinal Virtues." *Journal of Moral Theology* 8, no. 2 (2019): 1–24.

———. "Beatitude and the Beatitudes in the *Summa Theologiae* of St. Thomas Aquinas." *Josephenum Journal of Theology* 17, no. 2 (2010): 233–49.

———. "Can Christians Possess the Acquired Virtues?" *Theological Studies* 72 (2011): 558–85.

———. "Habitual Ordering in Aquinas." *Nova et Vetera* 19, no. 4 (2021): 1289–1321.

———. "Moral Virtue, the Grace of God, and Discipleship." In *Gathered for the Journey: Moral Theology in Catholic Perspective,* edited by David McCarthy and Theresa Lysaught, 198–215. Grand Rapids, MI: William B. Eerdmans, 2007.

———. "A New Look at the Last End: Noun and Verb, Determinate Yet Capable of Growth." *Journal of Moral Theology* 8, no. 2 special issue (2019): 95–113.

———. "Revisiting the Relationship between Infused and Acquired Cardinal Virtues: Lessons from Thomas Aquinas on Dead Faith." In *Being, Goodness, and Truth: Proceedings of the Society for Medieval Logic and Metaphysics,* vol. 16, edited by Gyula Klima and Alex Hall, 3–16. Cambridge: Cambridge Scholars Press, 2019.

———. "Thomas's Categorizations of Virtue: Historical Background and Contemporary Significance." *The Thomist* 74 (2010): 189–235.

McCabe, Herbert, OP. *The Good Life.* London: Continuum, 2005.

McDowell, John. "Deliberation and Moral Development in Aristotle." In *Aristotle, Kant, and the Stoics,* edited by Stephen Engstrom and Jennifer Whiting, 19–35. Cambridge: Cambridge University Press, 1996.

McInerny, Daniel J. *The Difficult Good: A Thomistic Approach to Moral Conflict and Human Happiness.* New York: Fordham University Press, 2006.

McKay (Knobel), Angela. "The Infused and Acquired Virtues in Aquinas's Moral Philosophy." PhD diss., University of Notre Dame, 2004.

Meinert, John. *The Love of God Poured Out: Grace and the Gifts of the Holy Spirit in St. Thomas Aquinas.* Steubenville, OH: Emmaus Academic Press, 2018.

Miller, Christian. *Moral Character.* Oxford: Oxford University Press, 2013.

———. "Virtue Cultivation in Light of Situationism." In *Developing the Virtues: Integrating Perspectives,* edited by Julia Annas, Darcia Narvaez, and Nancy Snow, 157–83. Oxford: Oxford University Press, 2016.

Millgram, Elijah. *Practical Induction.* Cambridge, MA: Harvard University Press, 1997.

Miner, Robert. "Aquinas on *Habitus.*" In *A History of Habit: From Aristotle to Bourdieu,* edited by Tom Sparrow and Adam Hutchinson, 67–88. Lanham, MD: Lexington, 2013.

———. "Non-Aristotelian Prudence in the *Prima Secundae.*" *The Thomist* 64 (2000): 401–22.

———. *Thomas Aquinas on the Passions: A Study of Summa Theologiae Ia–IIae 22–48.* Cambridge: Cambridge University Press, 2011.

Mirkes, Renée. "Aquinas's Doctrine of Moral Virtue and Its Significance for Theories of Facility." *The Thomist* 61, no. 2 (1997): 189–218.

Murphy, Mark. "Consent, Custom, and the Common Good in Aquinas' Account of Political Authority." *Review of Politics* 59, no. 2 (1997): 323–50.

Newton, Lloyd. "The Virtual Presence of the Cardinal Virtues." In *Being, Goodness, and Truth: Proceedings of the Society for Medieval Logic and Metaphysics,* vol. 16, edited by Gyula Klima and Alex Hall, 17–34. Cambridge: Cambridge Scholars Press, 2019.

O'Connor, Edward. "*Instinctus* and *Inspiratio.*" In *Summa Theologiae, Vol. 24: The Gifts of the Holy Spirit, Ia–IIae 68–70.*

———. "The Evolution of St. Thomas's Thought on the Gifts." In *Summa Theologiae, Vol. 24: The Gifts of the Holy Spirit, Ia–IIae 68–70.* Cambridge: Cambridge University Press, 2006.

———. "The Scriptural Basis for the Doctrine of the Gifts," In *Summa Theologiae, Vol. 24: The Gifts of the Holy Spirit, Ixia 68–70,* 80–87.

Osborne, Thomas. "Perfect and Imperfect Virtues in Aquinas." *The Thomist* 71 (2007): 39–64.

———. "The Threefold Referral of Acts to the Ultimate End in Thomas Aquinas and His Commentators." *Angelicum* 85 (2008): 715–36.

———. "What Is at Stake in the Question of Whether One Can Possess the Natural Moral Virtues Without Charity?." In *The Virtuous Life: Thomas Aquinas on the Theological Nature of Moral Virtues,* edited by Harm Goris and Henk Schoot, 117–30. Leuven, Belgium: Peeters, 2017.

Pasnau, Robert. *Thomas Aquinas on Human Nature.* Cambridge: Cambridge University Press, 2001.

Peterson, Christopher, and Martin E. P. Seligman, eds. *Character Strengths and Virtues: A Handbook and Classification.* New York: APA and Oxford University Press, 2004.

Pieper, Josef. *The Four Cardinal Virtues.* Notre Dame, IN: University of Notre Dame Press, 1966.

Pinckaers, Servais, OP. "Aquinas's Pursuit of Beatitude: From the *Commentary on the Sentences* to the *Summa Theologiae.*" In *The Pinckaers Reader: Renewing Thomistic Theology,* edited by John Berkman and Craig Steven Titus, 93–114. Washington, DC: Catholic University of America Press, 2005.

———. "Beatitude and the Beatitudes in Aquinas's *Summa Theologiae.*" In *The Pinckaers Reader: Renewing Thomistic Theology,* edited by John Berkman and Craig Steven Titus, 115–29. Washington, DC: Catholic University of America Press, 2005.

———. *La vie selon L'Esprit.* Luxembourg: Editions Saint-Paul, 1996.

———. "Morality and the Movement of the Holy Spirit: Aquinas' Doctrine of *Instinctus*." In *The Pinckaers Reader: Renewing Thomistic Theology,* edited by John Berkman and Craig Steven Titus, 385–99. Washington, DC: Catholic University of America Press, 2005.

———. *Sources of Christian Ethics.* Washington, DC: Catholic University of America Press, 1995.

———. "Virtue Is Not a Habit." *Cross Currents* 12, no. 1 (1962): 65–81.

Pinsent, Andrew. *The Second Person Perspective in Aquinas's Ethics: Virtues and Gifts.* New York: Routledge, 2011.

———. "Who's Afraid of the Infused Virtues?: Dispositional Infusion, Human and Divine." In *The Virtuous Life: Thomas Aquinas on the Theological Nature of Moral Virtues,* edited by Harm Goris and Henk Schoot, 73–96. Leuven, Belgium: Peeters, 2017.

Porter, Jean. "Moral Virtues, Charity, and Grace: Why the Infused and Acquired Virtues Cannot Coexist." *Journal of Moral Theology* 8, no. 2 (2019): 40–66.

———. *Nature as Reason.* Grand Rapids: William B. Eerdmans, 2005.

———. *Perfection of Desire.* Milwaukee, WI: Marquette University Press, 2018.

———. "The Subversion of Virtue: Acquired and Infused Virtues in the *Summa Theologiae.*" *Annual of the Society of Christian Ethics* 12 (1992): 19–41.

———. "The Unity of the Virtues and the Ambiguity of Goodness: A Reappraisal of Aquinas's Theory of the Virtues." *Journal of Religious Ethics* 21, no. 1 (1993): 137–63.

———. "The Virtue of Justice (IIa–IIae qq. 58–122)." In *The Ethics of Aquinas,* edited by Stephen Pope, 272–86. Washington, DC: Georgetown University Press, 2002.

———. "Why Are the Habits Necessary?: An Inquiry into Aquinas's Moral Psychology." *Oxford Studies in Medieval Philosophy* 1 (2013): 113–35.

Rhonheimer, Martin. *The Perspective of Morality: Philosophical Foundations of Thomistic Virtue Ethics.* Washington, DC: Catholic University of America Press, 2011.

Romero, Miguel. "The Happiness of 'Those Who Lack the Use of Reason.'" *The Thomist* 80 (2016): 49–96.

Russell, Daniel. *Practical Intelligence and the Virtues.* Oxford: Oxford University Press, 2009.

Ryan, Peter, SJ. "Must an Acting Person Have a Single Ultimate End?." *Gregorianum* 82, no. 2 (2001): 325–56.

Salzman, Todd, and Michael Lawler. *Virtue and Theological Ethics: Toward a Renewed Ethical Method.* London: Orbis, 2018.

Scotus, John Duns. *Duns Scotus on the Will and Morality.* Edited by A. Wolter. Washington, DC: Catholic University of America Press, 1986.

Sherwin, Michael, OP. *By Knowledge and By Love.* Washington, DC: Catholic University of America Press, 2011.

———. "Infused Virtue and the Effects of Acquired Vice: A Test Case for the Thomistic Theory of the Infused Cardinal Virtues." *The Thomist* 73, no. 1 (2009): 29–52.

Smith, Christian. *What Is a Person?: Rethinking Humanity, Social Life, and the Moral Good from the Person Up.* Chicago: University of Chicago Press, 2010.

Snow, Nancy. "Notes Toward an Empirical Study of Virtue." In *Aristotelian Ethics in Contemporary Perspective,* edited by Julia Peters, 130–44. London: Routledge, 2012.

———. *Virtue as Social Intelligence.* London: Routledge, 2009.

Solomon, David. "Internal Objections to Virtue Ethics." *Midwest Studies in Philosophy* 13, no. 1 (1988): 428–41.

Sorabji, Robert. *Emotion and Peace of Mind: From Stoic Agitation to Christian Temptation.* Oxford: Oxford University Press, 2000.

Spezzano, Daria. *The Glory of God's Grace: Deification According to St. Thomas Aquinas*. Ave Maria, FL: Sapientia, 2015.

Stichter, Matthew. "Virtue as a Skill." In *Oxford Handbook of Virtue*, edited by Nancy E. Snow, 57–81. Oxford: Oxford University Press, 2018.

Stroud, James. "*Instinctus* and the Gifts of the Holy Spirit: Explaining the Development in St. Thomas' Teaching on the Gifts of the Holy Spirit." *Journal of Moral Theology* 8, special issue 2 (2019): 60–79.

———. "Thomas Aquinas' Exposition of the Gifts of the Holy Spirit: Developments in His Thought and Rival Interpretations." PhD diss., Catholic University of America, 2012.

Sullivan, Ezra, OP. *Habits and Holiness: Ethics, Theology and Biopsychology*. Washington, DC: Catholic University of America Press, 2021.

———. "Seek First the Kingdom: A Reply to Germain Grisez's Account of Man's Ultimate End." *Nova et Vetera* 8, no. 4 (2010): 959–95.

Ten Klooster, Anton. *Thomas Aquinas on the Beatitudes: Reading Matthew, Disputing Grace and Virtue, Preaching Happiness*. Leuven: Peeters, 2018.

Tessman, Lisa. *Burdened Virtues: Virtue Ethics for Liberatory Struggles*. Oxford: Oxford University Press, 2005.

Titus, Craig Steven. "Moral Development and Making All Things New in Christ." *The Thomist* 72, no. 2 (2008): 233–58.

———. "Passions in Christ: Spontaneity, Development, and Virtue." *The Thomist* 73, no. 1 (2009): 53–87.

Torrell, Jean-Pierre, OP. *Saint Thomas Aquinas, vol. 2: Spiritual Master*. Translated by Robert Royal. Washington, DC: Catholic University of America Press, 2003.

———. *Thomas Aquinas, vol. 1: The Person and His Work*. Translated by Robert Royal. Washington, DC: Catholic University of America Press, 1996.

———. *Thomas Aquinas, vol. 2: Spiritual Master*. Translated by Robert Royal. Washington, DC: Catholic University of America Press, 1996.

Uffenheimer-Lippens, Elisabeth. "Rationalized Passion and Passionate Reality: Thomas Aquinas on the Relation between Reason and the Passions." *Review of Metaphysics* 56, no. 3 (2003): 525–58.

Vogler, Candace. *Reasonably Vicious*. Cambridge, MA: Harvard University Press, 2009.

Ward, Kate. *Wealth, Virtue, and Moral Luck: Christian Ethics in an Age of Inequality*. Washington, DC: Georgetown University Press, 2021.

Weisheipl, James, OP. *Friar Thomas D'Aquino: His Life, Thought, and Works*. New York: Doubleday, 1974.

White, Leo. "Instinct and Custom." *The Thomist* 66, no. 4 (2002): 577–605.

Whitmore, Andrew. "Dispositions and Habits in the Work of Saint Thomas Aquinas." PhD diss., Catholic University of America, 2018.

"William Whittaker's Words." https://archives.nd.edu/words.html, accessed May 24, 2021.

INDEX

ABOUT THE AUTHOR

William C. Mattison III is the Wilsey Family Associate Professor at the University of Notre Dame. He also serves as Senior Advisor: Theological Formation at Notre Dame's Alliance for Catholic Education (ACE) program, preparing K–12 Catholic school teachers of religion and helping form Catholic school leaders in how mission informs all aspects of education. He previously spent ten years on the faculty of the Catholic University of America's School of Theology and Religious Studies, including three years as associate dean and one year as interim dean. He has published six edited volumes as well as several single-authored books including the popular undergraduate ethics text *Introducing Moral Theology: True Happiness and the Virtues* (Brazos, 2008); the scholarly monograph *The Sermon on the Mount and Moral Theology: A Virtue Perspective* (Cambridge, 2017); and the forthcoming wider-audience spirituality book tentatively titled *Encountering Jesus in the Gospels* (Emmaus Road, 2022).